Praise for *The Beat Hotel*:

SO-AVR-169

"[The Beat Hotel was] a potent interzone of deep culture, unvarnished self-indulgence, and unbridled creativity. . . . Barry Miles knows his Beats, and he is a generous and salubrious host. *The Beat Hotel* . . . is packed with visceral history, making for a nicely decadent read."
—*Philadelphia Weekly*

"Barry Miles uncovers a vein of gold in this history."
—*Milwaukee Journal Sentinel*

"Miles exposes this previously overlooked existence of the Beat artists with accounts of their correspondence and far-out experiences with their European contemporaries. *The Beat Hotel* fills a biographical hole in Beat history."
—*Bookpage*

"Part scholarly study and part gossip-fest . . . An entertaining narrative about important writers now considered American literary heroes."
—*Publishers Weekly*

"Engrossing and enlightening . . . in particular [as to] how the experience affected them by providing a productive context for creativity."
—*Booklist*

"A sliver of Paris in the late '50s and early '60s."
—*Oregonian* (Portland)

"Miles . . . paints a vivid picture of literary life along the Left Bank in the late 1950s and early 1960s. . . . This is fun reading, especially for those steeped in the Beats."
—*Library Journal*

The Beat Hotel

Also by Barry Miles

William Burroughs: El Hombre Invisible
Ginsberg: A Biography
Paul McCartney: Many Years from Now
Jack Kerouac: King of the Beats

The Beat Hotel

Ginsberg, Burroughs, and Corso
in Paris, 1958–1963

Barry Miles

Grove Press
New York

Copyright © 2000 by Barry Miles

All rights reserved. No part of this book may be reproduced in any form or by any electronic or mechanical means, including information storage and retrieval systems, without permission in writing from the publisher, except by a reviewer, who may quote brief passages in a review. Any members of educational institutions wishing to photocopy part or all of the work for classroom use, or publishers who would like to obtain permission to include the work in an anthology, should send their inquiries to Grove/Atlantic, Inc., 841 Broadway, New York, NY 10003.

Published simultaneously in Canada
Printed in the United States of America

FIRST PAPERBACK EDITION

Library of Congress Cataloging-in-Publication Data
Miles, Barry, 1943–
    The Beat Hotel : Ginsberg, Burroughs, and Corso in Paris, 1958–1963 / Barry Miles.
        p. cm.
    Includes bibliographical references (p.).
    ISBN 0-8021-3817-9 (pbk.)
    1. American literature—20th century—History and criticism.   2. Beat generation.   3. Burroughs, William S., 1914—Homes and haunts—France—Paris.   4. Ginsberg, Allen, 1926—Homes and haunts—France—Paris.   5. Americans—France—Paris—History—20th century.   6. Corso, Gregory—Homes and haunts—France—Paris.   7. Paris (France)—Intellectual life—20th century.   8. Authors, American—France—Paris—Biography.   9. Authors, American—20th century—Biography.   10. Beat generation—France—Paris.   I. Title.
PS228.B6 M55 2000
810.9'944361'09045—dc21
    [B]   00-020187

Design by Laura Hammond Hough

Grove Press
841 Broadway
New York, NY 10003

01 02 03 04   10 9 8 7 6 5 4 3 2 I

To Allen, Bill, Brion, and Ian

Contents

Introduction

The Beat Hotel is no more. The ground-floor façade of 9, rue Git-le-Coeur has been rebuilt, and the building—once a decrepit rooming house with hole-in-the-floor toilets shared by all the residents—is now occupied by the Relais-Hôtel du Vieux Paris, with wall fabrics by Pierre Frey, individual room safes, nineteen television channels, direct-dial telephones with modems, minibar, and white marble bathrooms complete with hair driers and terrytowel robes. The narrow street, however, is little changed; each morning to this day water runs down the gutters in a complicated medieval street-cleaning system controlled by rolls of rags placed strategically at various drains, where water either bubbles up or swirls away. The ancient gray walls on either side are still chipped and patched, unchanged these forty years. The drains whiff a bit, as ever, and at the end of the lane the view across the Seine to the Palais de Justice and the thin tower of Ste. Chapelle has altered little in hundreds of years.

Nine, rue Git-le-Coeur, the Beat Hotel, is one of those legendary addresses, along with the Hotel Chelsea in New York and the Chateau Marmont in Hollywood—these are the addresses of international bohemia. There were more: the Mills Hotel and the Albert in New York, the Swiss American and the Hotel Wentley in San Francisco, the Tropicana Motel in Hollywood; these were places where artists and poets lived, addresses mentioned in poems, glimpsed in blurred avant-garde movies, used as the titles of huge dripping abstract paintings, the care-of addresses on mimeographed poetry magazines, scribbled suggestions for lodging at which to stay if you ever made it out of Britain.

I was sixteen when I went to art college in England in 1959, but I had already heard of the Beats and within a matter of months I had obtained some of their writings. I was immediately attracted to their ideas and knew that these were the people I had to meet; the days of artists in garrets were long over but these people seemed to be continuing the tradition. To my regret I never visited the Beat Hotel when it was up and running. By the time I got a passport it had closed in 1963. For years I had heard travelers' tales from friends, usually students who had hitchhiked to Paris in the best *On the Road* tradition. Fellow art students, friends, and older flat-mates would arrive back from Paris, smoking Gitanes or Gauloises, a fresh copy of *Naked Lunch* hidden in their shirt in the hope that customs would not find it and confiscate it.

Paris itself was an exotic location in those days. It had bars that stayed open later than the 10 P.M. closing time then in force in England. French cigarettes were stronger and more fragrant, the Metro had first- and second-class seats. One listened in astonishment to descriptions of the hole-in-the-floor toilets, open-air pissoirs, and the ladies who ran the public lavatories. Visitors described student bistros and casual jazz clubs; London had only one jazz club—Ronnie Scott's—and that was prohibitively expensive. They described the easygoing sex and the freely available drugs, and though we knew they must be exaggerating, it sounded a good deal more interesting than life in Britain. Everyone said the Beat Hotel was the place to stay, but if it was full, or the owner did not like the look of you, there were plenty of other, equally inexpensive places within a few blocks. Some people had actually managed to meet William Burroughs, Gregory Corso, Brion Gysin, or Allen Ginsberg—already legendary names.

My own involvement with these individuals began in 1964 when I started corresponding with William Burroughs, who was then living in Tangier. I was putting together a literary anthology called *Darazt* and wrote asking for material. He sent me a manuscript and we kept in touch. I met Allen Ginsberg the following year when I was managing a bookshop in London and arranged for him to read at the store. He needed somewhere to stay in the center of London and moved in with my wife and me. This was when the famous poetry reading at the Royal Albert Hall was being organized and Ginsberg was joined by Lawrence Ferlinghetti, Corso, and dozens of others to read before an audience of seven thousand or so people in July of 1965. Corso and Ferlinghetti made frequent visits to my flat to see Ginsberg, and by the end of the summer, when they all moved on, I had become friendly with them all. Later that year Burroughs moved to London and so I got to know him as well.

Over the subsequent years I worked closely with all of these writers. I produced an album of Allen Ginsberg singing William Blake's *Songs of Innocence and Experience* and lived for a year on his farm in upstate New York, cataloging his tape archives; Gregory Corso was also living there at the time. I wrote Ginsberg's biography and edited an annotated text edition of "Howl." I saw him whenever I was in New York and he frequently stayed with me on visits to London. Allen was always generous with his time, and though I had already interviewed him about the Beat Hotel for my biography, he was happy to answer more specific questions about it for this book. My working involvement with William Burroughs was closest in the 1960s and early '70s when he lived in London. I published numerous articles by him in underground-press publications. I also cataloged his archives, coauthored his bibliography for the University of Virigina Bibliographical Society, and wrote a short biography of his life. During my last visit to William's home in Kansas, I tape-recorded an interview with him for this book. Over the years we had often talked about his time at the Beat Hotel, which he regarded as a high point in his life, and he was always happy to revisit those times and recount the stories again.

By the 1980s, the Beat Generation was no longer regarded as a threat to the American establishment, its surviving members sufficiently old not to give further offense, and so they were accepted, with only slight reluctance, into the American academy. When Allen Ginsberg and William Burroughs died—four months apart in 1997—they both were canonized in *The New Yorker*, a sure sign of establishment recognition. The Beat Generation had become America's Bloomsbury Group, its first homegrown literary movement, complete with its own canon of books, memoirs, volumes of letters, albums of photographs, biographies, and scholarly studies.

American Puritanism and Prohibition as well as a strong dollar abroad had caused previous generations to choose self-imposed exile, usually in Paris. Between 1903 and 1939 Paris was home to virtually every American writer, poet, or composer of note: Ernest Hemingway, e.e. cummings, Gertrude Stein, Ezra Pound, Aaron Copland, Virgil Thomson, Paul Bowles, John Dos Passos, F. Scott Fitzgerald, Walter Piston, Henry Miller, to name some of the most noted—a virtual roll call of the Modernist movement. After World War II Paris was more expensive for Americans, and the United States had, in any case, developed its own arts centers. However, for African-Americans the lure of Paris continued into the 1940s and '50s as a place of shelter from racism, prejudice, and segregation at home, including writers such as Richard Wright, Chester Himes, and James Baldwin, and jazzmen Sidney Bechet and Bud Powell.

Some American writers continued to live in Paris: Ned Rorem, James Jones, George Plimpton and *The Paris Review* crowd, and, of course, the Beats, but with few exceptions, such as William Burroughs, theirs was not permanent exile; a year or two abroad at the most and then they returned to the States. The Beats went to Paris to be free not from racism—they were primarily from white middle-class college-educated backgrounds—but to escape the conformism and Puritanism of America after the war. Many of them were gay, and they could lead a freer life in France, and most of them were using illegal drugs. In the '50s the French police knew little about drugs, and were, in any case, much too preoccupied with the terrorist attacks in Paris provoked by the independence struggle in Algeria to seriously care about the activities of a few British or American tourists.

For a brief period, from 1958–63, the Beat Hotel in Paris was the site of the largest concentration of Beat Generation activity. Most of the founding members of the movement lived there at one time or another. The only major Beat figure not to set foot in the rue Git-le-Coeur was Jack Kerouac. In many ways, what the Beats staged in Paris

was a second round of their activities in mid-'50s S[...]
1955–56 Allen Ginsberg, Peter Orlovsky, Jack Kerouac, and Greg
Corso—though not Burroughs—were at the center of what came to be
known as the San Francisco Poetry Renaissance. It was then that
Ginsberg wrote "Howl" and gave its first performance. In 1957–58
Ginsberg, Orlovsky, Corso, and William Burroughs—though not
Kerouac—became the central figures in the Beat Hotel.

It was there that Ginsberg wrote some of his best-loved poems,
including "To Aunt Rose," "At Apollinaire's Grave," and a long section of "Kaddish," his great elegy to his mother, Naomi, who died in
a mental hospital. It was there that Corso wrote his famous poem,
"Bomb," shaped on the page like the mushroom cloud of an atomic
bomb. It was in Paris, too, that Corso composed most of the other poems
in his popular book *A Happy Birthday of Death.* It was in the Beat
Hotel that Burroughs completed *Naked Lunch* and where Brion Gysin
invented the infamous Cut-up technique. Burroughs, Gysin, and others
produced two collaborative books of Cut-ups there: *Minutes To Go*
and *The Exterminator,* and Burroughs went on to write the first of his
Cut-up novels, *The Soft Machine,* and much of the second, *The Ticket
That Exploded,* in his room in the hotel. In room 25, Gysin and Ian
Sommerville built the first Dreamachine, a means of employing flickering light at the alpha frequency to create visual hallucinations. Gysin
and Sommerville together formulated the first multimedia light shows
and body projections, precursors of psychedelic rock shows half a
decade later. Filmmaker Antony Balch shot a quarter of the footage
for his film *Cut-ups* in the hotel and among its surrounding streets.
This is an amazing inventory of activity focused within and around
just one building, a creative epicenter that has been virtually overlooked
in the majority of studies on the Beats.

The Beat Generation had a worldwide impact, like the Lost Generation preceding it, but I believe this has not been sufficiently appreciated in the United States. The 1995 exhibition at the Whitney
Museum in New York, *Beat Culture and the New America, 1950–
1965,* for instance, was divided simply into "East Coast" and "West
Coast." This awkward national arrangement of material meant that

they had no effective way to present the work of William Burroughs, who spent all but a few months of that fifteen-year period of time living in Mexico City, Tangier, Paris, and London. Nor did they present any of the Beats' overseas activity—no Dreamachine, no *Olympia* magazine, no foreign Beatnikery—with the consequence that the work of Brion Gysin was almost entirely overlooked and, instead, many little known West Coast artists had huge amounts of wall space devoted to their work.

I am not alone in thinking that the international aspect of the Beat Generation has been underappreciated. Allen Ginsberg spent years of his life traveling to all parts of the planet, spreading the word and developing internationally solid ongoing contacts with poets, writers, and artists who were of similar mind. Ginsberg felt strongly that the Beat Generation was an international phenomenon, that it embodied an approach to life, a set of beliefs that transcended national barriers, and in virtually every country he was able to find a local "Beat" scene: the circle of writers and poets surrounding Simon Vinkenoog in Amsterdam; the group involving Carl Weissner and Udo Breger in Germany; Miguel Grinberg's *Eco Contemporaneo* group in Buenos Aires; Sergio Mondragón and the *El Corno Emplumado* folks in Mexico City; Pradip Choudhuri and the writers of the Hungry Generation in Calcutta. His travels were paralleled by those of Lawrence Ferlinghetti, Michael McClure, and some of the younger poets associated with the Beats, such as Anne Waldman and John Giorno, who read at summer arts festivals in many European countries and elsewhere, sharing the stage with local poets, writers, and translators who were mining the same vein.

This book is an attempt to fill this gap in Beat Generation history. At the Beat Hotel the members of the original New York faction of the Beat Generation were hard at work, and many of the ideas first formulated there went on to have an impact not only in art and literature but in the wider culture: the credits on CNN now move faster than the edits in Antony Balch's *Cut-ups*, which was regarded at the time as unwatchable; Burroughs, Gysin, and Sommerville's performances were among the earliest "Happenings," and Burroughs's and Sommerville's Cut-up tapes, with the sounds of radio static and pneumatic drills mixed with read text, were definite precursors of Industrial music. Cut-ups themselves were later used by rock artists such as David Bowie, who used the technique in writing his *Diamond Dogs* album. Here were people experimenting with drugs, with psychic phenomena, with new models of community. The sixties were just beginning; a new generation of young people had arrived, a postwar generation that required maps to investigate for themselves the new areas and possibilities that were being presented. The residents of the Beat Hotel were making the first sketches of unexplored terrain—sometimes they explored dead ends, and at other times the trail was more dangerous than they thought, but they were leading the way.

I also want to tell the story of Brion Gysin and Ian Sommerville, who, in other circumstances, would have a higher profile in the history of this movement. Like Carl Solomon, Herbert Huncke, Harold Norse, and Neal Cassady, they too played their significant parts in Beat Generation history. Finally I wanted to write a tribute to my friends. Walking the ancient streets around the rue Git-le-Coeur, researching this book, I felt an enormous sadness at the loss of Ginsberg, Burroughs, Gysin, and Sommerville, all of whom I had known and worked with since the mid-1960s. I deeply miss them all.

It seemed at one point that Bill Burroughs's influence was at work as I wrote this book, for there occurred an example of synchronicity and coincidence that he would have enjoyed. I had written a passage within which Allen Ginsberg took Alan Ansen to a small bar on the rue de la Huchette, and a half hour later I wrote a paragraph about Bernard Frechtman, Genet's translator. When researching a book, I always try to use contemporary maps of the period I am dealing with but I was unable to find my 1960 Paris map to see if the rue de la Huchette was as close to the hotel as I remembered. I happened to have Kenneth Tynan's copy of the *Michelin Paris Index and Plan*, dating from 1973—given to me by Kathleen Tynan after Ken's death, and as yet unopened by me—and when I turned to the page I wanted, there was Ken's place marker with a note to himself: "Caveau de la Huchette. 5 rue de la Huchette. 9.30 Bnd Frechtman." Voices speaking to us from the past.

1 9, rue Git-le-Coeur

I view life as a fortuitous collaboration ascribable to the fact that one finds oneself in the right place at the right time. For us, the "right place" was the famous "Beat Hotel" in Paris, roughly from 1958 to 1963.
Brion Gysin, *The Third Mind*

In the 1950s the Left Bank, or Latin Quarter, was to Paris what Soho was to London, Greenwich Village was to New York, and North Beach was to San Francisco: an inexpensive central neighborhood where writers and artists could meet and spend their nights talking or drinking, where basic accommodation was cheap and the local people were tolerant of the antics of youth. The maze of small streets between the Blvd St. Germain and the river Seine housed dozens of small, low-priced residential hotels, home to many of the students from the nearby Sorbonne. The University of Paris was seven hundred years old and it was a long-established tradition for students to live in small hotels in the surrounding streets. There were also art students and models from the École des Beaux Arts on the quai Augustins as well as many established artists whose ateliers were tucked away in small courtyards and side streets, recognizable by their north-facing skylights. Bohemians and students lived side by side with a large working-class population of old-time city dwellers, the true Parisians who filled the food markets on the rue de Buci or the covered market at Mabillon each morning and returned home with their produce long before the young bohemians had even sipped the first coffee of the day.

Inexpensive and run-down, the area around the rue Saint Séverin was a traditional center for *clochards*—tramps, bums—who once had a street of their own, the rue de Brèvre, in the days when the area near Place Maubert was frequented by boatmen and tawsers. In the '50s there were an estimated 10,000 such folk in Paris, both men and women, sleeping under bridges, on manhole covers in the public squares, wrapped in rags, warmed by the sewer heat, lying huddled against the exhaust vents of the Metro where the stale warm air was expelled.

The Latin Quarter was an area of dusty used bookshops, avant-garde art galleries, antiques shops, dealers in ethnological artifacts, and the tiny cramped offices of radical publishing houses and small presses specializing in experimental literature and the arts. Along the Seine the booksellers displayed tattered prints and well-thumbed books in boxes clamped to the river wall, which could be locked shut at night. All around the rue de Seine and Place St. Michel there were bookshops that featured titles in Surrealism, 'Pataphysics, medicine, the occult, alchemy, and Asian mysticism. These were sometimes hidden in court-yards or on the higher floors of buildings, known only to aficionados.

There were artists' cafés, like the Palctte, where one could meet a gallery owner to plan a show, hire a model, or buy drugs. There were dozens of inexpensive restaurants such as the Café des Arts on the rue de Seine where art students sat in rows on benches; there was just one fixed-price three-course menu, and all the red wine you could drink stood in liter flagons on the bare wooden refectory tables. One café, Chez Raton, was so small that the bread was kept in baskets hanging from ropes above the tables and you had to wind them down to get some. Chez Jean, in a passageway off Blvd St. Germain, was one of the few restaurants in Paris to still have sawdust on the floor. Some-times a cellist or guitarist played there. It was full of tough characters but the bohemian crowd liked to gather there too, and an uneasy truce was maintained. There were many cheap Chinese, Vietnamese, and North African restaurants in the neighborhood, particularly around Place Maubert and the rue de la Huchette.

Each night Blvd St. Germain was the scene of the greatest prom-enade in Paris as people made their way from Place Maubert to Place St. Germain des Pres and back again, past the grand cafés: the Brasserie Lipp, the Café aux Deux Magots, the Café de Flore, filled with existentialists and wealthy tourists watching and being watched. Some promenaders would stop off at the Pergola just behind the Mabillon Metro station, which had a 500 fr menu and was open all night. It was the principal gathering place for male and female homosexuals. Some of the young men wore lipstick and powder, and some of the more masculine women dressed as men. The Pergola also attracted the late-night student crowd, including many residents from the Beat Hotel, two streets away.

The Beat Hotel was located at 9, rue Git-le-Coeur, a narrow medieval lane running down to the Seine from the rue St. Andre des Arts to the quai Augustins in the oldest part of the Latin Quarter. In the thirteenth century the street was called rue de Gilles-le-Queux or Guy-le-Queux (Guy the cuisinier, or cook). It was known also as rue Guy-le-Preux. Over the centuries this transformed into Git-le-Coeur, which Brion Gysin claimed was a pun on the street name made in the early seventeenth century by Henri IV, the first Bourbon King of France, whose mistress lived on the street. The King passed by one day and remarked *"Ici git mon coeur"* ("Here lies my heart"). Like many of Gysin's stories, it is probably untrue, but it sounds just fine.

An alternate story, found in *Nichol's Guide to Paris,* claims that the street name commemorates the murder of Etienne Marcel, Provost of the Merchants and one of the fathers of Paris. On the night of July 31, 1358, he was assassinated in this street by Jean Maillart, a mercenary in the pay of the Dauphin Charles; the word *git* means "lies," as on a tombstone inscription: *"ci-git,"* or "here lies."

As in many of the old lanes in this quarter, the buildings are four stories high, usually leaning out over the street on the ground floor, then sloping quite steeply back away from the street on the three higher floors. Numbers 5, 7, and 9 were built in the late sixteenth century, originally encompassing the mansion of Pierre Séguier, marquis d'O, which later belonged to the Duc de Luynes, the uncle of Racine. In 1933 Monsieur and Madame M. L. Rachou, a provincial couple from Giverny, near Rouen, northwest of Paris, bought number 9 to run as a hotel. Brion Gysin, who became very friendly with Madame Rachou during the years he lived at the hotel, said that they had only the *gérance*, or management, of the hotel and did not own it, which is very probable as it is hard to imagine how the couple could have found the money to buy such a large building. Monsieur Rachou, acting as janitor and bellhop, was a huge, silent man, slow and patient with his guests. Madame was tiny and energetic, her short arms habitually folded over her pale blue housecoat with its round smocked collar—the sort that workingwomen wore throughout the nineteenth century, except on Sundays. She ran the small bistro on the ground floor and registered the guests.

The Rachous enjoyed the company of artists and writers and encouraged them to stay at the hotel. Madame Rachou would sometimes allow artists to pay with paintings, none of which she kept, not thinking for one moment that they would ever be valuable. Her affection for artists stemmed from her youth, when, at the age of twelve, she began working in a country inn at Giverny only a short walk from Monet's studio. After a morning's work on a series of paintings of grain sacks or haystacks, Monet would stroll down to the inn to have lunch with his old friend Camille Pissarro. Madame Rachou once asked Brion Gysin, "And what became of his son, the young M'sieu Pissarro?" Brion did not know but told her that there was a big retrospective of Pissarro's paintings on at that very moment in Paris and offered to take her, but she was too busy with the hotel for such distractions.

Madame tended the bar and her name, J. B. Rachou, was painted on its glass door in the slanting calligraphic hand of an old-fashioned master sign painter. The Rachous never gave the hotel a name, preferring instead simply to label the entrances: above the left-hand door was a sign HOTEL and above the glass door and front of the café: CAFE VINS LIQUEURS, which was enough. For twenty-four years, through the Occupation and the hard months after Liberation, when food and fuel were even more scarce than they were under the Germans, they kept the hotel open, although the couple was barely able to make a living.

Then in September 1957, Monsieur Rachou was killed in an automobile accident in the town of St. Germain, just outside Paris. The

Rachous had recently bought a secondhand Citröen DS, and Monsieur Rachou had driven out to the country to collect some friends and drive them back to the hotel for a Sunday lunch. In St. Germain a car had run into him at a crossing, killing him and seriously injuring his four friends. Madame Rachou was devastated but she had little choice but to carry on. A hotel, of course, cannot be neglected for more than a few days.

Because she was so small, Madame had to stand upon an upturned wine case behind the traditional zinc-topped bar in the bistro in order to serve. There were lace curtains at the wide glass window and several spindly aspidistra plants, their bladelike leaves always brown at the ends. The bistro had a cracked tiled floor with three marble-topped tables on slender cast-iron legs where she served breakfast of coffee and croissants. This was not included in the rent, it was not that sort of hotel; the 40 centimes for a coffee had to be paid on the spot.

She served large, inexpensive lunches of cassoulet or rabbit stew but after the death of her husband she no longer opened the dining room in the back except for occasional private parties for police lieutenants and other *fonctionnaires*. This was a class 13 hotel, the lowest on the scale, which meant it had to meet the minimum legal health and safety requirements and that was all. After the war, as part of the same clean-up of Paris that had closed the brothels, many of the small class 13 hotels in the neighborhood had been boarded up by the police for contravening long-ignored regulations. This was one of the reasons there were so many *clochards* on the streets. Madame Rachou, however, had been on good terms with the police since before the Occupation and intended to keep it that way.

She was a classic concierge. From her perch on the oversize wine box she could monitor her domain: the narrow hotel hallway to her right was visible through a paneled glass door and her back dining room, separated from the bar by a curtain, had a window facing the stairs that showed the legs of anyone coming in or out—ideal for grabbing the ankle of a welching lodger attempting to sneak out. Next to the hall doorway, facing the bar, was Madame's control panel of electrical switches; the number of the corresponding room was identified by a small enamel plaque. Above each was a small flashlight bulb that glowed when the light in that room was turned on. Each room was supplied with 40 watts, just enough for a dim 25-watt lightbulb and a radio or record player. The electrical system was archaic: it was extremely sensitive and periodically plunged everyone into darkness if someone overloaded the circuit. When a bulb flared on her control panel Madame knew that someone was using an illicit hot plate and would rush upstairs to confront the offender. The power could be increased to 60 watts but naturally there was a small surcharge for this service. Rather than pay the extra, most residents cooked on small two-burner gas or oil stoves, which they'd bought themselves. The gas stoves ran on individual meters and Madame always seemed to choose the most inconvenient time to arrive in the company of the meter reader.

The forty-two rooms had no carpets or telephones. Some were very dark, as their windows looked out onto the stairwell inside the building and so received only indirect lighting from the grimy landing windows. The corridors sloped at strange angles and the floors creaked and groaned. The ancient wooden doors had a handle in the middle instead of the side. Each landing had a Turkish *chiotte:* a traditional hole-in-the-floor toilet with a raised footprint-shaped platform on either side upon which to position your feet while you squatted. Torn sheets of newspaper hung on a nail in lieu of toilet tissue, though many residents bought their own and carried it with them. There was a bath on the ground floor but advance notice had to be given so that the water for it could be heated. Naturally there was a small surcharge for this service. Brion Gysin maintained that if you put your head under the water in the bath, you could hear the gurgling of the Bièvre, the underground river that enters the Seine a few blocks east of the rue Git-le-Coeur, across from Notre Dame—a claim he enlarged upon in his novel *The Last Museum.* Like everything else in the building, the plumbing was ancient, and it was consequently subject to backups, clankings, fiercely loud vibrations, and leaks. There was radiator heat all week and hot water only on Thursday, Friday, and Saturday.

The curtains and bedspreads were washed and changed each spring, and the bed linen a little more frequently—in theory, at the beginning of each month. After the death of Monsieur Rachou, Madame employed a janitor, Monsieur Duprés, who occasionally wandered through the hotel with the apparent intention of cleaning the rooms and making the beds. He was often accompanied by a collection of small children and, like Madame, inevitably chose just the wrong moment to walk into a room. Some of the walls were very thin, little more than hardboard partitions, and sound traveled in mysterious ways, sometimes blaring from the waste pipe in the sink.

The front door was never locked or controlled, but Madame Rachou had an uncanny, almost clairvoyant knowledge of everything that went on both in the hotel and in the street outside. She could "hear" trouble—a strange footstep, an unusual creak—and was able to materialize at the door to protect her residents from creditors, con men, or occasional visits from the police. No matter what time of night, she would appear stone-faced in her white nightgown: *"Monsieur? Que voulez-vous?"* Not even the police were a match for Madame. In 1962, during the Algerian crisis, a spotty-faced young *flic* (cop) was on duty across the street, guarding the house of an ex–police chief on the OAS (Organisation Armée Secrète) death list who was expecting a bomb or assassin's knife at any moment. The *flic* saw an attractive young American woman enter the hotel and followed her up to her room, whereupon Madame Rachou appeared and drove him from the hotel with a barrage of abuse, her tiny arms flapping and her blue-rinsed hair luminous in the dimly lit corridor.

Still, she could not control visits from the immigration inspectors. As William Burroughs has described: "The 'police of foreigners,' the immigration police made passport checks from time to time, always at eight in the morning, and would often take away some guest whose papers were not in order. The detainee would be back in a few hours, having paid—not a fine—but a tax, attendant on the application for a *carte de sejour;* though few had the time and patience to fulfill the complex bureaucratic regulations required to obtain this coveted document." Most of them, including Burroughs, undertook the expedient of a brief trip to Brussels or Amsterdam every three months so that they could begin their three-month allowance afresh upon each reentrance of France.

The culture of bohemia is a very French one. In fact Henri Murger, author of *Scènes de la Vie de Bohème*, claimed that true bohemians could exist only in Paris. Britain was less tolerant of unorthodox behavior. London produced eccentrics and aesthetes but had no tradition of bohemian poverty. Byron and Shelley had found life easier on the continent in the nineteenth century. When he was released from the Reading jail, Oscar Wilde moved to Paris to live out his life.

The rue Git-le-Coeur has always had its bohemian residents. In 1930 Dorothy Wilde, Oscar's wild niece, lived at number one, and Lord Gerard Vernon Wallop Lymington, ninth Earl of Portsmouth, used to have rooms high in the eaves of the same building, where, in the late 1920s, he used to smoke opium with Caresse and Harry Crosby. In the '30s Brion Gysin lived in a beautiful apartment on the corner of the quai, never thinking he would return to the same street two decades later.

The rue Git-le-Coeur was also the setting for the famous arrest of e.e. cummings. At 3 A.M. on a July morning in 1923, John Dos Passos, Gilbert Seldes, and cummings were headed for "the Calvados joint on rue Git-le-Coeur." When cummings paused to urinate against the wall, "a whole phalanx of gendarmes" materialized. He was arrested and taken to the police station on the quai Grandes-Augustins, where he was booked as *"un Américain qui pisse,"* and told to return the next morning for arraignment. Seldes telephoned his writer friend Paul Morand, the *Ministre des Affaires Etrangères*, who had the charges dropped. cummings was not informed of this development and he reported to the police station the next day. He was dismissed, but when he left the building he was confronted by a band of his friends carrying placards reading *"Reprieve le Pisseur Américain."* cummings was profoundly moved by their solidarity until he learned that their protest was all an elaborate joke.

The Rachous' hotel maintained the bohemian tradition of the *quartier.* There was a photographer in one of the attic rooms who had not spoken a word to anyone for two years, and an artist who had filled his room with straw. Among the whores, jazz musicians, and artists' models were characters such as the giant man from French Guyana who could barely squeeze through the narrow corridors, and an imperious Indo-Chinese lady who always dressed in silk and had a bamboo curtain at her door. The first of the so-called beatniks came in 1956: a Swiss painter everyone called Jesus Christ. He wore his thick dark hair long, almost to his waist, and left his beard and mustache untrimmed. He wore flowing robes of dirty white cotton and went barefoot in sandals even in the bitter cold of the Paris winter. As he could not afford to buy canvas, he painted on the walls, and, in turn, the ceiling and floor of his second-floor room. Monsieur Rachou was unconcerned, as he believed the paint would discourage bugs.

Unlike the hundreds of other run-down hotels in Paris that offered the bare necessities, the Beat Hotel was exceptional in the way that Madame Rachou encouraged artists to reside there and allowed her guests the freedom to live exactly as they pleased. You could take anyone back to your room, boy or girl or group, provided that they signed the *fiche* guest register if they stayed overnight. The police insisted on this. In every other respect, the hotel was just as squalid and dirty as its neighbors. There were rats and mice, the rooms and stairs were filthy, the toilets stank, and the corridors reeked with stale cooking odors. The artist Jean-Jacques Lebel lived nearby on the rue de l'Hotel Colbert and often visited the American Beats there. "It very often smelled very bad in that place," he recalled, "because a lot of people were cooking in their room, and there was Dixie Nimmo, who was a Jamaican fellow, he would cook with a lot of garlic and oil and stink up the whole place. And there were a few old French people who had been there since three centuries who would cook with a lot of grease and the place stank. . . . The rats were on the ground floor, not on the top floor, and it's only when the Seine would come up that the rats would come up out of their holes. And when there's junkies around there's rats. It was a ghastly thing, an atmosphere a bit like the *Naked Lunch*."

The first of the Rachous' guests to gain celebrity was the African-American writer Chester Himes. His first story, "To What Red Hell," was published in 1934 by *Esquire* when Himes was serving an eight-year term in the Ohio State Penitentiary for armed robbery. His first novel, *If He Hollers Let Him Go*, was published in 1945 to critical acclaim, but his follow-up, *Lonely Crusade*, was too brutally honest about the conditions under which black people were living in the United States and was not so well received. He arrived in Europe in 1953 and remained abroad, living mostly in Spain, until his death in 1984. His French translator, Marcel Duhamel, suggested that he try his hand at detective novels, which were very popular in France at the time. He created a pair of African-American Harlem detectives, Digger Jones and Coffin Ed Johnson, whose exploits over a series of eight novels made Himes a star in France, though he remained relatively unknown in his own country. It wasn't until 1970, when director Ossie Davis made Himes's 1965 book *Cotton Comes to Harlem* into a successful film, that Himes was brought to the greater attention of American audiences.

At first Himes experienced outright racism when he tried to find a hotel room in Paris. In his autobiography he described hotel-hunting in 1954: "The Hotel Welcome overlooking the Odéon, a favorite of the young white Americans, set the pattern. They said they couldn't rent to *noirs;* their clients wouldn't like it. The first nine hotels we tried turned us down because I was black. The majority of the proprietors unequivocally gave that as the reason." Many of the Americans on the Left Bank had brought their prejudices with them and expected the hotels to operate with the same color bar that they were used to back in the States. Eventually Himes sent his young white girlfriend to a hotel that had already claimed to be *complet.* She was given a room and they moved in. He traveled in France and Europe and, on his return to Paris in the spring of 1956, he had the good fortune to encounter Madame Rachou. He moved into the hotel with his young German girlfriend, Marlene Behrens. It was one of the few hotels where a black man was able to live with a white woman, much less one half his age, without opprobrium.

They lived in the front on the second floor above the proprietors in a room equipped with a marble-topped dressing table, which doubled as both a kitchen and dining table complete with a gas ring. It was a small room almost filled by the bed but a giant battered armoire with a full-length mirror gave the room the illusion of space. It was here that Himes worked on portions of *Mamie Mason*, and it was here that he wrote *The Five Cornered Square*, which he finished on January 18, 1957. He completed *A Jealous Man Can't Win* on May 3 of the same year. He was a fast worker. After M. Rachou's death, Marlene spent a lot of time consoling Madame Rachou, sitting with her at the bar, sympathetically listening to her stories of the old days. She had been a child in Germany during the war and Madame's stories about the German occupation of Paris were an education to her. Himes and Marlene left for Palma, Majorca, in October 1957, a few weeks before the first of the Beat Generation writers moved in.

The new arrivals were never to know what the hotel had been like with the solid presence of Monsieur Rachou or that Madame Rachou was broken-hearted. She continued with her life, but now she relied more heavily on her guests for companionship, treating them as a substitute family. In the evening she would sit talking endlessly to her tenants over cups of watery espresso, Mirtaud the hotel cat curled on her lap, until the bar closed at 10:30 and she pulled down the iron shutters.

With the arrival of the Beats that October, the hotel entered another phase, and for about the next six years it was home to a sustained burst of creative activity equal to that which they had achieved recently in San Francisco. There, the presence of Allen Ginsberg and Jack Kerouac had catalyzed the poetry scene, creating what came to be known as the San Francisco Poetry Renaissance—a loose grouping of poets including Gary Snyder, Michael McClure, Lawrence Ferlinghetti, Philip Whalen, Richard Brautigan, and others. (It was presumably named after the Harlem Renaissance, since there had been no previous literary movement in San Francisco.) A series of poetry readings, beginning with the now legendary Six Gallery reading on October 7, 1955, when Ginsberg first read "Howl," brought the San

Francisco poets to the attention of Richard Eberhardt, who wrote an important article on the scene for the *New York Times*. This, coupled with the fortuitous seizure of copies of Ginsberg's *Howl and Other Poems* for obscenity, focused nationwide attention on the poets of the Bay City. More readings were organized, and coffee bars began to feature live poetry. Poets collaborated with jazz musicians in late-night clubs. Suddenly there was a vibrant, active literary scene, with Ferlinghetti's City Lights Bookshop, publishers of the popular and prestigious Pocket Poets series, which included Ginsberg's *Howl*, as its center.

Ginsberg, however, did not remain to bask in his fame. He returned to New York City and went from there to Tangier to assist William Burroughs with the manuscript that eventually became *Naked Lunch*. Just as *Howl* hit the mass media, Ginsberg was on his way to Paris to set up a new headquarters at the Beat Hotel, accompanied by his boyfriend Peter Orlovsky and poet Gregory Corso. The cheap rent and permissive atmosphere fostered a climate of freedom and creativity unfettered by financial concerns. As non–French speakers, they had no involvement with French culture and the issues of the day, nor were they restricted by rules with which the French lived, simply because they were ignorant of them. As Jean-Jacques Lebel put it, "They were on an island, isolated in this magic little paradise full of rats and bad smells. But it was paradisical because it gave them the green light to be themselves without having to confront America." The Beat Hotel offered the freedom to be idle or to work with passionate intensity, to while away the day in cafés or to talk through the night. It was a place where ideas could be developed in a community removed from conventional morality in the manner of the residents of the famous Impasse du Doyenné, the first bohemian colony.

Close to where the Louvre pyramid now stands, in the corner of the Carrousel, was once a group of dilapidated buildings on a dead-end street where, in the 1830s, a miniature, self-contained bohemian colony existed in the ruins of the priory of Doyenné, a few arches and columns of which still remained standing. There Théophile Gautier, Gérard de Nerval, Arsène Houssaye, Edouard Ourliac, and many other writers and painters lived and worked, surrounded by Gothic furnishings, tapestries, and fabrics, looted during the Revolution, which could still be bought cheaply from curiosity shops. Nerval called the community *la Bohème galante* and wrote a book with this title describing their lives. Here Ourliac worked on *Suzanne*, the book that made his name. Gautier wrote *Mademoiselle de Maupin*, Houssaye wrote *La Pécheresse*, and Rogier illustrated Hoffmann's *Tales*.

There was a strong strain of eroticism in these writers' works, which marked Gautier and his friends apart from other writers and artists of the time, and at the Impasse du Doyenné, orgies were a popular entertainment. An orgy provides the theme for Gautier's *Les Jeunes France*, in which a group of young men gets together to organize a colossal feast. There was one celebrated occasion when Gautier and his friends knelt before a woman and in complete darkness drank punch from human skulls. When they held a fancy dress ball in 1835, Camille Corot painted two large Provençal landscapes over the paneled walls of Nerval's rooms. *La Bohème galante* attracted famous visitors such as Eugène Delacroix, Alexandre Dumas, and Petrus Borel, anxious not to be left out of the latest thing. This was the tradition that the rue Git-le-Coeur continued and, like l'Impasse du Doyenné, for a few brief years the Beat Hotel was the center of the literary avant-garde.

Even though the hotel was cheap and the dollar strong, the tenant students and writers had to get money from somewhere. One of the main forms of employment for impoverished Americans living on the Left Bank was writing pornography for Maurice Girodias's Olympia Press, an English-language publishing house producing books that would have been illegal if published in the United States or Britain.

About one third of the Traveller's Companion series in Olympia's catalog consisted of suppressed works of literature banned in Britain and America: Oscar Wilde's *Teleny*; J. P. Donleavy's *The Ginger Man*; Vladimir Nabokov's *Lolita*; Jean Genet's *The Thief's Journal*; Lawrence Durrell's *The Black Book*; Henry Miller's *Sexus*, *Plexus*, and *The World of Sex*; the Marquis de Sade's *Bedroom Philosophers*, *The 120 Days of Sodom, The Story of Juliette,* and *The Story of Justine; The Story of O* by Dominique Aury (a.k.a. Pauline Réage); the *Kama Sutra* and John Cleland's *Fanny Hill.* There were even a number of titles lacking in sex altogether, such as Raymond Queneau's *Zazie dans le Métro* and Samuel Beckett's *Molloy* and *Watt.* But to the visiting British and American tourists the distinctive green paperback wrappers of the Traveller's Companion series represented "pornography," and works of literature were snapped up indiscriminately and hidden away at the bottom of the suitcase alongside other Olympia titles like *Sin for Breakfast, Until She Screams,* and *With Open Mouth.*

Girodias referred to them as "DBs," or dirty books, and would often announce titles that did not yet exist in his catalog. If enough orders came in for a title, then he would commission one of his writers to produce it. Throughout the '50s and early '60s, Olympia produced over a hundred DBs, virtually all written under pseudonyms by Americans, a great many of whom were in some way connected to the Beat Hotel.

When tourists got fed up with literature and wanted more DBs, Girodias thoughtfully provided several more imprints for them, which he called the Atlantic Library, Othello Books, the Ophelia Press, and Ophir Books, all of which published titles refreshingly untainted by literary merit. Of these the Ophelia Press was the most grand, with titles such as *The Ordeal of the Rod, Iniquity, The English Governess, Under the Birch, Lust, Without Shame, The Whipping Club,* and *Whips Incorporated,* which left the reader in no doubt as to the subject matter of the books. Many dozens of writers were kept busy turning out DBs to suit all tastes.

The Left Bank's primary outlet for these titles was the English-language bookshop the Librairie Anglaise, at 42 rue de Seine. It was owned by a beautiful, petite Frenchwoman named Gaït Frogé who loved American writing and American writers. She was from Brittany and spoke English with a cultured British accent. The tiny shop was almost triangular, in a crooked sixteenth-century building at the intersection of the rue de Seine and the rue de l'Echaudé. The room was filled by a huge table that took up nearly the whole space, so it was very hard to walk around the shop. It was piled high with dusty self-published volumes of poetry and little literary magazines, a treasure trove for rare-book hunters.

Olympia Press books were Gaït's specialty and were best-sellers in her shop, but she kept few of them on the shelves, just enough to let customers know she had them. She never bothered to lock the door at night even though the little green-covered Traveller's Companion series and the more pornographic Ophelia Press editions were quite expensive and obvious targets for a shoplifter or nighttime thief. She kept most of them in a cupboard by the till, available upon request. The more literary Olympia titles, such as those Girodias published by William Burroughs, written during his years at the Beat Hotel, were often launched with publication parties at the shop, held in the tiny *cave*, the shop's medieval barrel-vaulted basement, with candles in wine bottles and rather damp walls. Girodias paid for the wine and invitation cards. When Charles Henri Ford and Parker Tyler's *The Young and Evil* was published by Olympia in June 1960 (though originally published in Paris in 1933 by Girodias's father), Gaït did a special display of photographs of the authors and filled the window with copies of the book.

The shop was cramped and overcrowded, books piled on other books, posters for exhibitions and readings filling the door and window, empty wineglasses balanced on wobbly piles of cheap American paperback thrillers, two-year-old copies of *Encounter* magazine shelved next to the latest slim volume from a local poet. Gaït lived above the shop, and customers often found the till unattended and the store silent but for the vigorous squeaking of the bedsprings upstairs. When Burroughs moved to Paris in 1958 Gaït became one of his greatest supporters. In 1960, when Two Cities, the publisher of *Minutes To Go*, could not afford to pay the print bill of $300, she took over the project, paid the bill, and launched the book from her shop. She also released a spoken-word album called *Call Me Burroughs*, produced by Ian Sommerville, on which Bill read from *Naked Lunch* and other later texts, recorded in her *cave*.

There were many Americans and Britons visiting or living in Paris in the late 1950s and early '60s, and they were well catered to by bookshops selling English-language titles. There was Stock on Place de Théâtre-Français; Brentano's on Avenue de l'Opéra; the five branches of Flammarion; and on the rue de Rivoli, Galignani and, ten doors down the street, the strictly conservative W. H. Smith's, where English tea was served. But all these sold mostly best-sellers and technical books to the large community of diplomatic and military residents; the younger literary and student crowds were catered to by the two English-language bookshops on the Left Bank, one of which was the Librairie Anglaise or English Bookshop (it was known by both equally). The other shop was the Mistral, at 37 rue de la Boucherie, another ancient building, situated across the Seine from Notre Dame and next door to the ruins of St.-Julien le Pauvre. Its proprietor, and consequently Gaït's archrival, George Whitman, was American, but had been in France since 1946 when he came over to work resettling war orphans. He drifted into bookselling, and in 1951 he bought the Mistral building with money from an inheritance, transforming what had been an Arab grocery into a combination bookshop, youth hostel, and social club. Upstairs he had a reading room with beds where visiting writers and poets were welcome to stay, free of charge, for up to a week and, like the Librairie Anglaise, the shop was used as a meeting place and mail drop by many of the expatriate Americans. Competition between the two shops was intense. Frogé claimed that Whitman was working for the CIA—"How else can you explain his long absences from the shop?—and she claimed that Whitman told people that she took drugs.

The English Bookshop was the more "literary" of the two, and the only one to sell Olympia Press books. Despite impassioned pleas from Girodias and arguments from Olympia's authors, Whitman refused to stock Olympia Press titles, perhaps fearing that he would encounter problems with the police. This was unlikely, as even Brentano's stocked Olympia titles; they had a discreetly hidden shelf of Traveller's Companions, and Americans always knew where it was. Many would enter the shop and head straight for it, ignoring all the other books.

The Mistral was much larger than the English Bookshop and had more room for poetry readings. The inhabitants of the Beat Hotel visited them both; they were about the same distance from the hotel. The Mistral was in the same direction as the Olympia Press and you could spend all day there, sitting around reading books, without George complaining, whereas the Librairie Anglaise was just a few doors from the Palette, on the corner of the rue de Seine and the rue Jacques-Callot, which in those days was a major hangout for drug dealers. Each excursion had its obvious advantages.

Many of the occupants of the Beat Hotel did not venture more than a few blocks from the rue Git-le-Coeur from one month to the next; virtually everything they needed was on hand. There were dozens of cheap restaurants within a few blocks and some of the residents had regular positions in them as guitar players or entertainers of some sort. The area was filled with jazz clubs and late-night cafés. The art college was two blocks away for those women in the hotel who worked as models, and most of the Americans who made their living street-selling the Paris edition of the *New York Herald Tribune* rarely strayed farther than Blvd St. Germain in their search for customers. Drugs were generally supplied to your door in the hotel, but were also easily obtainable from the Algerian and Moroccan cafés around the rue Saint Severin and from the Palette. The wonderful food market on the rue de Buci was a few minutes' walk, and late-night shopping was available on the rue de la Huchette. Here there was a grocery called Ali Baba where people from the hotel could buy food up to 2 A.M. for a late meal; the fruit displayed outside was protected from passing thieves by string netting. To many of the residents, the area seemed like paradise.

2 Kaddish

My hand writes now in a room in Paris Git-le-Coeur
                    Allen Ginsberg, "At Apollinaire's Grave"

On October 15, 1957, Allen Ginsberg, Peter Orlovsky, and Gregory
Corso arrived in Paris where Madame Rachou had a room waiting for
them at the Beat Hotel. They had been in Paris earlier in the summer
but the hotel was full; none of the other available hotels allowed cooking so they had decided to go to Amsterdam until a room became free.
The day they returned, there was a power strike. There was no gas or
electricity and the Metro was not running. Candles were selling on the
street for 35¢ each. Nonetheless they were happy to be back and to
settle at last at a fixed address after months of traveling. Allen, Peter,
and Gregory squeezed into room 32 on the top floor under the roof,
which leaked when it rained. They unpacked their knapsacks and
stowed their things in the armoire, which had two large drawers beneath its ornate mirrored door. They washed their nylon shirts and
woollen socks in the streaked sink, and Allen scrubbed his corduroy
jacket, stained from traveling. They hung the washing on the filthy
black window frame. There was a romantic view of medieval roofs and
chimneys of the rue Git-le-Coeur, and five buildings down, at the end
of the street, they could see the Seine with the row of booksellers along
the quai and, in the middle of the river, on the Ile de la Cité, the solid
towers of the Palais de Justice. A large gray bird "with rat's eyes" stared
in at them from the eaves. The poets were finally in a Paris artist's
garret. The bed had two mattresses, piled one atop the other, and it
sagged in the middle. There was a two-burner gas stove and a small

round table covered with oilcloth by the window. The discolored plaster walls were very thin and they had to be quiet after ten o'clock because the couple next door had to rise early and get to work.

Allen wrote, "Peter needs a shave. I need a bath. Gregory needs a new personality. The room needs a thicker wall—so we could yell at night and eat green butter on the wall. Is that a spider on the ceiling? A snail? A snail that leaves a silver track behind. Peter looks like a great lousy bum. But dont make great monstrous noise eating those snails lest the neighbors who work all morning wake and gnash thru the paperthinwall." Someone's radio could be heard playing from the plug-hole in the sink. Madame Rachou told Peter that when he boiled water he must open the window, otherwise the walls would get wet from the steam and fall in. She promised them a cheaper room in a week or so where they could make as much noise as they wanted. They bought cooking pots and pans and soon found the daily open-air market on the rue de Buci, a few streets away, with its inviting displays of seafood, fresh fruit, and meticulously arranged vegetables. Allen was the chef and made beef stew, beans, big pots of spaghetti, lentil soup, and steamed mussels. He claimed French mussels did not need cleaning. At night, the three slept together in the big groaning iron bed.

Within three days of getting back to Paris, Gregory had acquired an eighteen-year-old girlfriend and a long black cloak with a royal blue silk lining, which he wore when he went to meet her. Gregory had a talent for finding wealthy young women who were prepared to give him money, or at least enough to buy the groceries, so they never starved. With his Italian good looks he rather resembled a young Sinatra, and with his vehement proclamations of himself as a poet, young women found him an immensely attractive and romantic figure.

Gregory Corso had been the first among the Beats to reach Paris and he had had a fine time there. He left New York on February 24, 1957, on the *S.S. America*. One of his girlfriends, already in Paris, had discovered the great-grandson of Shelley (one assumes a number of "great"s were left out of this appellation), and Gregory hoped to meet him. In Paris Gregory quickly found where the writers and artists liked to meet and introduced himself. He met both Marlon Brando and Jean Genet this way. He and Genet had both been in jail as adolescents and had enough in common to develop a rapport, albeit a stormy one based largely on trading insults: Gregory would accuse Genet and the French in general of decadence and Genet would expiate his dislike of Americans and their inability to speak French. Genet enjoyed the friendly banter well enough to arrange for Gregory to stay in a friend's apartment for the summer, but when the friend returned he found that Gregory had painted pictures on the living room walls and threw him out. Allen wrote about the episode to Lawrence Ferlinghetti: "[Corso] says he sees Genet & had big argument with him about Gregory painting in oils on some friends apartment walls—so Genet insulted American boors & Gregory called him a frog creep, or some such Gregorian scene."

Despite being broke Gregory had made a number of trips out of town, including one to Nice, where he saw Picasso at the opening of an exhibition of Joan Miro's paintings. Gregory yelled at the artist in French, "I'm starving, I'm starving . . ." and got into a garbled conversation before being dragged away by Picasso's minders. He continued around the coast to Barcelona, where he somehow got ahold of a pistol. On his return to Paris he began waving his gun at the Americans sitting outside the Café aux Deux Magots, screaming, "Why did you all let me starve, you bastards?" The police arrested him as drunk and disorderly—which he was—and let him go the next morning.

Gregory was impetuous and gregarious, unimpressed by fame and status, and he had a forthright manner that people often found rude and intrusive. He saw poetry as his vocation, saving him from a life of crime. Gregory was a true New Yorker. He was born in 1930 in the heart of Greenwich Village above a funeral parlor at the corner of Bleecker and MacDougal Streets, which was then a part of Little Italy. He had no memory of his sixteen-year-old mother, who had abandoned him when he was a baby and was thought to have returned to the mountains of her native Lombardy. (They were finally reunited sixty years later.) His seventeen-year-old father felt unable to bring him up and Gregory was placed with a series of eight different foster parents, all over the city. When he was eleven years old his father remarried and took him back, but when the United States joined the war his father was drafted into the Navy. Gregory ran away from home a year later and lived on the streets. At one point in 1942 he was so hungry that he smashed the window of a restaurant and broke in, looking for food. He was caught on the way out, convicted of robbery, and sent to the notorious Tombs prison on Foley Square, a place with a terrifying reputation that was closed in 1947. Gregory later recalled, "I went there because I stole a radio . . . to TOMBS at the age of 12! For five months I stayed there, no air, no milk, and the majority were black and they hated the white and they abused me terribly, and I was indeed like an angel then because when they stole my food and beat me up and threw pee in my cell, I, the next day would come out and tell them my beautiful dream about a floating girl who landed before a deep pit and just stared."

When he was released, he still had nowhere to go. Cold and hungry, he broke into a youth center to sleep but was caught by the night watchman and sent straight back to the Tombs. Prison life was hard on the child and he fell ill. All the social services were stretched to the breaking point during the war, and the Tombs infirmary couldn't cope, so Gregory was sent to Bellevue Hospital to recover. Bellevue was overcrowded and understaffed. In the canteen one day Gregory flicked a piece of bread across the room, accidentally hitting a patient in the eye. In the uproar that followed, Gregory was placed in a straitjacket and held on the fourth floor for three months, among the seriously ill mental patients, until his health had recovered enough for him to be returned to the Tombs. When he was released he was fifteen years old, streetwise, tough, rebellious, and alone on the streets. "I lived with Irish on 99th and Lex, with Italians on 105th and 3rd, with two runaway Texans on 43rd etc.," he later wrote, "until 17th year when did steal and get three years in Clinton prison."

He was smart and one day he realized that walkie-talkies could be used to great advantage in robberies. He planned a heist and got away with it until one of the gang began spending too much money. Gregory was traced to Florida and, in 1947, he was given three years in the Clinton state prison in Dannemora, New York, up by the Canadian border. It was at Clinton that he discovered poetry and classical culture. He read voraciously, determined to educate himself. He started at the beginning with the classical era of the Greeks and Romans, which was to remain a significant influence upon his poetry. In fact, he later dedicated his book of poems *Gasoline* "to the angels of Clinton Prison who, in my 17th year, handed me, from all the cells surrounding me, books of illumination."

Gregory told biographer Neeli Cherkovski, "I had the best teachers. There were some guys in prison. I was seventeen when I went in and I was nineteen when I got out. You dig it? Those are big years. I was a problem in society. So you know what I got in Dannemora? Stendhal's *The Red and the Black* and my Shelley. That's a good thing in life to find Shelley when you're a kid, when they got you locked away for being a menace. . . . You make the time your own. I used it to get the literary gems. I even read the dictionary in jail and learned all the words." Using an enormous, turn-of-the-century dictionary, Gregory started at *A* and methodically learned all the words, even those described as archaic.

Gregory was released in 1950, just before his twentieth birthday, and he now regarded himself as a poet. He later reported, "Went home, stayed two days, left family forever, but returned at night to beg their forgiveness and retrieve my stamp collection." He got a job in the Garment District and shortly afterward he met Allen Ginsberg. A friend of Gregory's was working as an artist, drawing portraits for the customers in a lesbian bar called the Pony Stable on Third Street at Sixth Avenue in the Village. Gregory was visiting him there when Allen stopped by. Gregory had a big sheaf of poems with him and was telling everyone who would listen that he was a poet. This was a common occurrence in the Village at the time, but Ginsberg noticed that the poems were all professionally typed, which was unusual, and, since he was also sexually attracted to the young man with tousled hair and flashing black eyes, he went over and introduced himself.

Ginsberg was surprised to find that the poems were good. There was one—now lost—that contained a line that Allen always remembered: "The stone world came to me, and said Flesh gives you an hour's life." Allen was impressed and began talking excitedly about his friends, who were also writers. They exchanged life stories and Allen asked him about his sex life. Gregory told him of a fantasy he had about one of his neighbors. He was living in a small furnished attic room on West 12th Street off Sixth Avenue and from his vantage point he was able to see everything that went on in the apartment of a young woman on the fourth floor of an apartment building opposite. He would masturbate as he watched her undress in front of her mirror, take a bath, use the toilet, and make love to her boyfriend, who visited every night. Gregory fantasized about crossing the street, knocking on her door, and introducing himself.

Allen was astonished because, as he heard the details of Gregory's story, he realized that it was his girlfriend, Dusty Moreland, that he was describing and that the boyfriend was himself. "You want me to introduce you?" Allen asked, mysteriously. "I have magical powers." The next day he took Gregory to meet her. Gregory later commented, "My first lay when I got out of prison."

Allen took him to meet Jack Kerouac and introduced him as a poet. "What's poetry?" asked Kerouac. "Everything," Gregory replied. Allen also took him to visit Mark Van Doren, a Pulitzer Prize–winning English professor with whom he'd studied at Columbia University, whom Allen still regarded as a sage and referred to as "The Chinaman." Gregory was overjoyed to be taken seriously as a poet and basked in the attention Allen was giving him. Gregory later wrote, "Through him I first learned about contemporary poesy, and how to handle myself in an uninstitutional society, as I was very much the institutional being. Beyond the great excited new joyous talks we had about poetry, he was the first gentle person and dear friend to me."

In 1952 Gregory struck out by himself and went to Los Angeles, where he landed a job with the *Los Angeles Examiner*, cub reporting once a week and working in the file morgue the rest of the time. Seven months later, perhaps inspired by stories told by Kerouac and Ginsberg, who had both served time in the Merchant Marine, Gregory shipped out on the Norwegian Line to South America and Africa. When he returned to Greenwich Village he stayed on and off in Ginsberg's Lower East Side apartment; by this time Corso had become a core member of the Beat Generation. In 1954, with Ginsberg away in Mexico, Gregory's girlfriend, Violet Lang, took him to Cambridge, Massachusetts, where fifty students from Harvard and Radcliffe clubbed together to raise the money to publish his first book of poems, *The Vestal Lady on Brattle*, in 1955. In addition he continued to build a name for himself as a poet by publishing in literary magazines such as the *Harvard Advocate* and the *Cambridge Review.*

Gregory was twenty-seven when he arrived in Paris for the summer of 1957. He had gone from Cambridge to San Francisco where Ginsberg was having great success with his poem "Howl," and went with him and Orlovsky to Mexico City to join Kerouac for the summer of 1956. When he got to Paris he was working on the final selection of poems for a new book called *Gasoline* to be published by Ferlinghetti in the same City Lights Books Pocket Poets series as Ginsberg's *Howl and other Poems.* Although he was constantly broke and living off his various girlfriends, Corso's years at the Beat Hotel would prove a very creative period, during which he would write much of his best work.

Gregory was followed to Europe by Jack Kerouac. Jack had left New York before him, on February 15, but had gone first to Tangier to meet up with William Burroughs. Jack was not very good out of America. By 1957 he was an alcoholic and spent his time living in the outer suburbs of New York with his mother. He had already written most of the books upon which his fame would rest—*On the Road; The Subterraneans; Doctor Sax; Visions of Cody; Visions of Gerard; Mexico City Blues*—but had yet to find a publisher for them. Though he was convinced of his own genius, he was growing progressively more disillusioned as the years passed and his talent remained unrecognized. The furor surrounding Ginsberg's "Howl" had encouraged Jack into thinking that their group might finally be discovered and also made him jealous of Allen's success. He did not have long to wait before *On the Road* was published, bringing him both fame and unwelcome notoriety.

Jack, Allen, Peter, and Gregory had planned to go first to Tangier to help Bill organize and type the manuscript of *The Naked Lunch* (published in the United States as *Naked Lunch* and forthwith referred to without the article), and then the four of them, excluding Burroughs, would spend the summer exploring Europe just as they had spent the previous summer together in Mexico City. Burroughs himself had no interest in exploring Europe. He had been living in Tangier since 1953, and had in any case traveled widely in Europe before the war, first visiting France in 1929 with his family and later studying medicine in Vienna. For the others it was their first time and they were anxious to see everything.

Jack had disliked the primitive sanitary arrangements and the foreign food in Mexico City and it had taken a lot of persuading to get him to make the trip to Morocco. He disliked Tangier for the same reasons and complained bitterly when he found that Arab whores cost $3 when he had been used to paying only 10¢ in Mexico. He was frightened of the Arabs, despite Burroughs's assurances that no one had run amok for months. Jack experienced a sudden homesickness for America, for Wheaties at breakfast and a kitchen smelling of pine cleaner. Most of all he wanted to see his mother. He abandoned his plan to explore Europe with the others and made a perfunctory trip to Paris and London before sailing back to the United States with the intention of getting a small house in the Bay Area, somewhere close to San Francisco, and living there with his mother.

During his few nights in Paris, Jack met up with Gregory, who was then living with a French girl named Nicole. Jack spent one night in their room, unable to sleep for the sound of their lovemaking, but the next night Nicole's concierge refused to allow Jack to stay. The Beats had not yet discovered the Beat Hotel and Jack never did stay there, despite reports to the contrary in various Kerouac biographies. Gregory, as usual, was starving and made the notoriously parsimonious Jack pay for drinks and food, something Jack complained of bitterly to his friends afterward. Gregory later wrote Jack, contesting his allegations: "I dint get you drunk and make you spend 5 thousand francs because when I first met you you were drunk sitting at Bonaparte in fact whenever I met you you were drunk, yes, drunk, and now you are trying to blame your drunkenness on me! Why must everybody blame everything on me? But I will announce to the world of dream that you lied when you said that I made you drunk! I did not make you drunk! You made yourself drunk! True, I did encourage you to spend a lot of money on food for me, but why not? I deserve to eat! Have I not devoted my entire life to beauty? Thus should I not eat? Should I not at least on straw sleep?"

Meanwhile, Allen Ginsberg and Peter Orlovsky made their departure from Manhattan on March 8, like Jack on a Yugoslavian freighter, going first to Tangier via Casablanca to see Burroughs. But already the plan to recreate Mexico City was not working out. Jack returned to America shortly after Allen and Peter arrived in Tangier and Gregory was already in Paris. So Allen and Peter left Burroughs in Tangier and made their way to Venice, where they stayed with poet Alan Ansen, an old friend from New York. Ansen was a tall, heavy man with a manic laugh and effeminate mannerisms. He graduated summa cum laude from Harvard, an astonishingly erudite classics scholar, quoting Herodotus in Greek, Tacitus in Latin, and referring familiarly to Goethe. He had been W. H. Auden's secretary and had known Ginsberg since 1948 when he was a part of the San Remo bar crowd in the Village. He moved to Venice in 1953 in search of the cheapest European country with the most available boys. Ansen was to become a Beat supporter in the wings: offering accommodation, secretarial help, occasional financial assistance, and writing laudatory reviews of their work (his essay "Anyone Who Can Pick Up a Frying Pan Owns Death" in the first issue of *Big Table* in 1959 was not only the first on Burroughs's work but remains one of the best).

Ansen would recall Ginsberg and Orlovsky's stay with some amusement: "Peter and Allen drove Peggy Guggenheim from the flat by tossing a dirty towel, which hit her by mistake, and almost did the same with a young Dutch painter, Guy Harloff, by showing off with Paul Goodman in manic mood expatiating on the joys of the Lido dunes. It was Harloff who introduced them to 9, rue Git-le-Coeur, later famous as the Paris Beat Hotel." Harloff was already living at the Beat

Hotel and recommended it to Allen as somewhere cheap and perfectly located in the Latin Quarter, where they could cook in their room and where the landlady turned a blind eye to drugs and unusual sexual behavior.

Allen immediately wrote to Gregory, asking him to reserve a room for them. But the hotel was full of Americans visiting Europe for the summer and he was told that he could come back in a month when something would be available. Since Gregory could not afford a regular hotel, and had managed to antagonize a fair number of people by bouncing checks and owing back rent, he set off for Amsterdam, leaving a letter at the American Express office for Allen and Peter, who were arriving in Paris shortly, explaining that the room would not be available until October 15, and that in the meantime they should join him in Holland.

On September 16, 1957, Ginsberg and Orlovsky arrived in Paris from Italy. There was little in their outward appearance to indicate that here were two notorious members of the Beat Generation. Unlike the weekend beatniks wandering the streets of Greenwich Village in goatees and sandals, carrying a pair of bongos in one hand and *Howl* in the other, Allen and Peter looked like the thousands of other young people who were then roaming across Europe with rucksacks. Their hair was a little long by the standards of the time in that it nearly reached their collars, but they were clean-shaven and, though not wearing ties, wore perfectly normal hard-wearing work clothing. It was Allen's eyes that set him apart; people often comment on how intense Ginsberg's stare was in those days, his large brown eyes absorbing everything. Allen and Peter were gregarious, always talking to strangers, asking questions, inquisitive, anxious to hear someone's life story or the history of an old building. People sometimes found the intensity of Allen's inquiries a little off-putting, but Peter's friendly good nature, with his high Russian cheekbones, big smile, and quirky sense of humor, usually relaxed them and they were welcomed by most of the people they met.

Allen had always wanted to see Paris and it lived up to his expectations. He wrote his father, "Just got here—greatest scene in

Europe for sure. May take short trip a few days to Amsterdam and return—places to live hard to find here, I'm not settled yet, sleeping in RR stations and hotels." Allen and Peter spent their first night on a bench in the Gare de l'Est. Allen slept fitfully and woke to scribble a few lines: "Waking all night / I wrote out these doublets / Six o'clock six o'clock / the RR station gets noisy."

They eventually located a hotel room for 700 francs ($1.75) a night for them both near the Place Pigalle—more than they were hoping to pay but they made up the difference by finding cheap restaurants. After two nights they found another hotel at the same price on the Left Bank overlooking the great façade of Notre Dame and the bookstalls along the Seine. In the meantime, Allen saw as much of Paris as he could on limited funds. He spent several days in the Louvre and took in all the tourist sites, writing to Kerouac, "We went up Eiffel Tower, beautiful dream machine in sky—greater than I imagined." In his role as literary agent for his friends, he also ran a few errands. One of these was to deliver the manuscript of Burroughs's *Interzone* to the Olympia Press. This was the working title of the book we now know as *Naked Lunch*, but when Maurice Girodias saw the condition of the manuscript he was not impressed. Girodias stated, "It was such a mess that manuscript! You couldn't physically read the stuff, but whatever caught the eye was extraordinary and dazzling. So I returned it to Allen saying, 'Listen, the whole thing has to be reshaped.' The ends of the pages were all eaten away by the rats or something . . . Allen was very angry at me."

Allen also contacted Bernard Frechtman, the translator of Jean Genet's books and Genet's onetime literary agent, who had been given a copy of the *Interzone* manuscript by Kerouac when he'd passed through Paris a few months earlier. Frechtman had translated the work of Antonin Artaud and other Surrealist work and later got to know Burroughs, but he had not been very impressed by Kerouac, who was probably drunk when he went to see him. Jack was irritated at Frechtman's response, partly because he had carried the heavy manuscript all the way to Paris from Tangier. He wrote to his friend John Clellon Holmes, "NO ONE wants anything to do with it not even Bernard Frechtman (translator of Genet) to whom I took it in my ruck-sack in Paris." Frechtman received Allen cordially enough, but despite having had possession of Bill's manuscript for more than three months, the only part he had read was "The Word" chapter, which he had not liked. Allen was disgusted and took the manuscript back, yet Frechtman later became a friend and often dropped by the hotel. He was living in Genet's old apartment, and during their meeting Allen looked around with ill-disguised curiosity.

Allen and Peter visited Guy Harloff at the Beat Hotel and it looked absolutely ideal. Harloff arranged for them to meet Madame Rachou and she confirmed that a room with a stove would be free on October 15, which was a month from then. Since none of the other hotels with vacancies would allow them to cook, they decided to visit Gregory in Amsterdam, and return when their room was ready.

Kerouac's *On the Road* was published on September 5, 1957; someone showed Allen Gilbert Millstein's review in the *New York Times*, which heaped extravagant praise upon the book and was to make Kerouac famous. Previously Jack had been grumbling to Allen that people kept introducing him as "the guy that Ginsberg's 'Howl' is dedicated to," but now he had fame of his own to contend with. Allen wrote him, "We saw *Times* Sept 5 review, I almost cried, so fine & true—well now you don't have to worry about existing only in my dedication & I will have to weep in your great shadow—what is happening in N.Y.—are you being pursued—is there a great mad wave of Fame crashing over your ears?"

Kerouac was being pursued mercilessly and the hangers-on and groupies accelerated his alcoholic decline. The problem was that people expected him to be like Dean Moriarty, the book's hero, a pool-hall hustler, womanizer, and car thief who could charm the pants off anyone and often did. But the Moriarty character was not Kerouac, of course, but a portrait of his friend Neal Cassady, with whom Kerouac was obsessed. Jack envied his easy way with women, his wide-eyed cowboy good looks, and his superb handling of an automobile. Though he bore a striking resemblance to Cassady and was handsome in the classic brooding manner of the era's film stars, Kerouac held an unfavorable view of himself as a short, stocky, hairy, thick peasant. His strict Catholic upbringing had made him ashamed of his body and shy and uneasy with women. While Jack attempted to deal with his newfound fame by drinking and carousing, Allen and Peter were preparing to join Gregory in Amsterdam.

The poets spent their last night in Paris, until 7 A.M., wandering around Les Halles, looking at the meat market, astonished by the indifference with which butchers in bloodstained aprons carried huge trays of livers or staggered by with half-carcasses of beef on their backs, the whole noisy nighttime spectacle watched over by the Gothic magnificence of the church of St. Eustache. Allen wrote a long description of the scene in his journals, which he called "Apocalypse at Les Halles": "Carts full of lungs carts full of liver carts full of hearts / Carts full of heads / The lungs shaking and quivering . . ."

They took the first train of the day to the Netherlands to join Gregory, going first to Rotterdam, where they explored and went to museums before continuing on to Amsterdam. There they slept on a huge carpet on Gregory's floor on Reijnier Vinkeleskade, on the Amstel Canal in the southern part of the city. He had a large steam-heated room so they were very comfortable. It was another city for Allen and Peter to explore and they rushed from the Rembrandthuis to the Rijksmuseum to the Stedelijk Museum, admiring the northern Renaissance visions of Vermeer and Rembrandt and the blazing light and energy in the art of van Gogh; by Peter's count, they saw 105 van Goghs. They walked the humpback bridges and quiet canals lined with weeping willows and seventeenth-century houses. Food was cheap; a large roast beef sandwich, cheese, and beer totaled 12 cents. Virtually everyone spoke English and Gregory had already made contact with the art and literary scenes. They spent long nights talking and smoking pot in the student bars and bohemian cafés with poets and editors of literary magazines.

Allen, Peter, and Gregory met the poet Simon Vinkenoog in the Bohemia jazz club after a friend of Vinkenoog's told him that he must go and meet these American poets. Simon became a lifelong friend of Ginsberg, and in 1965 translated "Howl" into Dutch while in the Utrecht House of Detention for six weeks on a marijuana charge. He was the editor of *Podium* magazine and was a friend of Jackson Pollock and Robert Lowell. Now he wanted to publish the Beats. Simon, tall and thin, with striking blond hair and boundless energy, strode the streets looking like the character Victor Lazlo from *Casablanca*. In the course of the day, he would buy all the quality daily papers from France, Germany, Britain, and Holland, and, like a true European, sit faultlessly translating from Dutch or German to English, exclaiming and denouncing, buying another paper to see what the French thought about it.

It didn't take Allen and Peter long to find the red-light district in Amsterdam Centrum. Allen had a very rosy view of it when he described it to Kerouac: "Huge red light district neat & clean & quiet— girls sit like mannequins in windows, like Dutch dolls in dollhouses, on ground floor, windows bright & clean, they sit in chairs & cross legs & knit quietly waiting for customers on quiet streets—whole blocks & blocks of girls in bright ground floor windows—like a heaven—and they don't yell at you or grab your arm—just go on with knitting— Neal would go mad." Prostitution was legal in Holland, and conditions in the Amsterdam red-light district were better than most, but many of the girls were still controlled by pimps and their lives were often desperately sad.

Peter was pleased to see these women in windows because he was beginning to think there was no sex in Europe. He had been unable to pick up a girl in any of the cities they had visited so far; however, he and Allen did go to a whorehouse in Venice and he and Jack went with some whores in Tangier. Peter couldn't wait to settle in Paris and concentrate on finding a girlfriend. Though Peter was Allen's "wife," as Ginsberg sometimes called him, his preference was for women. His fantasies were always of women, even when he was in bed with Allen, and throughout his and Allen's long relationship, Peter usually had a girlfriend who lived with them. They both felt that sex was a way of spreading love and believed in having as many sex partners as possible, often by organizing orgies. This was an aspect of the Beat Generation philosophy that was picked up later by the hippies in their quest for sexual freedom.

As Ginsberg traveled Europe, back in San Francisco *Howl and Other Poems* had been seized May 21, 1957 by the police as obscene, and his publisher, Lawrence Ferlinghetti, taken to court. The American Civil Liberties Union took up the case and there seemed little doubt as to a favorable outcome. The case hinged on whether or not the poem was protected by the constitutional guarantee of freedom of speech despite its containing a few so-called obscene words. All literary San Francisco was buzzing.

At first Allen had written to Ferlinghetti with lots of suggestions for publicity and support for the trial, but everyone in San Francisco was so excited and busy that they neglected to keep him informed and he never knew if his suggestions had been taken up, to whom he should write, or what articles had appeared in the press. At first he went daily to the American Express office in Paris to look for news, and pored over *Time* and *Newsweek* for reports, but he was too far away to play any kind of active role, and the trial became very unreal for him. Ferlinghetti did write him from time to time, and his old girlfriend Sheila Boucher sent him information. Meanwhile, all the press attention caused *Howl* to sell and sell and, by the end of the trial, Ferlinghetti had gone back to press three times and had over 10,000 copies in print.

Mail took some time to reach him from California but Allen assumed that all was well and wrote his father, Louis, "I haven't heard news of the Trial recently, perhaps it's over now. *Time* is supposed to have a story soon." He was pleased to be distanced from the affair, knowing that had he been there it would have taken up every waking hour of his day. City Lights's lawyer Jake Ehrlich had decided to use local expert testimony and brought forward a succession of literary figures to testify to the literary merit of the work. He presented Mark Schorer and Leo Lowenthal from the University of California at Berkeley; Walter Van Tilburg Clark, Herbert Blau, and Arthur Foff, all from San Francisco State College, as well as poet Kenneth Rexroth, novel-

ist Vincent McHugh, *San Francisco Examiner* book editor Luther
Nichols, even a literary adviser to the U.S. Army.

There had been some concern when Judge W. J. Clayton Horn
was appointed to preside because he had recently achieved a certain
notoriety by sentencing five women shoplifters to watch the movie *The
Ten Commandments* and requiring them to write him an essay on what
they had learned from the film. But Judge Horn's handling of the case
was exemplary; he read all the relevant case histories, including the
trial of James Joyce's *Ulysses*, and identified the constitutional aspects
of the case, namely that to be considered obscene the book had to be
shown to have no redeeming social importance whatsoever.

It was in Amsterdam that Allen heard Judge Horn's verdict. On
October 4 the judge had pronounced *Howl* to be not obscene. Judge
Horn said, "I do not believe that 'Howl' is without redeeming social
importance. The first part of 'Howl' presents a picture of a nightmare
world; the second part is an indictment of those elements in modern
society destructive of the best qualities of human nature; such elements
are predominantly identified as materialism, conformity, and mecha-
nization leading toward war. The third part presents a picture of an
individual who is a specific representation of what the author conceives
as a general condition. 'Footnote to Howl' seems to be a declamation
that everything in the world is holy, including parts of the body by
name. It ends with a plea for holy living. . . . The theme of 'Howl' presents 'unorthodox and controversial ideas.' Coarse and vulgar language
is used in treatment and sex acts are mentioned but unless the book is
entirely lacking in 'social importance' it cannot be held obscene." He
concluded, "In considering material claimed to be obscene it is well to
remember the motto: *Honi soit qui mal y pense*," and found the de-
fendants not guilty.

Allen was naturally delighted with the decision, though it was not
unexpected, and wrote to Ferlinghetti asking if there was anyone he
should write thank-you letters to, and thanking him for all his trouble.
Allen enclosed a huge list of people who would run articles on the
decision and who could be prevailed upon to review City Lights's books,
since it was now a famous publisher.

Whenever he settled anywhere for more than a few days, Ginsberg was immediately busy, writing and receiving dozens of letters each week. One of his tasks in Amsterdam was dealing with *Evergreen Review*. *Evergreen* was about to publish his long poem about Mexico, "Siesta in Xbalba," and had also released a spoken-word album on its Evergreen Records label, containing an extract from "Howl," read by Allen. It was a poor reading and Allen was ashamed of it. Ferlinghetti did a deal with Fantasy Records in Berkeley to release an entire album of Allen reading his poems and had made arrangements for him to record it in a studio in Paris. While in Holland, Allen also continued in his role of literary agent. In the past he had been responsible for the publication of Kerouac's first book, *The Town and the City*, and for getting Burroughs's first book, *Junkie*, published. He had a great belief in the genius of his friends and was indefatigable in his promotion of their work.

In Amsterdam he dealt with Ferlinghetti and City Lights on the matter of proofs, cover copy, and the selection of poems for Gregory's second book of poems, *Gasoline*. As soon as he arrived in Amsterdam he wrote asking Ferlinghetti for a list of the poems to be included so that he could write an introduction, and asked for all unused poems to be returned to him. He praised Ferlinghetti for publishing the book in the face of opposition from many of the San Francisco poets who disliked Gregory's manner: "I know everybody puts Gregory down there and am glad you dont, I am amazed by his genuine genius & originality. . . . Gregory says right color for *Gasoline* cover is bright solid red letters on white background. Have you used this already? (Red border?, white label like mine, red letters on label) Is it possible to get a red explosive & solid like an Esso sign?"

Allen wrote to Kerouac for a cover note for Corso to accompany his introduction, saying, "We unite & give him send off—for he is sure to be generally put down unless people are *made* to dig him. Everybody in S.F. according to Ferl puts him down as a 'showman' & for that reason Ferl won't even publish 'Power.'" The poem "Power" was a matter of some contention between Ginsberg and Ferlinghetti. Ginsberg regarded it as Corso's greatest poem. Ferlinghetti, however, thought that it could be construed as fascist, particularly by the San Francisco literati, and refused to include it in the book. Allen was convinced that Ferlinghetti was wrong and cunningly got around Ferlinghetti's prohibition by quoting extensively from "Power" in his introduction, pointedly describing it as "unpublished." (It was subsequently published by New Directions in Corso's next book, *The Happy Birthday of Death.*)

Kerouac responded positively with a blurb, saying Gregory "rose like an angel over the rooftops and sang Italian songs as sweet as Caruso and Sinatra, but in *words.* 'Sweet Milanese hills' brood in his Renaissance soul, evening is coming on the hills."

Autumn was closing in and, after two weeks in Benelux, Allen, Peter, and Gregory boarded a train at Amsterdam Central Station; soon the canals and old houses gave way to low green fields, drainage ditches, and cows under the huge sky of south Holland, where everything was still and green except the windmills turning furiously in the breeze.

Once they were settled in the Beat Hotel they began to explore Paris. They took the funicular railway up to Sacre Coeur at dusk and looked out over Paris from the terrace as the lights blinked on all over the city, then wandered back down through the narrow streets of Montmartre, past its tiny vineyard on the rue St. Vincent and its cafés and squares. They often visited nearby Notre Dame just across the Seine to marvel over the rose windows. They found that smoking pot gave an increased intensity to the color of the north rose, which is mostly of blue stained glass dating from 1270, and depicts the Virgin surrounded by concentric circles of Prophets, Kings, Judges, and Patriarchs. They walked beneath the flying buttresses, squatting like spider's legs around the nave, and paid the old lady in the ticket office a few francs to climb the tower to see Viollet-le-Duc's gargoyles. Gregory wrote a poem about them: ". . . It's the way they're placed / Outstretched gargy necks / screammouthed haunched pensivity . . ."

They went to Sainte-Chapelle to see the shocking brilliance of the blue stained glass. They visited the Rodin Museum and returned repeatedly to the Louvre but, before they could embark on serious museum-going, Allen came down with Asian flu and spent almost two weeks in bed with a bad cough, taking sleeping pills to try and rest. They ran out of money but were saved by a check for ten dollars sent by Allen's father and a loan from Gregory's girlfriend. Eventually Peter's monthly Veterans Administration pension money came through and they were able to pay the rent. Peter had been discharged from the army for mental instabilility; he called his pension his "mad money."

Peter's enjoyment of exploring Paris with Allen was marred by disturbing news from his mother concerning his brother Lafcadio. His family had a history of mental illness and his elder brother, Julius, was in a mental hospital. Lafcadio, his younger brother, often behaved very strangely but Peter was determined that he should not be confined to a hospital. Allen and Peter had looked after Lafcadio in San Francisco and had taken him with them to Mexico City the previous summer, though whether he was aware that he had even left the States is debatable. When Allen and Peter left New York for Tangier, Lafcadio went back to Northport, Long Island, to live with his mother and twin sister, Marie. He made one attempt to live independently, in July, when he moved back to the city to live with Allen's ex-girlfriend Elise Cowen at her apartment on East 4th Street, but that didn't work out, and Elise, who was herself mentally unstable, left for the West Coast.

Lafcadio moved back home to the converted chicken-coop where the Orlovsky family lived, but Katherine, his mother, found it increasingly difficult to cope with him. During one argument he hit her and she retaliated by throwing a large metal bottle opener at him, which cut his arm almost to the bone. Peter worried that Lafcadio was going to end up in the mental hospital with Julius and decided that he had to return and look after his mad family: protect his mother and sister, be the older brother that Lafcadio needed, and try to get Julius out of Central Islip Hospital where he had lived for six years. Allen remembered Peter's waking up one morning in late November, weeping and saying, "Julius is in the hospital and I can't just leave him there and enjoy myself here, stay around the world enjoying myself. I've been away a year already."

Neither Allen nor Peter had enough money for Peter's boat fare, but Allen was owed $225 by Kerouac, who had borrowed Allen's merchant seaman savings in order to get to Tangier. Now that *On the Road* was a best-seller, Jack was due to receive a big royalty check, yet though he knew of Peter's dilemma he was loath to send any money to Allen before it arrived in case he ran short himself. To Allen's irritation he kept mentioning the money in his letters but never sending it. His latest letter told Allen that he would pay him in January when his next royalties came through. Peter went to the U.S. Embassy to apply for a Veterans Administration loan. They forwarded the paperwork to the appropriate people, but warned him that it might take several months to complete the process.

The summer visitors had left and, as promised, Madame Rachou moved Allen and Peter to a better room. They were given room 25, on the third floor, next door to Guy Harloff, the painter who was responsible for getting them into the hotel. A Dutchman who held an American passport, Harloff was over six feet tall with long black hair slicked back with hair cream. If he was not painting, he read Henry Miller and had loud drunken arguments with his girlfriend, Sharon Walsh, sometimes breaking the furniture. But he was kind to Allen and Peter and often gave them food; on the day they arrived he presented them with a pound of English bacon and a packet of English butter. Peter was impressed with his style, writing to the poet Ron Loewinsohn that Harloff "always has girls at candlelight night in bed and cooks good food." Harloff came from a well-off Dutch family who provided him with a generous allowance, which was why Madam Rachou was prepared to give him credit at the bar and allow him to owe back rent.

When Burroughs arrived in 1958, Harloff spent a lot of time trying to convince him of the virtues of Communism with little discernible effect. Burroughs said of Harloff, "He was always putting on this proletariat act, 'We impoverished artists,' and all this crap. I noticed he had credit all around the quarter. His parents turned out to be very wealthy. He was well provided for. So that was just an act. The French people don't extend credit unless you have the means. His paintings looked like cigar bands. People used to collect cigar bands, oh yes, they're quite pretty, with all that gilt. Well that's exactly what they looked like. Some of them were huge."

The new room was a great improvement. It appeared to have changed little since the nineteenth century, though the walls were considerably older than that. To reach it, they first took a gas-lit staircase, which in turn led to an eighteenth-century staircase, and finally reached a set of rooms that were probably originally used by well-to-do people who lived far from Paris and who would take them for a few months at a time when they visited the capital. Room 25 was in the front of the hotel and had two windows with long drapes overlooking the street. The walls were whitewashed. There was a big bed, a large wardrobe with a built-in mirror, a sink, and a worktable. It was one of the few rooms in the hotel to have a gas range. They stowed away their knapsacks and unpacked their clothes; Allen took his red portable Royal typewriter from its carrying case, arranged his piles of notebooks and manuscripts on the worktable, and, tacking his portrait of Rimbaud to the wall, he made himself at home.

The coverage of the *Howl* trial in *Life* magazine stimulated a great deal of journalistic interest in the Beat Generation but it was the publication of Jack's *On the Road* in September that really caused the press furor over the Beats. In addition to the attacks from the literary establishment and articles in the popular press equating them with juvenile delinquents, there was great interest in the writing they were producing. Allen got the first inkling that he might be able to not only get by but actually make a living as a writer. That summer in Venice there had been a check for $100 from City Lights, his first royalty payment on *Howl*. Because of the trial, the third edition of 2,500 had sold out and Ferlinghetti had ordered a fourth printing, which meant that Allen could expect a further royalty check of between $100 and $200. He was also receiving money from *Evergreen Review*, *Partisan Review* had paid him for two poems, and Citadel Press wanted to include "Howl" in an anthology of Beat writing. His brother, Eugene, and his father sent him small sums to tide him over until his next royalty check, and Bill Burroughs promised to send him something. Allen thought that he could survive in Paris until Christmas at that rate, which was when Kerouac, in theory, was to pay back the $225. Meanwhile, Peter had his regular $50 a month from the V.A.

Jack wrote from New York to say that both Viking Press and Grove Press wanted to publish *Howl and Other Poems* in hardback. In Jack's opinion *Howl* needed proper distribution because "It had not even begun to be read." Even though City Lights could not afford to capitalize on the trial or place ads to tell people where they could get the book, Allen decided to stay with the small press that had taken the risk to publish him in the first place. All the publicity over *Howl* and the Beats led to a huge volume of mail, so that at the beginning of September, before the trial was even over, Allen complained to his father, "Correspondence mounts and is being a bad problem now. Too much publicity at this point. I'm beginning to think 'Howl' too slight to support so great a weight of bull." In the same letter he sent his father the clover leaf he had picked at Shelley's grave in Rome, "Just like any clover anywhere I guess—I cried when I saw Keats' stone tho . . ."

Ginsberg's correspondence with his father, Louis, ranged over a wide variety of issues, and always included long descriptions of the places he visited as well as comments on political issues of the day. His views on the launch of the Russian Sputnik on October 4, 1957, for example, were interpreted by Louis as being pro-Russian. Allen wrote, "Sputnik I & II greatest story since discovery of fire has everybody here delighted. The side issue of America taking the Fall finally is too bad but seems inevitable, like the future is not ours, American, any more, as we used to think." And in his journals Allen wrote, "It seems unimportant that it be America to surpass the earth, to moon, now that Russia has begun—As if America already had betrayed its promise of great spiritual victory—so now already's beggared materialistically. What promise? To lead world to Fraternal Freedom full of comradely hip judgement. With this we surpass in poetry, to enrich world." But as a socialist who firmly rejected Communism, Louis felt that Allen should be upset that Russia was leading the space race. As

Louis got older, he became more conservative politically, and their correspondence was often heated. However, much of it was good-natured argument concerning poetry, line length, Williams, and Whitman.

In September, Louis asked Allen about his identity as a Jew, pointing out that Allen had investigated virtually every religion except the one that was his cultural heritage. Allen replied that he did not like being regarded as a "Jewish" poet. In later years, he would avoid, whenever possible, being interviewed by Jewish magazines or appearing in anthologies of Jewish poets. In answer to Louis's letter he said, "I tend not to want to identify myself with Judaism (I mean, nor with Buddhism either). This because it gives me a theoretical abstract identity, other than the actual self, or no-self, that I am. In other words, I'm not really a Jew any more than I am a Poet. Sure I'm both. But there is a nameless wildness—life itself—which is deeper. I dig Buddha doctrinally (and some Hassidistic sayings which are similar to Zen sayings) because he realizes, says, all conceptions of the self which limit the self to a fixed identity are obviously arbitrary—and lead to illusory conflict. . . . But as with Buddhism, Judaism also seems bound & fixed to old institutional anachronisms, which have become rule and organisation, to which I feel unsympathetic. Dietary restrictions, some conceptions of eye for eye justice, Grandma pinching Eugene, a closing down of selfhood into doctrinal Judaism rather than an opening of self into nameless wildness—soul is soul, neither Jewish nor Buddhist. So finally it even begins dawning on me to stop thinking of myself as an American. And often in the dead of night I wonder who this fiction named Allen Ginsberg is—it certainly isn't me." Ginsberg was later to revise this opinion and, from the early 1970s, he declared himself a Buddhist.

Allen began to investigate French poetry and found that his command of French had improved considerably in the short time they had been in the country. At the Gallerie La Hune bookshop on Blvd. St. Germain he discovered works by poets associated with the Cubist and Surrealist movements: Max Jacob, Robert Desnos, Pierre Reverdy, Henri Pichette, Léon-Paul Fargue, Blaise Cendrars, and Jacques Prévert. He told Kerouac, "All personal and alive . . . I want to improve French & dig them, none translated, and all fine fellows, I can see from the pages of loose sprawled longlined scribblings they've published for 50 years." He was amazed to find that there were books and pamphlets by Vladimir Mayakovski and Sergei Essenin translated into French that were as yet unknown in English, and believed the former was a particularly great writer. He wrote to Louis recommending him as "a major world poet like Lorca or Eliot—first great voice of the new Oriental age to come."

Allen ran a few errands for Ferlinghetti, who wanted to publish a book of poems by Jacques Prévert in translation but had been unable to get permission. Allen offered to visit Prévert's representative and was astonished at the difference between Prévert's agent and the literary agents he knew in New York. The office was on the Ile Saint Louis in a sixteenth-century *hotel privée.* A maid in a black dress showed him into the book-lined study of the respectable elderly lady in charge, who was playing with her poodle. Allen made four visits, and though the lady was charming and courteous, nothing ever seemed to get done and Ferlinghetti still did not receive the letters he was expecting. Eventually the matter was sorted out and *Paroles* by Jacques Prévert was published as number nine in the Pocket Poets series, the volume following Gregory's *Gasoline.*

It did not take long for Allen, Peter, and Gregory to discover that the heroin in Paris was better than what they could get in Mexico or with Bill Burroughs in New York. The main connection in the hotel was a man called Hadj, a name that meant that he had made the pilgrimage to Mecca. He was popular because he offered a very good deal. Allen told Jack, "So pure horse we sniff it, simply sniff, no ugly vaginal needles, & get as good almost a bang as main line, but longer lasting and stronger in long run." Pot was easy to get and very cheap—"for Louvre visits."

Every building and street was a delight to Allen, who was an inveterate museum-goer and sightseer. He loved the shabby sixteenth-century buildings in his *quartier,* the unexpected little squares, the busy market streets, and the water running in the gutters twice a day to clean them. He examined the wonderful scrolly detail of Hector Guimard's Métro entrances, designed in 1900 in the purest Art Nouveau style. Paris was the perfect city for walking but Allen often got no farther than the Tabac St. Michel, a favorite with Beat Hotel regulars, or one of the nearby outdoor cafés on Blvd St. Germain, which was then still cobbled and looked much as it did when Baron Haussmann built it a century before. Allen was often accompanied by Peter on his walks but Gregory, who had already explored the city on his own that summer, was usually out with one of his various girlfriends, often returning to their room at the hotel early in the morning.

Allen enjoyed walking to the middle of Pont des Arts, the spindly iron bridge spanning the Seine from the Louvre to the Institut de France, built originally only for pedestrians, who could sit in chairs among boxed orange trees. It was a quiet haven from which to contemplate the fishermen on the Ile de la Cité and the fabulous Paris skyline. Another favorite place to sit and look at life was the Luxembourg Gardens, laid out in formal Italian style but peculiarly French in atmosphere, filled with students from the nearby University of Paris reading or sunning themselves on the benches. People gathered in clusters, perched on the heavy iron park chairs, while children enjoyed donkey rides or sailed their yachts on the round pond. There were marionettes and band concerts, old men playing cards and games of *boule*, and the thwack of a tennis ball could occasionally be heard on the nearby courts.

Allen was always keen to see literary sites, and made a point of visiting all the literary cafés: the Dôme, Deux Magots, Brasserie Lipp, Flore, Rotonde, Closerie des Lilas, and La Coupole. He particularly liked Le Select on Blvd Montparnasse with its huge awning and scrolled neon sign, once home to Radclyffe Hall and Lady Una Troubridge, Picasso, Kiki de Montparnasse, André Gide, and Max Jacob. Whenever he could afford it he would sit outside and nurse a coffee, observing the passing sights. During his time at the Beat Hotel, Chester Himes wrote several of his books sitting outside the Select, cutting an impressive figure in his gabardine raincoat, crew cut, and little mustache. He looked as if he were impersonating one of the detectives he was writing about. Many of the hotel residents used to gather there during the day to plan their evenings. On November 13, Ginsberg wrote to Kerouac, "I sat weeping in Cafe Select . . . last week writing first lines of great formal elegy for my mother—

> *Farewell*
> *with long black shoe*
> *Farewell*
> *smoking corsets & ribs of steel*
> *Farewell*
> *communist party & broken stocking*
>   *. . .*
> *with your eyes of shock*
> *with your eyes of lobotomy*
> *with your eyes of stroke*
> *with your eyes of divorce*
> *with your eyes alone*
> *with your eyes*
> *with your eyes*
> *with your death full of flowers*
> *with your death of the golden windows of sunlight.*

I write best when I weep, I wrote a lot of that weeping anyway and got idea for huge expandable form of such a poem, will finish later and make a big elegy, perhaps less repetitious in parts, but I gotta get a rhythm up to cry."

The fifty-six lines he wrote in the Select were to become "Kaddish Part IV," where they appeared with very few changes: a few repetitions eliminated and some images combined to give a tighter rhythm. Most of "Kaddish" was written in one very long session on his return to New York, but the idea for the poem had its origin in Paris. Though not as famous as "Howl," it is widely regarded as Ginsberg's best poem.

Allen had been reading the work of André Breton and this section of "Kaddish" is clearly influenced structurally by Breton's poem *"L'Union libre"* ("Free Union"), first published in June 1931:

My wife with a belly like a giant claw
My wife with the back of a bird fleeing vertically
With a back of quicksilver
With a back of light
With a nape of rolled stone and wet chalk
    . . .
My wife with a sex of seaweed and ancient sweets
My wife with a sex of mirror
My wife with eyes full of tears

"Kaddish" is the biography of Naomi Ginsberg, Allen's mother. Naomi had a severe case of schizophrenia, or *dementia praecox*, as it was then known. When he was a child Allen often had to stay home from school to look after her while she heard voices and prowled furtively around the apartment, convinced that Allen's grandmother was plotting to kill her. Naomi's madness was the dominant theme of Ginsberg's childhood and had a profound effect on him. In a poem in his Beat Hotel journals is the line "[I] realize, walking in reverie downstreet / that I love my mother, and she put me down / all thru my childhood, with her paranoia . . ."

Naomi was a member of the Communist Party and on her good days sometimes took Allen and his brother, Eugene, to cell meetings in Paterson, New Jersey, where they lived. Allen grew up in an atmosphere of political activism—of marches, rallies, pamphleteering, and letter-writing campaigns. His father was a schoolteacher and a published poet, with two books to his name. He was a Socialist, and he and Naomi had frequent quarrels over political issues. Naomi was a practicing naturist and often walked around the apartment naked. She was not attractive: she was overweight and her belly was scarred from operations. Allen maintained it was the sight of his mother that made him a homosexual, and complained that it was usually women who looked like her who were attracted to him.

When Naomi's illness got too bad, she would go away, first to a private nursing home and then, later, to the big state mental hospitals of New Jersey and New York, where she was given insulin shock treatment and finally a lobotomy. In "Kaddish" Ginsberg tells the entire harrowing tale, sparing no details. Naomi and Louis had divorced, so when it came time for the family to authorize her lobotomy, this painful task lay with Allen; his elder brother was away by this time. Naomi died in 1955 in Pilgrim State Hospital in Long Island, New York. The last time Allen visited her there she did not recognize him.

Allen had been planning an elegy for his mother for several months. Her death, shortly after he had written "Howl," which in some ways was also addressed to her, had so affected him that it was the obvious subject for his next major work. One of his Paris journals opens on page one with the heading "Elegy for Mama," and the journals contain long passages, filling many pages, that did not make it into the final version of the poem: ". . . I have no mother's belly left to crawl back to under the covers she's in the grave, she's a void—a longing for what was once not void but trembling weepy insane flesh . . ."

These sections prefigure the exceptionally long extended lines that make up most of "Kaddish," but other early notations for the poem use the shorter line of the section Allen sent to Kerouac:

> *Mother, what should I have done to save you*
> > *Should I have put out the sun?*
> > *Should I have not called the police*
> > *Should I have been your lover*
> *Should I have held your hands and walked in the park*
> > *at midnight for 60 years?*
> *I am a poet, I will put out the sun*

The madness of his mother was the great tragedy of Ginsberg's life, and it shaped and formed his ideas and attitudes. It gave him a certain fatalism, an awareness of the transitory nature of things. This, possibly combined with the influence of his parents' left-leaning idealism, meant that Allen never became materialistic; for instance, he read voraciously but gave books away and never kept first editions—books were to be read and not collected. Fashion, gourmet food, fine wines, antiques, furniture design, cars, all the bourgeois pleasures failed to provoke his interest. He was fascinated by madness and extremes of feeling and self-expression. Given a choice of which letters to read first, he would put aside correspondence from friends and begin with a ten-page letter written on lined paper in smudged colored chalks sent by an unknown fan.

Dealing with his mother's madness had left Allen with an enormous reservoir of tolerance for antisocial behavior and craziness to the extent that he rarely ever noticed abnormal behavior unless it was extreme. He felt an empathy with disturbed people, the muttering drunks on the Bowery, the old lady talking loudly to herself, people who heard voices, the downtrodden and the homeless, and he was attracted to them. His association with Jack Kerouac and William Burroughs when he was at college in the early '40s introduced him to a bohemian world of drug dealers and petty thieves. At that time he had befriended a small-time thief and male hustler named Herbert Huncke, whose behavior was so "heinous" that the cops on Times Square called him The Creep and sometimes threw him off the Square in disgust. Huncke would steal from anyone, no matter how down-and-out they were, and invariably took advantage of friendship. Allen allowed Huncke to move in on him, steal his belongings, and eventually, in 1947, get him busted for possession of stolen goods. As a result Allen spent nine months in the Columbia Presbyterian Psychiatric Institute while Huncke went to jail. Huncke was to spend a total of eleven years of his life in jail, but he eventually became something of a Beat Generation legend, and, encouraged by Allen, he wrote a series of short stories, published as his autobiography and titled *Guilty of Everything.*

Allen himself had heard voices. One afternoon, when he was a student at Columbia, in a top-floor apartment looking out over the rooftops of Harlem, he experienced an auditory hallucination of William Blake's ancient voice reading poetry to him across the vault of time. For several days afterward, he saw reality with a shuddering intensity, observed the armoring that people surround themselves with, witnessed their sadness and fear, their crushed hopes and expectations. He felt such powerful waves of compassion and understanding for the human condition that it made him fear he was going mad like his mother. This vision, or perhaps partial nervous breakdown, was to dominate his life for many years, strengthening his attachment to those outside society, the insane, the criminal, the rejected. For him junkies and thieves were saints and angels—"angelheaded hipsters"—and they became the subject matter of "Howl" as well as other poems. Allen's own lifestyle also placed him outside normal society: he was homosexual, he used heroin and marijuana, and he was regarded by the authorities as a threat to the American Way of Life. For Allen Ginsberg, the Beat lifestyle was not a pose; for him it was the only life that made any sense, it was the only life possible.

3 **Expatriates**

The disturbing effects of a sudden change of environment on even the tolerably well-educated are always and everywhere apparent. On their first arrival in Paris young English and American men will behave as they would never dream of behaving at home. Young women, too, one is forced to add. It was ever so.

Aldous Huxley, *Jesting Pilate*

Bill Burroughs, still in Tangier, wrote frequently to Allen, often twice in one week. He was still adding new passages and sections to his book, such that it no longer resembled the original manuscript that Allen had delivered to Maurice Girodias on his arrival in Paris. Bill sent Allen copies of all the revisions and new material so he could continuously update Girodias's copy—a hapless task. In mid-November Allen gave the latest version of Bill's manuscript, now called *Naked Lunch*, to Mason Hoffenberg, an "adviser" for Olympia Press who had just co-authored *Candy* with Terry Southern for Girodias. Hoffenberg was amazed by Bill's writing and pronounced it the "greatest greatest book" he had ever read. He assured Allen that Olympia would take it on his recommendation, and Allen gave a sigh of relief, thinking the book would be published at last. Meanwhile Bill sent Allen another thirty pages to add to the manuscript, telling him that there were a further hundred pages to come. Yet, though he looked through the manuscript a second time, Girodias still rejected it on the grounds that there was no sex in it, despite Southern's claim that the title referred to an American tradition not dissimilar to the French *cinq a sept*, when Frenchmen visit their mistresses in the hours before dinner. Girodias also objected to the drug references, something Olympia had not previously had to contend with as subject matter in their books.

On November 24, 1957, Peter wrote his first poem, which he titled "Frist Poem." Peter's eccentric spelling was retained when it was published and is partly responsible for its charm—"I look for my shues under my bed" or "I drink a hole bottle of wine with my eyes shut." It was written just as Peter spoke—as William Carlos Williams said about Orlovsky's work, "Nothing English about it—pure American." On December 27, he wrote "Second Poem," which is largely about their room in the Beat Hotel: "Is there any one saintly thing I can do to my room, paint it pink / maybe or instal an elevator from bed to the floor, maybe take a bath on the bed? / . . . There comes a time in life when everybody must take a piss in the sink—here let me paint the window black for a minute." The poems were described by Allen as "Both unmistakably his own weird surreal style & both exact & great round poems. New poet actually to be sure!" Europe inspired Peter to write. His first attempts were in Cannes, when he and Allen were on their way to stay with Alan Ansen that spring. There he wrote the long scroll entitled "One Line Scrapbook," which appears in his City Lights Pocket Poets volume, *Clean Asshole Poems & Smiling Vegetable Songs.*

Peter was happy because there were lots of young women in the hotel. They also met two French shopgirls who took a liking to them. Peter wrote to Jack Kerouac, "Allen & Gregory have erections pointed at 2 french girls all 4 on the iron bed bouncing, Gregory going out to score for H, let me tell you theres fucking in the house tonight." Alas, this time it was not to be. Gregory returned with the dope and, later in the letter, which was written over several days, Peter commented that he had read 120 pages of Jean Genet's *Thief's Journal* "wile Allen & Gregory were trying to fuck with limp hard ons because of the dope." They stayed up all night talking, and when the girls left to go to work, Allen, Gregory, and Peter took a walk to the part of Paris where Gregory thought Genet now lived, but they were unable to find him.

Twenty-five years later, remembering the girls, Allen said, "They were the first real French people we met. . . . One of them, Françoise, was really hung up on me. I didn't realize the consequences, I didn't take it seriously. I didn't realize it was real. It's apparently a big neurotic problem of mine, not recognizing genuine affection. I thought anybody in love with me must be crazy! Since I'm gay anyway and I've been living with Peter, that if anybody gets fixated on me there must be some misalliance or misjudgment of some sort. I didn't see it, as I might now, as an indication for an open situation, more as a fixed obsession on her part. So I probably hurt her a great deal. Being so closed off. She was very young. I was thirty by then."

Allen wrote to his old friend Lucien Carr, using an abbreviated code (x for sex, and T for tca [marijuana]): "We're crowded & have usual choice collection of interesting screwballs dropping in for supper, X, T, heroin or whatever's on menu. Also making time with two french shopgirls & Peter makes ladies of the streets." Peter would go off alone to the wine warehouses half a mile away on the quai Saint Bernard where the prostitutes gathered next to the Port au Vin and serviced the men handling the great barrels of wine. They looked older than they were—working-class girls who drank the cheapest *vin ordinaire*, dressed in black high heels, nylons, and skirts to mid-calf, with their hair sprayed into shape.

One of the many people who showed up at room 25 was the English translator Simon Watson-Taylor. Watson-Taylor was a member of the College of 'Pataphysics, the French literary group founded in honor of Alfred Jarry, and was a translator of French avant-garde and Surrealist literature into English. He had somehow obtained their address and wanted to meet someone who could explain the Beat Generation to him. When he arrived, Allen and Peter both had bad colds and were tucked up in bed sniffling, surrounded by Kleenex. He entered the room and burst out laughing at the state they were in. Watson-Taylor was very amicable and took them both out for a good meal. He knew Marcel Duchamp and many of the Surrealists and was able to recommend many books and authors to Allen.

November came and the streets were cold. The rue Git-le-Coeur was sheltered but a vicious wind cut along the river. To visit the little *tabac* on the quai des Augustines near Picasso's old studio meant turn-

ing the corner into an arctic gale. Allen usually awoke about midday
and frequently spent the afternoons walking the cobbled streets alone,
looking at the winter rain on the cobblestones, cold sunlight on gray
walls, the statues and plaques commemorating dead artists and states-
men and heroes. He would climb the *butte* of Montmartre to the row
of ramshackle wooden studios on the rue Ravignan, dubbed "Bateau
Lavoire" by Max Jacob, where Picasso, Juan Gris, Kees van Dongen,
and their poet friends lived before the Great War.

Allen often took long walks along the river and examined the
jumble of used books and prints for sale at the bookstalls on the quais
beneath the branches of the plane trees. There he found all the Olympia Press editions of Henry Miller and Genet that were banned in the
United States. Allen was unaware that the poet Guillaume Apollinaire
had written pornographic novels and was delighted to find copies of
Amorous Exploits of a Young Rakehell and *The Debauched Hospodar*.
After they had all read them, Allen sent the books, one at a time, back
to his parents in Paterson. His father had remarried after his divorce
from Naomi and Allen told his stepmother, Edith, "OK for you to read
them if you're not shocked but don't burn them they're expensive and
rare in the US."

These books inspired Allen to reread Apollinaire's poetry, and
toward the end of November Allen and Peter went in search of his
grave at the Père-Lachaise cemetery. Père-Lachaise, opened in 1804,
is a vast, picturesque garden, an overcrowded jumble of mausoleums
and statuary in every conceivable style, filled with huge trees and
winding footpaths, the final resting place of Sarah Bernhardt, Oscar
Wilde, Honoré de Balzac, Gérard de Nerval, Théodore Géricault,
Frédéric Chopin, Colette, and Marcel Proust among thousands of
others, the celebrated and the unknown. Allen and Peter walked
quietly hand in hand through the winter trees and fantastic statuary, following the street names until they found Apollinaire's grave.
The headstone was a menhir, or standing stone, a rough, thin slice
of granite, taller than Allen, incised with his full name—Wilhelm
Apollinaris de Kostrowitski—and two of his poems. There was a jam
jar filled with daisies and a cheap gift-shop ceramic rose on the tomb.

Allen sat on the mossy roots of the tree next to the grave and smoked a cigarette, watching an ant walk over his corduroy sleeve, Apollinaire's *Alcools* in his pocket. He laid a copy of *Howl* on the gravestone for Apollinaire to read in Heaven. This same division held the grave of the poet Henri de Régnier, one of the founders of Symbolism, and in the next division lay Proust. After a while, Allen and Peter looked around the rest of the cemetery.

Back at the rue Git-le-Coeur, Allen and Peter's visit to Père-Lachaise inspired a typical Beat Hotel prank. A painter named Howie, who had listened to Allen talking about the cemetery, was about to return to the States and, in early December, the night before he was due to leave, he got drunk and decided he wished to take Baudelaire's gravestone with him as a souvenir. He recruited helpers from around the hotel, including Allen, and they all piled in a cab and went to Montparnasse cemetery on Blvd Raspaïl, where Howie climbed the wall and disappeared into the darkness. The others waited for a while, then walked down the Blvd Montparnasse to the Café Select to wait for him. Howie arrived eventually, saying that the wall was too high and that the tombstone, which he never found, was probably too heavy anyway.

Because it was so cold, they spent less time exploring and sightseeing. Gregory bought some oil paints and brushes and began to paint abstract pictures on canvas paper tacked to the hotel wall. He bought a sketchbook and did a series of humorous and lighthearted line drawings. Peter bought some colored crayons and drew strange red angels sitting in red trees. Allen was too shy to try, even though his journals often contained expressive pen-and-ink drawings. They found one excursion they could make and keep out of the wind: on December 7, Allen, Peter, and Gregory spent the afternoon walking underground in the Paris catacombs for a mile, starting from Place Denfert-Rochereau. The vaulted passages were stacked with human bones and skulls like logs stored for a winter fire, moved there in the 1780s because the cemetery at Les Halles was filled to overflowing. Peter described the scene to Robert LaVigne: "Eerie haunting damp and partly sweet odor from millions of leg bones & skulls piled up neatly along the tunnel way. All

that death in a small place. I felt I was dead myself walking there—
Gregory stole a leg bone & its now laying next to Rimbaud on the wall."

Allen usually cooked supper in the room for himself and Peter,
and Gregory if he was around, and the evenings were spent reading
and writing, with occasional expeditions. Allen made many visits to
the Musée Guimet on Place de l'Iéna, looking at the Indian miniatures
and Tibetan tankas, and mentioned it several times in his journals—
"The stone of Scone sits like winged victory / In Musée Guimet's in-
testines." They went several times to the Chinese Ballet and, when they
could afford it, to Gregory's favorite café, the Bonaparte, on Place St.
Germain, which was the preferred meeting place for their growing circle
of friends and acquaintances. Jean-Paul Sartre lived in the apartment
building above the café, but strangely the Beats were never interested
in the existentialists and did not read their books. Ginsberg wrote, "I
thought, and still do, that existentialism was an intellectual practice
rather than a physical practice. It was a theory of being spontaneous,
and theory of confronting the void, but they weren't out there. And
even when they went out there to do it, it was in purely political terms
which involved a tremendous amount of aggression and hatred." Despite his political involvement Allen professed to share Kerouac's de-
tached view of life, often claiming it as the official Beat Generation
line. Kerouac proposed complete noninvolvement, or as Allen termed
it, "the lambiness of non-existence, the lambiness of illusion." Kerouac
went further; he was sympathetic to the American far right and a great
supporter of Senator McCarthy. He saw existentialism as a communist plot. Kerouac writing in 1963 stated, "In the long run men will
only remember the lamb. Camus would have had us turn literature
into mere propaganda, with his 'commitment' talk. . . . Myself, I'm
only an ex-sailor, I have no politics, I don't even vote." For Ginsberg,
who was not an academic, existentialism was too European, too intellectual. Many years later, when he was teaching poetry at Brooklyn
College, Ginsberg still had not read any literary theory or made any
attempt to engage with the critical discussions concerning textual
analysis and deconstruction that were then raging in English depart-
ments across the country.

On November 16, Alan Ansen arrived in Paris to spend three weeks visiting Allen and Peter. They took him to the Café Le Royal, a homosexual meeting place on St.-Germain-des-Pres. The café was described by a later resident of the hotel, Harold Norse, in his poem "Green Ballets": "Shlepping from St. Michel along the pissoir route to the Flore . . . the cold whipping into the make-up of the hopefuls at the terrace tables. Across the street at the Café Royale gray old swindle—worse there is—the Youth Swindle. Blade-sharp hustlers. Gray old fag swindle. It's an insult when they regard you from under age on show. Sweeping coiffures, every dyed hair counted, every advantage price-tagged. To your disadvantage, dig? Makes you feel old & sin. Can't join the Youth Club now."

Ansen preferred the scene on the rue de la Huchette across from Place St. Michel, where the students and young people hung out in the basement jazz clubs and bars like Chez Popov and the Caveau de la Huchette. Allen and Peter took Alan to their favorite rue de la Huchette bar, where runaway high school boys with shoulder-length hair and wispy d'Artagnan beards stood in corners with their even younger-looking girlfriends, none of them able to scrape up the 40 francs (10¢) needed for a glass of red wine.

Ansen took a great liking to Gregory and his work and invited him to come and stay in Venice whenever he wanted. At that moment Gregory was not in need of a patron because he had met a rich Mexican girl in the Louvre and she had somewhat eased his financial crisis. She even had a car and promised to drive them all to Chartres. Gregory was writing really well and Allen wrote a glowing description of his work to Lawrence Ferlinghetti, commenting on his penury and saying, ". . . in his poverty too marvellously, how he gets along here hand to mouth, daily, begging & conning & wooing, but he writes daily marvellous poems. . . . Gregory is in his golden inspired period like in Mexico, but even more, & soberer solemner, calm genius every morning he wakes and types last nites 2 or 3 pages of poems, bordering on strangeness, now he's even going further . . ."

Though Ferlinghetti had accepted Gregory's book *Gasoline*, he and Gregory were now replacing poems in it, having decided that the selection of poetry was not quite right. Allen now had certain reservations about the book, even though he had written an enthusiastic introduction when they were in Amsterdam. He told Ferlinghetti, "I'm glad you dug the new Gregory poems, 'Coit Tower' is certainly approaching something really great like Fern Hill. I was depressed when I finally saw his proofs because I really do think he's one of the greatest poets in US but it wasn't in the book. I like his short poems, but I dig his genius best in the long wild incomprehensible blowing, the pure phrasing—His life is too unstable for him to sit down for long cool afterthoughts & assembling of book properly—it should have had more long poems . . . I hadn't realized in Amsterdam how much crap like 'America' fragment had crept in & short meaningless poems. But almost everything now is near perfect—strangely he's best when he's serious I mean, not when he's being Little Gregory writing about his dollies. I'm glad it's all OK to rip up & delay the book again to include 'Coit Tower.'" Ferlinghetti had reached the same conclusion and did revise the book to include Gregory's new poems, though he still refused to include "Power."

Though Gregory's work was becoming more spontaneous, with less rewriting and fixing, he was still not a convert to Kerouac's belief in total spontaneity. Jack insisted on spontaneous composition—that nothing should ever be changed, not even the punctuation. Jack wrote poems by the yard, their composition time determined only by his typing speed, whereas Gregory believed that the poet should be a craftsman, should know how to construct a poem. It was a long-standing disagreement between them and a frequent subject of debate when Gregory was discussing poetry.

Irritated that Jack had criticized his work methods in a letter, Gregory replied with his own criticism of Jack's recent poems, referring him back to Shelley: "When I look at your poem I know to myself that this poem was written with the fast finger, well all I can say is that if beauty were to pass my window I would her to move slow slow slow, not shot, whiz, tennis ball, was that beauty? O why didn't she linger? I guess for those who have never seen beauty before should be satisfied with the shot, but I, like you, who have seen her, would now prefer examination—ergo, you write not for me but for the lack, and of course that is your way and that is good, that is why I prefer your prose which is poetry better than your poetry which is almost bullet . . . whiz." He ends by saying, "You, who have written a book of verse in an hour, can write 24 books in a day . . . no, I'm sorry Jack, but poetry is Ode To The West Wind."

Thanksgiving came and Allen's father sent him $15 so they were able to fry a chicken to celebrate the holiday. Allen was snowed under with correspondence and complained that he had no time to work on his own poetry—a situation that would persist for the rest of his life. Some of his friends inundated him with letters, making Allen feel guilty—by mid-November he owed Robert LaVigne six letters. Letters arrived from Michael McClure, Philip Whalen, Lawrence Ferlinghetti, Allen's family, Neal Cassady, Ron Loewinsohn, and Jack Kerouac, and he received unsolicited poetry manuscripts by the score from all over. He received letters from unknown young businessmen who had read about him in *Life*, one of whom congratulated him on being free, on leaving the rat race, and complained that he had "lost his soul." Allen told his father, "Spend or waste a lot time answering strange letters, everything from Jesuit appeals to Christ in me to young poets who write in on toilet paper."

The latter referred to LeRoi Jones, then living in the Village, who had been very influenced by "Howl" and was thinking of starting a new literary magazine called *Yugen*. In his autobiography, Jones wrote,

> Wanting to be as weird to him as I thought he was to me, I wrote him a letter on toilet paper, sent to the 9 rue Git-le-Coeur address, asking was he for real. He sent me back a letter, also written on toilet paper, but the coarser European grade that makes better writing paper. He told me he was sincere but he was tired of being Allen Ginsberg. (The notoriety was just starting.) He signed the letter and had a drawing under his signature of a lineup, a parade of different beasts and animals, all with halos over their heads in some weird but jolly procession.

Allen sent LeRoi four short poems and suggested that he contact Philip Whalen, Gary Snyder, Corso, Burroughs, and Kerouac. Whalen sent him work immediately, and Allen mentioned the magazine in his wide correspondence. Jones wrote, "He was the poetry advertiser of that age, the role that Ezra Pound played during the 20s, hipping people to each other, trying to get various people published." He described Ginsberg's letters as being like "quick courses in contemporary American poetry."

Allen was very keen to get Jones to publish Kerouac's poetry, as Ferlinghetti had just rejected Jack's *Book of Blues* for City Lights. And early in November, Allen had received a group of poems from Ray Bremser, via Bordontown Reformatory, which he liked enough to pass along. Suddenly LeRoi was at the center of Beat Generation small-press publishing and the magazine, *Yugen*, which he edited with his girlfriend Hettie Cohen, became one of the most influential of all the Beat periodicals.

Once Jones had published the Beats in his magazine, Allen began to suggest other poets he should publish. According to Jones, "Ginsberg also hipped me to the San Francisco School (old and new, some of whom were known as the Beats), the New York School (Frank O'Hara, Kenneth Koch, John Ashbery, James Schuyler) and a host of other young people. Older poets like Charles Olson and Robert Duncan. Trendsetters like Robert Creeley and all kinds of other names. Kerouac and Burroughs of course. John Wieners, Ron Loewinsohn, Paul Blackburn, Denise Levertov, Ferlinghetti, Jack Spicer . . ." Allen was in contact with all of them, putting them in touch with one another and with editors, sending poems and receiving news.

In December, Allen wrote the first draft of "At Apollinaire's Grave," which was to become one of his most anthologized poems. Like many of Ginsberg's poems it is universal, addressing eternal verities, and specifically dated; for instance, he mentions President Eisenhower's visit to Paris for the NATO conference. Ike left on December 19 and Allen wrote, "So let it be the airport at blue Orly in the winter day /

and Eisenhower winging home to his American graveyard." Though at the time Ginsberg did not feel he was producing much in the way of poetry because he was so busy socializing and writing letters, he later found that he had accumulated a large body of work during his stay in Paris. By situating himself in the Beat Hotel, he was removing himself from the constant bombardment of images from the mass media, all-pervasive in daily city life back home. Paris supplied its own equivalent, but it was a foreign culture and most of the messages went unheeded because he didn't know the language sufficiently well, or understand the references.

Though he was removed from the immediate effects of American culture, Allen recognized that his work fell within a literary tradition and that he was influenced on an unconscious level by conventions, parental views, and by the values of American society, despite his making a conscious effort to strip away preconditioned notions. He would no doubt have agreed that his past experience governed what Walter Benjamin called the "overtaxing of the productive person in the name of . . . the principle of 'creativity,' in which the poet is believed on his own and out of his pure mind, to have brought forth his work." At the Beat Hotel, Allen, Gregory, and the other residents lived in a micro-climate of their own creation, self-referential and hermetic. It was an ecosystem that fell within the emerging drug culture, with its background in jazz and the avant-garde, its roots firmly planted in the bohemian tradition.

That Christmas, Thomas Parkinson came to Paris. He was a professor of English at Berkeley and had been a member of Kenneth Rexroth's anarchist circle in the Bay Area in the 1940s. Allen knew him from his year in San Francisco. Parkinson had received a Guggenheim award and he and his wife, Ariel, had moved to London in order for him to write on Yeats and Pound. Allen contacted him in London inviting him to visit. When the couple arrived at the Beat Hotel, Allen showed Parkinson the manuscript of the first part of "Kaddish," which in Parkinson's memory was written in red ink to "simulate blood running out onto the page, his own and his mother's."

Allen and Gregory accompanied Parkinson around Paris and he was particularly impressed by the Musée Gustave Moreau. Parkinson invited Allen to stay at their house in Hampstead, and also to contribute to a series of programs on American poetry that he was recording for the BBC Third Programme. Allen wanted to go but was still awaiting Kerouac's $225. He wrote to Louis, "I may go over there in February if Jack ever sends that money. He mentions it (the money) in every letter and said originally he'd pay it Xmas, then January when he got his royalties, now he says royalties don't come till February and's left me broke waiting." Meanwhile Allen was being hounded by the owner of the local grocery over a small bill for milk and eggs.

It was too cold to go walking so Allen devoted much of his time to reading, trying to finish the more obscure Shakespeare plays that he had not yet read: *The Life of Timon of Athens*; *Pericles, Prince of Tyre*; and *Coriolanus*. He also read Balzac, Dickens, and the complete works of Vachel Lindsay given to him by Gregory, which prompted the poem "To Lindsay." He sampled various modern French poets but he made surprisingly little effort to contact any of the young French writers.

This was regrettable, as it was a high point in French culture: the Beats were living within yards of the cafés where Camus, Boris Vian, Sartre, and Simone de Beauvoir were holding court. They could have met Françoise Sagan, whose *Bonjour Tristesse* was then a worldwide best-seller, Brigitte Bardot, Juliette Gréco, and the young filmmakers of the French *Nouvelle Vague*, who could be found then on Paris's Left Bank. Eugène Ionesco was developing his Theater of the Absurd, and Fernando Arrabal and Arthur Adamov were producing new works on a regular basis. In fact, Adamov lived on the rue de Seine and was frequently ensconced at the Old Navy on Blvd St. Germain where many of the Beats hung out. Even Samuel Beckett was accessible and was often to be found at the Falstaff bar.

But the Americans preferred their own company, content to celebrate their own genius. They were living in a Paris of dreams—a fantasy of James Joyce and his *Ulysses*, Sylvia Beach, and Ezra Pound, not the actual Paris of thirty years later, which has now become just

as mythic. Allen spent his time reading Russian poetry and applied to
the Soviet Embassy for a grant to travel to Moscow. Using a French
dictionary, he began making rough English translations of Essenin's
poems from the 1922 French versions by Franz Hellens and Marie
Miloslawsky in *La Confession d'un voyou.*

Kerouac's agent, Sterling Lord, was in Paris over the New Year and
took Allen, Peter, and Gregory to supper with some of his friends. Lord
described the first night of Jack's series of readings at the Village
Vanguard, and how smashed he was. Kerouac was reading his work
accompanied by a jazz combo but was too nervous and too drunk,
stumbling over words, sweating heavily, and the open-ended residency
closed in only one week. Allen made arrangements for Lord to offer
Howl to foreign publishers.

Allen had no money with which to celebrate New Year's Eve.
Instead of seeing in 1958 with his friends in a café, he wrote a catalog
poem about the sink in his hotel room, describing the long chain attached to the plug, his and Peter's toothbrushes, the black abrasive
pad used to scrub the cooking pots, and listing the many activities he
performed standing before it. Gregory was off with his girlfriend and
Peter now had his own group of friends, but later in the evening someone gave Allen a lift to Place Pigalle in Montmartre to see the groups
of people kissing one another at midnight, twice on each cheek, a cere-
mony destined to last for hours in so big a crowd. He walked all night,
musing "under the noisy stars," heading south toward the red-light
district around Les Halles where revelers staggered drunkenly in the
street, then crossed back over the river to the Left Bank. He felt sub-
dued and anxious about his relationship with Peter, who was shortly
heading home. The United States Consul had finally accepted Peter's
need to return to the States to look after his family and had arranged
an assisted passage on the *Mauritania*, leaving January 17, 1958.

Gregory too, was leaving; he borrowed a 10,000-franc note from Graham, "the foggy hipster upstairs," and left Paris on January 4 to try
his hand at selling encyclopedias to GIs in Frankfurt. He also took a

folder of his drawings and paintings, hoping to sell them. He failed on both counts but he wrote an article on American poetry for the Dutch magazine *Literaire Passpoort* which put him in contact Walter Höllerer, the editor of the German literary magazine *Akzente*, who wanted a similar article for his magazine. Höllerer was a poet himself and had visited San Francisco and contacted the poets there. He said that he would find a translator for Gregory's *Gasoline* and also for *Howl and Other Poems*. He invited Gregory and Allen to give a poetry reading at Frankfurt University, offered them an apartment, and said that he would find a publisher for an anthology of San Francisco poets. He and Gregory did, eventually, coedit a bilingual anthology, called *Junge Americanische Lyrik*, which was published by Carl Hanser Verlag in 1961, one of the first European anthologies of Beat Generation writing. It included a 7-inch 45 rpm record of Allen, Gregory, and Ferlinghetti reading from their work.

Gregory had been seeing Joy Ungerer, a beautiful half-Indonesian girl who worked as an artist's model. She was amusing, vivacious, and very friendly. When Gregory took off for Frankfurt she climbed into bed with Allen and Peter. It is typical of the Beat attitude toward women that Gregory abused her openness by offering her to Kerouac as an inducement in a letter trying to get Jack to visit them all in Paris. The Beat Generation was virtually an all-male society wherein women had no role except as wives or "chicks." Their experience as wives was generally a disaster.

This sometimes cruel attitude is neatly summed up by Barbara Ehrenreich in her book *The Hearts of Men: American Dreams and the Flight from Commitment.* "The Beat pioneers were deeply, if intermittently, attached to each other," she wrote. "Women and their demands for responsibility were, at worst, irritating and more often just uninteresting compared to the ecstatic possibilities of male adventure . . . their adventures did not include women, except, perhaps, as 'experiences' that men might have. And in their vision, which found its way into the utopian hopes of the counterculture, the ideal of personal freedom shaded over into an almost vicious irresponsibility to the women who passed through their lives."

* * *

For several months Allen had been encouraging Bill Burroughs to come to Paris from Tangier. Bill felt that he needed further assistance with *Naked Lunch* and finally decided to make the move. On January 3, a vacancy opened up at the hotel. As rooms were much sought after, Allen took it on Bill's behalf, even though he had not heard from him for several weeks. It was a big room, cheaper than Allen's at $25 a month, with a gas pipe, so Bill could buy a five-dollar gas stove to make himself tea and cook meals.

Bill arrived by plane from Tangier on January 16, 1958, the day before Peter shipped out for New York. Allen and Peter were a little fearful about what would happen now that Bill was in Paris. Bill and Allen had had an intense three-month affair in New York back in 1953. Allen had found it mentally stimulating but it also worried him enormously because Bill appeared to be trying to absorb him in some kind of ultimate telepathic union—"schlupping," Bill called it. Allen described the affair twenty years later: "Schlupp for him, was originally a very tender emotional direction, a desire to merge with a lover, and as such, pretty vulnerable, tenderhearted and open on Burroughs's part." Allen went along with it because he regarded Bill as his teacher. But the intensity of the affair scared Allen and, when Bill began talking of taking him along to Tangier, Allen blurted out, "But I don't want your ugly old cock," which brought the affair to an end in no uncertain terms. Bill departed for Tangier, Allen to the jungles of Chiapas, Mexico. But Bill had remained obsessed with Allen and, even four years later, when Allen and Peter arrived in Tangier in the spring of 1957, Bill's fixation on Allen remained unabated.

He had built up a fantasy of him and Allen together. When Kerouac was staying with him in Tangier before Allen and Peter arrived, to Jack's horror Bill broke down in tears one evening because he wanted Allen so much, unable to hold in his feelings any longer. In fact, when Allen and Peter went to Tangier to stay with Burroughs it was with the specific intention of including him in their love circle and lovemaking, but it had not been a success. Bill had been contemptuous of Peter and constantly put him down, while at the same time maintaining that he was incapable of jealousy. Allen took offense at Bill's condescending attitude toward Peter and, one evening when they were all high on majoun, Bill's mockery irritated Allen so much that he ripped open Bill's khaki shirt with one of Bill's hunting knives. Not long after that Allen and Peter left for Spain.

Thus Bill's arrival, coincidentally timed with Peter's departure, was a cause for apprehension as Bill appeared to be just as captivated by Allen as ever. Both Allen and Peter were filled with doubts and trepidation when Peter left on the Boat Train the next evening for Le Havre. Bill and Allen saw him off at the Gare St. Lazare at 5:35 on a Friday evening. They all had coffee and pernod in a café. Allen and Peter kissed intimately as they parted, tears in their eyes, wondering what the future would bring and if they would ever see each other again.

Back at the hotel Allen fell into a deep depression, scared that Bill would claim him now that Peter was gone. He sat on his bed sobbing, then sniffed some heroin, which calmed him somewhat. Though he was apprehensive, he was genuinely pleased to see Bill again and they had sex, but afterward the usual arguments and misunderstandings arose once more, as they had in Tangier. Allen thought it was his duty to have sex with Bill for the sake of their old friendship but he felt that Bill was trying to take him over with the old schlupp routine again. Allen retreated to his room and smoked some pot, but he had recently been getting anxiety attacks every time he used it, so it was a bad choice of drug for him. Then Françoise, the French girl who was infatuated with him, arrived. She tried to get him to have sex with her, climbing all over his body. He felt great waves of paranoia and slumped back on the bed, silent and terrified.

At that moment there was a knock on the door, startling him. It was Gregory, back from his adventures in Germany with news of readings and anthologies and free apartments. Allen was delighted to see him; he was so reassuring and comforting, a familiar figure from the happy days when the three of them lived in the room together. "I also thought he would save me from sordid sorrows with Satanic Bill," Allen wrote Peter.

Allen and Peter had made a point of always sorting out their problems—Peter's worry that Allen would overwhelm and drown him, Allen's worry that Peter would withdraw his love—with heart-to-heart talks, revealing to each other all their worries and fears. Allen decided that he must do the same with Bill and the next day they sat down at the round table in Allen's room for a serious talk. First Allen expressed all his worries, then Bill explained what had been happening to him in Tangier during the six months since Allen and Peter had left.

Allen's departure had made Bill take a close look at himself. Each afternoon he sat on his bed and attempted to dispassionately examine his attachments and obsessions, working through every area of his life that was causing him pain. He stopped drinking and stopped writing and devoted more and more of his time to quiet thinking and meditation; essentially, he performed a course in self-analysis, repeatedly working over problems and fantasies until they were drained of energy and would fade. He concluded that Allen was right and that it was possible to extend love out beyond a personal attachment into a central well of energy, what Ginsberg called "a benevolent sentient center to the whole Creation" or "big peaceful Lovebrain." It was Bill's confidence in this that gave him the courage to conduct a thorough analysis of his whole life, including his troubled relationship with Allen. There were naturally many areas that he was unable to reach himself, and one of the reasons for his trip to Paris was to find a psychoanalyst who could remove the unconscious blocks that remained.

They talked through the afternoon and late into the night and established such a rapport that Allen almost trembled with excitement. This new closeness was similar to what he had with Peter but without the sexual vibration that accompanied it. They discussed sex, and Bill finally accepted that Allen was prepared to have sex with him but that his heart was not really in it. Bill said he would no longer pressure

Allen to go to bed, a position he had been heading toward in his self-analysis. Allen wrote Peter, "He no longer needs me like he used to, doesn't think of me as a permanent future intimate sex schlupp lover, thinks even he'll wind up maybe after difficulties with women." Allen felt a tremendous sense of relief. His dread that Burroughs had come to claim him disappeared and he awoke the next morning with "a great bliss of freedom and joy in my heart."

Allen felt sure that when Peter and Bill next met, there would be no more animosity between them. "Bill is changed nature," he told Peter, "I even feel much changed, great clouds rolled away, as I feel when you and I were in rapport. Well, our rapport has remained in me, with me, rather than losing it, I'm feeling to everyone something of the same as between us . . . I cried the other night realizing you'd gone, thinking that love would go away with you and I'd be alone without connection—but now I see Bill is really on same connection and I begin to feel connected with everything and everyone, the universe seems so happy."

Allen and Bill slept in their own rooms that night, both feeling happy. It was the first time Allen had been alone in bed for at least a year. He missed Peter and masturbated. Bill woke him in the morning and they had breakfast and talked some more. The new rapport was real. Delighted, Allen wrote Peter, "I changed too, no longer suspicious and worried of him. He doesn't even bother the cat." (In Tangier, Bill had made a habit of torturing the hotel cats. Bill's improved demeanor saved Madame Rachou's cat Mirtaud from his attentions.)

Allen was pleased that he and Bill were now discussing the very things that it had been impossible to talk about in Tangier. They talked about a new model for relationships, about finding a way to extend "Love bliss" to many other people without losing the essential intimacy of the partners. "We'll solve that problem too before we're done," Allen wrote Peter. It took almost a decade for the idea to spread but by 1967 tens of thousands of hippies were practicing the ideas that Allen and Bill had mulled over at Allen's kitchen table in room 25: a lifestyle based on free love, peace, and the use of consciousness-expanding drugs.

Allen explained his ideas about the need for openness between people and the need to love everyone in a letter to his father, and received a very touching reply from Louis describing his love for Allen's mother, Naomi. "I do what my nature allows me," Louis wrote. "True, in the beginning, when I loved a woman who grew incurably psychotic, I was handicapped, yet in my handicap I used the handcuffs as bracelets by letting my spirit soar and create poetry and also providing the best I could for Naomi. I did more than I could but the odds were against me . . . I hope you never know what it is to love a woman as I did and then have to lose her."

Bill explained his method of meditation and self-analysis to Allen, how he accepted any mean or horrible fantasies that came to mind as being a true part of himself and, instead of suppressing them, let them emerge and take shape so that he could analyze them. Allen thought that his own fear of marijuana was caused by his unwillingness to accept the paranoid and sordid perceptions that it sometimes brought on within him. He realized that he was shutting them out rather than experiencing them, so the next night he tried it Bill's way, intending to go along with whatever came up. Soon he had a masochistic fantasy of being fucked by Peter. This turned into a more horrible fantasy of being fucked by his brother and then by his father. He then realized that the masochistic dream of being fucked by his father had always been with him but had been too ugly for him to accept before then. He looked at it consciously for the first time and experienced a great feeling of new knowledge and liberation from it instead of again passing it off as unreal. He wrote Peter, "Just as between us, we cleared up hostility and doubts by bringing them out in the open, so inside myself I have been continuing the same process."

Allen's relationship with Bill deepened and grew more intimate. They were more relaxed around each other and, though they went to bed together a few times, Allen thought that they would end up with a nonsexual relationship because Bill decided he didn't really need sex anymore. Bill began a twice-weekly analysis with Dr. Schlumberger on January 28, intending to make sure that the improvements in his mental state achieved by his self-analysis in Tangier were lasting ones. His analytic sessions would last for nine months before Bill decided that no further progress was being made. The good feelings seemed to be breaking out all over because Bill also got along with Gregory for the first time and, in a fit of generosity, Gregory gave Bill the big leather coat that he had acquired in Germany. In return Allen and Bill paid Gregory's train fare to Venice and gave him a bag of heroin to take to Alan Ansen as a gift. Allen wrote his brother, Eugene, "Burroughs and Ansen never liked him before this year. He seems to have ripened in Europe."

Even Jack finally sent Allen the $225 he owed him. Allen had borrowed money from Bill in order to keep going and suggested they go together to the American Express at L'Opera to cash the money into traveler's checks. It was a fine day with a clear blue sky so they decided to walk, and afterward they visited "Pierre," who gave them a black-market rate for dollars. Allen told Eugene that Jack had paid him and said, "Sooner or later, when the shock of repaying me wears off, I'll maybe remind him to return the $25 you once advanced him to get to S.F. He's very funny about money, not that he's stingy but he has his mother's native French peasant parsimony which has served him well the last ten years."

Allen and Jack were still exchanging regular correspondence, though it must have been difficult for Ginsberg to maintain his happy mood when he received such letters as the one Kerouac wrote him on January 21: "When I feel happy and pure from weeks of studying sutras and praying, suddenly I open one of your letters (sometimes) and feel a nameless depression, as tho a black scum over my lucid bowl . . . Well you know you ARE a black bowl of sorrow . . . such depression." Kerouac's solution to Allen's worries was for Allen to adopt his own "apolitical" stand: "Why, for instance . . . don't you ignore war, ignore politics, ignore samara injust fuckups, they're endless . . . Allen, cool it. Rid thee of thy wrath, go lamby, isn't it a better thing to do in eternity to leave everybody alone good and evil alike and just pile along glad? Aha! our old 1946 argument!"

Jack believed that Allen should not revise his poems once he had written them and was annoyed that Allen and Alan Ansen had revised and changed Bill's text when they were in Tangier. Allen tried to explain to Jack, "I write so little painfully and revise and I can't get settled down to free expression and have nightmares about ever holding my piece. It's not that I don't really agree with you about method of writing—I don't have your football energy for scrowling endlessly on pages—I am nervous and fretful and have to force myself to sit down—at least lately—other seasons it's been more natural—I guess all this publicity is bad."

Grove Press sent Ginsberg an advance copy of Kerouac's new novel, *The Subterraneans*, and he read it the night he received it. He wrote Peter the next day, "It's very intimate and funny—tho Jack seems to reveal unconsciously that he avoids deep final relations with women on account of tie and fear with his mother, and doesn't completely understand it in the end of the book, and so suffers and turns to writing Buddhism on account of self-frustration of human love-possibilities." Ginsberg did not think it was one of Jack's better books, nor did his father, though Louis was more vehement in his opinions. He wrote Allen that it was "mutilated in its English, wretched abominable English sentence structure . . . wreck of the English language," and that he would flunk any pupil of his who mangled the language like that. Many of Kerouac's critics agreed with Louis.

Meanwhile, in Venice, Gregory used for himself all the junk intended for Alan Ansen, leaving only two meager allotments. When Ansen remonstrated with him, Gregory was furious and Alan threatened to repatriate him to Paris. Bill now said that he was not prepared to do much, or in fact anything, to help Gregory, and Joy Ungerer felt the same way. They were tired of Gregory never having any money to make his own way. However, when Ansen got over his irritation at Gregory, they became good friends.

Gregory was renowned for a remarkable ability to rub people the wrong way. The very first night he was in Venice he was thrown out of Harry's Bar because some Americans at the bar took exception to his long hair and sneakers. Alan lived a very comfortable life, as evidenced in the opening line of Gregory's poem "Venice, 1958": "I eat! and well!" He and Alan got some more heroin, which they took, and wrote chain-poems together. Alan was very impressed with *Gasoline* and wrote a favorable two-page review for *Partisan Review.* He was so impressed that he said, a bit rashly, that Gregory should be supported forever on the strength of it.

Alan introduced Gregory to Peggy Guggenheim. She was a good friend of Ansen's and he sometimes staged pageants at her palazzo. Despite her patronage of the arts, Guggenheim had a reputation by this time as one of the stingiest women in Venice—she served the cheapest wine at dinner and took a gondola to the other side of the island in order to buy the cheapest toilet paper for her guests. Nevertheless, Gregory clearly thought he might get his hands on some of the Guggenheim millions. They saw each other for a week and got drunk together. Peggy thought Gregory was wild, and when he "confessed" to her that he had been in prison she gave him a wristwatch (he had been late for an appointment because he didn't have one). But the problem was that Guggenheim wanted to get Gregory into her bed. Twenty-eight-year-old Corso felt more attracted to her thirty-three-year-old daughter Pegeen than to fifty-nine-year-old Peggy. Then Gregory made some remark about her daughter that Peggy found insulting and he was no longer welcome at the palazzo.

This sort of scenario had happened before with the other Beats. When Burroughs was in Venice in 1956, he and Ansen attended a soirée in honor of the British Consul at the palazzo. Alan explained to Bill that it was customary to kiss Peggy's hand. Bill was what he described as "country drunk" and brayed, "I will be glad to kiss her cunt if that is the custom." Unfortunately Guggenheim's man in attendence, Bob Brady, overheard the remark and practically swooned with outrage. Bill was banished from the premises. And of course there was the incident when Guggenheim visited Ansen in

1957, and was almost hit by a towel Peter had thrown to Allen. Guggenheim was deeply offended and refused to invite them to a party given in honor of Nicolas Calas. As Bill wrote to Ansen, "It was hardly on the cards that Peggy Guggenheim should find Allen and Peter congenial. However, it does seem to me she is being a bit unreasonable to move in admittedly bohemian circles and simultaneously demand conventional behavior."

However, by the time Gregory and Jean-Jacques Lebel took a house together in Venice for the summer of 1960, she had forgotten Gregory's remarks and relations were once more cordial.

4 **Bomb**

"It seemed like a nice place. Very cheap. I love those red tile floors, it was just a very nice place, old old old. Middle ages. And Madame Rachou was very nice."

William Seward Burroughs

With Peter gone, Allen began to look around for new sexual partners. When Peter and Allen were together, Allen was happy to extend the relationship to include women for Peter. Now Allen found himself without Peter, but with his girls still around. He wrote Peter that he "Saw Joy, had lone ball with her 2 nites ago, she came I didn't. Talked Françoise out of idealizing me. Told her to not come by except Fridays, hah that's over." Allen began to socialize more; he often hung out at Gaït Frogé's bookshop, and he went to a book launch at the Mistral and had dinner with Bernard Frechtman. Now that he could afford it, Allen wrote to Thomas Parkinson and made arrangements to visit London and stay with him. He spent the night before he left with Joy Ungerer and wrote to Peter, "Screwed Joy again and we both came together, she's a great girl. She loved you—she digs you—she thinks you're tremendously wise and deep—did you know? I mean she appreciates you. She's been meditating too—sort of cheerful asia-girl mystic."

Allen and Gregory saw a lot of Jean-Jacques Lebel, who was not only a friend but also acted as an interpreter. Lebel was born in Paris in 1936 but had been educated in New York, during the war, where he perfected his English. In New York he had three decisive encounters: Billie Holiday; and, through his father, the art historian Robert

Lebel, he got to know André Breton and Marcel Duchamp, both of whom had spent the war years in the United States. Jean-Jacques embraced Surrealism from an early age and had his first exhibition in 1955 in Florence at the Galleria Numero. He first met the Beats when Bill Burroughs did a reading in the basement *cave* of the Frogé's English Bookshop. Jean-Jacques remembered:

They thought I was American and they came up to me and said, "Man we have to score some hash, where can we go?" They asked my name and I told them and Gregory said, "That's a Frog name!" I said, "Yeah, I'm French!" and they couldn't believe it. Anyway, so we took the Metro and we went to the Bastille. At the Bastille there was a little Algerian place called Chez Madame Ali, and we used to spend a lot of time Chez Madame Ali. Ali was an Algerian fellow, and his wife was French, it was Madame Ali's place. It was on the Passage Thiere, near the Place Bastille. There was two rooms. The first room was tables and you would eat couscous and when you entered there you were stoned immediately because the thickness of the smoke was so heavy that you couldn't breathe without getting stoned, just breathing the air. We would buy little cubes of hash, as thick as a finger, for three francs. It was black stuff, coming specially from Khetama in Morocco, really good stuff. Madame Ali had a dog, and the dog was so stoned, he would always bump himself into chairs. The dog was totally out of his mind, he couldn't walk straight. To go from here to there he would go around the room. The dog was completely wrecked.

And the second room was a secret room, where they had meetings of the FLN, the Algerian underground—we were in the middle of the Algerian war you understand. And we were sitting there, getting stoned, all talking in English of course. And the Arab guys were stoned, looking at us, really weird, they could not understand why we were not speaking French and we were the only non-Moroccans, non-Algerians, in the place of course. Then all of a sudden, one day, *Crash!* The police come in with tommy guns, like in an old black-and-white cops movie. The French guys with trench coats and an old Citroën outside. "Face the wall!" We couldn't understand what the fuck was going on. So we were standing up against the wall with our arms up, and Gregory was the one who was really shitting his pants because he had needles and stuff. It took me ten minutes to understand. They weren't after us, or after the hash or anything, they were after the guys in the back room, who were having secret meetings. It was the FLN. That's where we were, can you imagine? They didn't bust us because they immediately saw we were not Algerians. I continued speaking English, they saw I was French. They asked us for our papers. They didn't even look in our pockets, or anything. They knew we weren't Algerians so they left us alone but the poor other guys, boy they got bashed on the head, they were bloody, so that's how I realized where we were.

Allen spent two weeks in London beginning February 2, when he crossed the Channel to Dover on the Boat Train. He was disappointed to find that there was no *old* London; the Great Fire of 1666 destroyed most of the medieval buildings, and two German bombardments plus the actions of property developers had done away with almost all of the rest except a scattering of churches, the Tower of London, and Westminster Abbey, where Allen saw Poets Corner and walked in the famous cloisters. London Bridge was a disappointment to him, "not much of a bridge, looks like any other bridge for cars, nothing beautiful about it," he told Peter, not realizing that the song was about the long-gone medieval bridge.

Simon Watson-Taylor, whom he had met in Paris, was working as a steward for the British Overseas Airways Corporation (BOAC) and was just about to fly off somewhere but arranged to see Allen on his return. Kerouac's school friend Seymour Wyse, whom Allen knew from the '40s when he ran Greenwich Records in the Village, was now in London, where he had a record shop of his own in Chelsea. He invited

Allen over and they spent all night talking. Otherwise, Allen didn't know enough people to have an active social life. He concentrated on seeing the sights and the museums. He found that London was filled with the works of Blake and Turner but most of all he was amazed by the Elgin Marbles, the Parthenon frieze taken from the Acropolis in Athens. He wrote Peter, "Elgin Marbles Naked Love in British Museum. Greatest thing in Europe."

Thomas Parkinson took Allen to the BBC to record a five-minute contribution to his series on modern American poetry. Evergreen had released an anthology album containing a recording of a very poor reading of "Howl," which Allen hated, and he felt nervous about reading now. Shortly after he began, Donald Carne-Ross, the producer, stopped the tape and ran excitedly into the studio shouting, "That's it! That's what poetry should be!" and asked if Allen would read the whole of "Howl" as well as "Supermarket in California" for a separate broadcast. This did wonders for Allen's confidence and he gave a slow, tearful reading, gradually building the tempo, imagining that he was talking directly to William Blake, becoming so emotional that his voice cracked a little and he almost broke down in tears. Everyone agreed that it was a great reading and Allen got drunk afterward with Carne-Ross, who said he would like to record Kerouac, Burroughs, and Corso.

When the producer went home, Allen felt sad and lonely. Watson-Taylor had just returned from his trip so Allen decided to visit him. In his drunken state he still managed to walk there, arriving at 7 P.M. Simon decided to cheer him up. "Went out on his Vespa motor scooter weaving fast round corners flying and balancing behind him ready to scrape my skull on the road for Death if it came to that," Allen wrote Peter. "Went into big bars and pubs and I talked to everybody beautiful all night and came home with Simon drunk, he invited me to sleep with him, he was drunk too, so we got naked and fell asleep in each other's arms without doing sexy except kiss in a big warm comfortable home bed." Watson-Taylor shared a house with George Melly, an artist, writer, and singer, and Allen very much enjoyed the atmosphere there. Melly was an expert on Surrealism and the walls were hung with a number of René Magrittes as well as a Paul Klee drawing, a Max Ernst, and various strange Dada objects. There were stuffed miniature dogs and a huge art library. Simon told Allen he could come and stay any time. Allen always liked him, and years later, in the '70s, Watson-Taylor stayed with him in Boulder and lectured on 'Pataphysics at the Naropa Institute.

Allen visited English poet Gael Turnbull in Worcester and took some of Turnbull's poems to send to Don Allen at *Evergreen Review.* Turnbull was a doctor, but he also found time to publish a very lively series of poetry pamphlets through his Migrant Press and had an enormous correspondence with poets all over the world. Turnbull drove Allen to Stratford-upon-Avon to see Shakespeare's grave. From there Allen took a train to Oxford where he read to a group of very enthusiastic students. He read "Howl" and Bill's "The City" from *Naked Lunch,* and from Robert Creeley's *The Whip,* as well as work by Philip Whalen and Denise Levertov. Allen told Peter, "I feel great again, communicating and crying in public—in front of the mild withdrawn English."

Parkinson also drove Allen to see Salisbury Cathedral and Stonehenge, where they walked among the fallen stones in the cold February wind. At St. Paul's Cathedral he climbed up to the Whispering Gallery in the dome and looked out over London. The area surrounding St. Paul's had been completely destroyed during the war and everywhere there were men clearing bomb sites and erecting new buildings. Allen tracked down poet Stephen Spender at *Encounter* magazine and gave him a set of City Lights books and Jonathan Williams's Jargon Society books to review. He also gave him a section from *Naked Lunch* but Spender rejected it, saying he had no interest in "wading through yards and yards of entrails."

Meanwhile, with Allen away Bill spent most of his time in Paris with John Balf and Mack Sheldon Thomas. They were both Texans, the former described by journalist Peter Lennon as being "of formidable scholarly capacity and decidedly un-Texan physique." Thomas lived in the Hotel Pax, a hotel similar to the Beat Hotel, located just around the corner on rue St. André des Arts. Shell, as Burroughs called Thomas, was a young writer trying to find his own voice by making the traditional pilgrimage to Paris. He had many things in common with Burroughs, including an interest in drugs and mysticism, and he was later to share in Bill's experiments with scrying and mirror-gazing. He and Bill became good friends and remained in contact until Bill's death.

The poet and editor Cid Corman came to visit and was disappointed to find Allen away. Bill received him in Allen's room, but just as they were talking, Madame Rachou came bursting in, accusing Corman of sleeping there. Bill assured her that this was not the case, and told Allen, "Graham and his beastly young hipsters keep blowing fuses with their machine and bugging the landlady ruins her disposition . . . and that kid Dick is somewhere in the house blowing fuses—he blew three yesterday with various electrical appliances." Bill felt depressed and took so much paregoric—an elixir of opium available legally from pharmacies in France—that he developed a light habit. He told Allen that he was making experimental use of it for his analysis, but on his return Allen insisted that he go to a doctor and get some apomorphine and kick the habit. Bill's life had been inconvenienced by the arrest of Zizi—one of Allen's and Bill's pot connections—and the closing down of his restaurant. Zizi continued to deal on the street but Bill didn't like scoring in public like that. However, he braved the possibility of arrest and got so high he didn't know which city he was in. He couldn't find his way home from St. Germain, two blocks away, and then he spilt jam all over his floor.

It was soon noticed that Allen's room was empty and Bill wrote Allen to say, "That kid Dick whatever was around trying to move into your room. 'NOOOOO' I brayed with inflexible authority. 'Don't like you and don't know you. I need two rooms. When I get tired of sitting in one I go and sit in the other.' Such crust. These Paris mooches would move right in and shove a man out of his own bed."

Bill became a great favorite of all the young pot-smoking Americans in the quarter and he never seemed bored with them, just sat in his room talking endlessly about junk, raising tomatoes in Texas, sword swallowers—a new interest—cancer, and viruses, while they marveled at this remarkable "hip gent." Bill had been hanging out with the younger crowd at the Café Monaco at the carrefour de l'Odeon where most of the regulars were American and English expatriates, painters, writers, and folksingers, who used it as a meeting place where they could leave and receive messages. There was a folksinger there named Darryl Adams who wore a ring through his ear, which was at the time highly unusual. Adams lived around the corner in the same hotel as Shell Thomas, but often visited Bill in his room in the afternoon to sit and talk while Bill made pots of English tea.

Bill reported, "Darryl was always going to see people when they were sailing and then staying on the boat. Well now this became very funny because the French are very tough on stowaways, they take your passport away etcetera. They tow the boat out, and when the tug boat comes back, if there's anybody left on there, that's their chance to get off. When Ansen left, Darryl stayed on the boat, but he had the sense to get off on the tug. There was a time when stowaways were fashionable. The first few times it happened. Oh yes, they'd spring out of the lifeboat at you, a life buoy around their neck, but that soon became a godammed nuisance."

Bill thought that this new American generation would be hip, and that they could slowly change the laws and attitudes back home. He told Allen he thought there might be some redemption for America, and that America might find its soul at last.

In February a friend of Shell's, an enthusiastic young New York actor named B.J. Carroll, known simply as B.J., moved into the room next door to Allen, along with his multilingual French girlfriend, who called everybody "Man." B.J. was very tall and rather tough-looking with his leather jacket, wild black hair, and big black beard. He smoked a lot of hash and quickly got to know Bill and Allen. He had held up a bookstore in San Francisco years before and said that he was horrified by the inhumanity and "bum kick of it" and had been "happy and good" ever since. He was first introduced to the Beat Generation through an article by John Clellon Holmes in *Esquire* magazine and told Allen, "You guys have really put it down! Us young are going to take off from there and really carry on the light and make it!" Allen thought he sounded like Peter. Allen took him to the Louvre for his first visit and they spent a lot of time together. Allen wrote Peter, "Another 4th successive all night up and walking or writing opiated or sober Seine sunrise gawkings with B.J., Peteresque ex-Hollywood angel talk fiend who woke up in hospital 2 mo ago with an infected asshole & big vision of heaven translating him from a Wild One to a Wilder One, now goes about Paris imitating Bill and accosting Germans on the street to talk about who are the young hip cats of Allemande . . . Also he started writing poetry last month & drags me out nights to stay up all joint night babbling in Halles & see sunrise over Notre Dame." As a consequence of all this carousing, Allen found himself living at night and not getting up until four in the afternoon. Bill remembered B.J.: "He became an actor, he always wanted to be an actor. I always saw him a fair amount in Paris, but after he came to America I never encountered him again."

Another new friend was a Dane named Lee, who was always surly when drunk. Shortly after they got to know him he got so drunk he fell and broke his arm. He had been trained to murder in the underground resistance in Denmark during the war and later fought in the U.S. Army and in Indochina. He said that he went to war because only in battle did men love each other and tell each other the truth—only then, he believed, were they true friends. He told them about a letter he had received a few days before from an old buddy in the army, enclosing 50,000 francs with a message telling him to get drunk on him because he was going to commit suicide. His friend's mother wired him shortly after that to say he had killed himself. Lee sometimes took Allen to his favorite cheap Chinese restaurant and they would go to bars together, but often Lee would get drunk at the Bonaparte and curse life and try to start fights, which Allen didn't like.

Allen missed Peter terribly and wrote to tell him that lines from Shakespeare's "Sonnet 30" kept popping up in his head: "But if the while I think on thee, dear friend, / all losses are restored and sorrows end." It was also at this time that he wrote the poem "Europe Europe": "I sit in my room / and imagine the future / sunlight falls on Paris / I am alone there is no / one whose love is perfect / mouth softer than angel / man has been mad man's / love is not perfect I / have not wept enough / my breast will be heavy / till death . . ."

On his return to Paris from London, Allen saw Joy again, but the sex was not very good because he had taken some of Bill's paregoric. Allen told her he would marry her to get her American citizenship if she needed it. "Maybe we Ball her in Manhattan," he told Peter. "Or maybe you marry her. Good girl—what a mystic, calm like pond water." After Joy left, Allen went out to the gay bar at the carrefour l'Odeon and got drunk and listened to the jukebox, surrounded by French and Arab boys. He wandered drunkenly around the bars and met up eventually with Darryl and B.J. He got even more inebriated and talked endlessly with them as they crisscrossed the nighttime streets. He smoked pot for the first time in weeks but was too drunk to really notice its effect. They finished up at the Bonaparte where Allen picked up an Arab boy. They had more to drink and the boy returned to the hotel with him but Allen fell flat on the bed, his head spinning, naked and drunk. He could see that the boy was only going to rob him. The boy took off his pants as if to come to bed but put on Allen's instead. He went through the drawers looking for money. Allen didn't care and was feeling too sick to get up. Allen told Peter, "I told him to take a few excess shirts I didn't want anymore, it was funny, he picked up my new (I bought in England) turtleneck gray wool sweater and the corduroy coat, I opened one eye and said I needed them, so he put them back, must have found my money in my watch pocket (3000 francs) ([$10]) and got dressed and walked out." The next morning Allen was tired and hungover. Bill said that Allen should have known better but, as Allen told Peter, "I have never picked up Arabs before and wasn't bugged by the practical loss hardly, tho a little sad no lovemaking kicks, ah, well, well, the world is full of sad monsters nobody has a good time like I wanted to, so nothing to do except to be good cheer and look for souls again anyway."

Ferlinghetti sent Allen the address of the Vogue recording studio in Paris, where Allen was supposed to make a recording of "Howl" for

Fantasy Records in Berkeley. He was to get an advance of $50. Despite spending hours and hours reading, and almost losing his voice trying to get it right, he was unable to come up with a satisfactory version in the clinical atmosphere of the studio and Fantasy had to wait until a good live recording was made in 1959 in Chicago before they could release the record. Allen explained to Ferlinghetti, "The idea of facing the microphone again is too much. I mean, I have tried but the feeling I have is awful—sort of like a young virgin boy who can't get it up in a whorehouse & freezes more and more." Whereas the BBC recordings had been excellent, the finality of making a record, in addition to the five-year recording contract and all the paperwork, conspired to dampen Allen's spirits. He was, however, able to make a short tape for the Canadian Broadcasting System, for which he received $35, helping to tide him over.

In March, Bill discovered the medical library in the rue Dragon, which had all the medical journals and textbooks Bill had ever dreamed of. Many of the details of obscure diseases that he discovered in his research were to end up in *Naked Lunch*. He and Allen began to read enormous volumes on the biology of schizophrenia and learned about experiments in which schizophrenic patients were given mescaline. They sat around for days talking about the implications of the research. One finding that Bill regarded as most significant was that schizophrenics never seemed to get cancer. Bill felt that this was a lead to a cancer cure and began clipping all the articles on cancer he could from *Time* and the *New York Herald Tribune*. Beyond this, Bill wasn't doing very much except sitting in his room, drinking tea; he consumed as much tea as Dr. Johnson is reputed to have drunk.

He would sometimes pass the time by composing occasional verse. One read:

> *There was a young man from Timbuktu*
> *Who fucked a fat old Jew*
> *He said, "It's not bad,*
> *It's just like dad,*
> *I'd fuck him again, wouldn't you?"*

He went to his analyst twice a week and waited for his life to change. He and Allen still made it occasionally but Bill had said that he wasn't much interested in sex anymore. He felt that something new was happening to him and that perhaps he would become celibate or take up women—he didn't know which. Over the next few years Bill did occasionally take a woman back to the hotel, though it was usually a disaster.

Bill's psychoanalysis was obviously uncovering a number of sexual problems, including the identification of a major trauma that had occurred when he was very young. Bill had had a great attachment to his Welsh nanny, Mary Evans, whom he knew as Nursy, to the extent that he would throw tantrums on Thursdays when she took her day off. Somewhere in his childhood memory there was a "murder" but he had not been able to reach back that far in his self-analysis. Back in the 1940s, Bill's analyst, Dr. Paul Federn, had finally cracked and yelled at Bill: "What IS this that has affected you your whole life?" But Bill just could not remember.

In July 1958, just after Allen had left Paris, Dr. Schlumberger identified the "murder" as a miscarriage. Bill wrote Allen, "Analysis is coming to a head. No doubt now: I witnessed a miscarriage, by Mary the evil governess, and the results were burned in the furnace in my presence." Bill later decided that this was not the case. Mary's boyfriend was a veterinarian and had allowed Bill to watch when he put down a couple of dogs. Bill had a memory of something he did with his older brother Mort when he was four years old. Mary had taken the two boys to see her boyfriend. Bill remembered being out-of-doors and one or two images: the man's grinning face; Mary saying "Come on, Billy. It won't hurt you," and his brother saying later, "Should we tell on Nursy?" Shortly afterward Mary Evans abruptly left the Burroughs family after an unexplained incident. Did the couple try to get young Billy to have sex with Mary, or to suck the boyfriend's cock? Bill was never able to find out what happened. Alan Ansen was of the opinion that Bill had been forced to suck the cock of the nurse's boyfriend and that Bill may have bitten the man. He cited a passage in *Naked Lunch* about "the white defenders," meaning his teeth, as an unconscious reference on Bill's part. It was something that Bill and his brother could not tell their straitlaced parents about.

Bill was born in St. Louis, Missouri, on February 5, 1914, in a bedroom at 4664 Berlin Avenue; the street name would be changed to Pershing shortly after the outbreak of the Great War. It was a pleasant middle-class neighborhood, and the house had a large front lawn and a substantial garden in the back. In addition to Mary Evans, there was a maid, a yard man, and an Irish cook who taught Bill how to call the toad that lived in the front yard. She would make a barely discernible humming sound and the toad would crawl out from under a rock by the front door.

In 1926 the Burroughs family moved to the prosperous suburb of Ladue, where Bill's father had built a white-frame house set on five acres of grounds. Bill attended the John Burroughs School—named after the naturalist, no relation—which he walked to each morning. Bill was named after his grandfather, William Seward Burroughs, the inventor of the adding machine and founder of the giant Burroughs Corporation. Bill's parents sold their shares in the company in 1929 and though they remained well-off, they were not millionaires, nor did Bill have the trust fund described by Kerouac in one of his books. His parents did, however, send him a monthly allowance of $200 after he graduated from Harvard in 1936, which continued until 1963, when he told them he was now earning enough from his books to live on.

Bill knew from an early age that he was homosexual. He developed a fixation on a fellow student, Kells Elvins, and though it never got physical they remained friends for life, sharing a house at Harvard, becoming citrus farmers together in Texas, and visiting in Mexico City, Tangier, Copenhagen, or wherever Bill happened to be over the years. It was at Harvard with Kells Elvins that Bill wrote the story "Twilights Last Gleamings," which first introduced his famous character Dr. Benway.

At the age of twelve, Bill read hobo and thief turned author Jack Black's autobiography *You Can't Win*, which had a tremendous affect on his thinking. "I first read *You Can't Win* in 1926, in an edition bound in red cardboard," he wrote much later. "Stultified and confined by middle-class St. Louis mores, I was fascinated by this glimpse of an underworld of seedy rooming houses, pool parlors, cat houses and opium dens, of bull pens and cat burglars and hobo jungles. I learned about the Johnson Family of good bums and thieves, with a code of conduct that made more sense to me than the arbitrary, hypocritical rules that were taken for granted as being 'right' by my peers." The book also provided for him a number of his characters: "Salt Chunk Mary" and the Johnson Family come from this book.

Bill was fascinated by the underworld and, protected by his monthly allowance, he began to move in those circles; taking small-time jobs as bartender, reporter, advertising copy writer, private detective working for Merritt Incorporated, and, his favorite job of all and one that he kept for eight months, working for A. J. Cohen Exterminators in Chicago. "I used to bang on the door real loud, 'You got any bugs, lady?' hoping to attract the neighbors so she might lie and say she didn't have any, and she would sign my book and I would get through my list early." Two of Bill's books were subsequently called *Exterminator:* a collection of Cut-ups, coauthored with Brion Gysin, called *The Exterminator*, published by Auerhahn Press in 1960; and *Exterminator!*, a collection of short stories published by Viking in 1973.

In New York in the early '40s, Bill met up with Jack Kerouac and Allen Ginsberg and, through them, was introduced to Joan Vollmer, who later became Bill's common-law wife. In 1945 he moved into her apartment on 115th Street along with Kerouac and Ginsberg—a legendary Beat Generation "commune" where many of the "routines" incorporated into *Naked Lunch* first had their genesis. Bill psychoanalyzed both Jack and Allen and together they acted out role-playing games, exploring the stereotypes of their own characters: Jack becoming the innocent American abroad wearing his father's straw hat, Allen playing the scheming art dealer, and Bill dressing up in drag and turning into a mad lesbian countess.

Many of Bill's roles were suggested by the layers of personality he was discovering in his own psychoanalysis. Bill had been in some sort of analysis off and on ever since 1939, when he cut off his little finger at the lower joint with a pair of poultry shears to try to impress a boyfriend. That incident landed him briefly in Bellevue, followed by a spell at the Payne-Whitney clinic. He read deeply into psychoanalytic theory and tried most of them. The ideas of Wilhelm Reich appealed to him most, and though he was never analyzed by a Reichian he did build an orgone accumulator, a device that Reich maintained could capture and concentrate what he termed "life energy." Bill swore by it and still had one in his garden at the time he died.

In 1945 Bill met Herbert Huncke, and a variety of petty thieves, who introduced him to heroin. He was busted and turned to heroin dealing while waiting for the case to come to court. His father bailed him out and in 1947 Bill and Joan moved to New Waverly, Texas, where on July 21, Joan gave birth to their son, William Burroughs III. They moved from Texas to New Orleans where Bill was busted once more, and rather than show up in court and face a jail sentence Bill moved himself and family to Mexico City.

There, in September 1951, Joan was killed in a shooting accident. Bill had recently returned from an unsuccessful expedition to the South American jungle in search of the hallucinogenic drug yagé. He had brought back a knife from Quito and wanted to have it sharpened. Bill later wrote, "The knife-sharpener had a little whistle and a fixed route, and as I walked down the street towards his cart a feeling of loss and sadness that had weighed on me all day so I could hardly breathe intensified to such an extent that I found tears streaming down my face. 'What on earth is wrong?' I wondered."

Back at his apartment, he began throwing back drinks and was soon joined by Joan. That evening Bill had arranged to meet someone at a friend's apartment hoping to sell him a gun. When Bill and Joan arrived at the apartment the man had not arrived but a party was in progress. Bill and Joan continued to drink. At one point Bill announced, "Let's do our William Tell act!" Joan placed a shot glass on her head. Bill, in his drunken state, picked up the gun, took aim, and fired. The shot missed the glass, which fell to the floor and spun around unbroken. Joan slumped to the floor, a bullet hole in her forehead. They never had a William Tell act and, in any case, as Bill later said, it was madness to shoot a glass in a crowded room, as the flying shards could have caused tremendous damage.

Bill never fully understood what happened. It was as if he was possessed by an evil spirit. His depression was caused by being rejected by his current boyfriend, who had accompanied him on the jungle trip, the story of which is told in his novel *Queer*. Bill was charged with "criminal imprudence," and after ten days in jail he was let out on bail. Some months later his lawyer was arrested for an unrelated murder and skipped the country. Bill was advised to do the same.

When he and Joan lived in New Orleans Bill had begun writing *Junkie*, the story of his experiences as a junkie in New York City. Now again he felt a great need to write, as he put it in an oft-quoted passage:

> I am forced to the appalling conclusion that I would never have become a writer but for Joan's death, and to a realization of the extent to which this event has motivated and formulated my writing. I live with the constant threat of possession, and a constant need to escape from possession, from Control. So the death of Joan brought me in contact with the invader, the Ugly Spirit, and maneuvered me into a lifelong struggle, in which I have had no choice except to write my way out.

He finished *Junkie* and Allen Ginsberg sold it to Ace Books in New York. It was published in 1953 as a paperback under the pseudonym William Lee. That same year Bill moved to New York and stayed with Allen. It was during this time that they had their affair, after which Ginsberg left New York to explore the jungles of Chiapas. Bill moved to Tangier, where he lived in Dutch Tony's male brothel and killed his sorrow with junk. Bill's "routines," humorous stories exaggerated and taken to the absolute limit of the imagination, which the 115th Street group used to act out, now became the subject of Bill's letters to Allen, and over the next few years most of the material that would eventually find its way into *Naked Lunch* was sent first to Allen as humorous inserts or as part of his actual letters. Bill always said he needed a recipient for his routines, and it was usually someone he was emotionally fixated upon. This was the material that Bill's friends had planned to go to Tangier to help him collate in 1957.

Allen used his time well at the hotel and was producing some of his finest work, though the increasing pressure of his correspondence meant that he had less time to devote to his poetry and journals. In March, Allen wrote his celebrated poem "The Lion for Real," causing Burroughs to comment, "Aha, so that's what's become of your heterosexual personality, the Lion." Allen was worried that people would misinterpret the poem as being a self-pitying lament over the problems of being homosexual but the only misinterpretation was when Diana Trilling mistakenly thought it was about her husband, Lionel, who had once been Allen's English professor at Columbia.

Allen also wrote "The Names," a poignant evocation of friends, more explicit than that in "Howl" and some of them dead, like Joan Vollmer: "Joan in dreams bent forward smiling asks news of the living / as in life the same sad tolerance, no skullbone judge of drunks . . ."

Allen spent several evenings with the poet and novelist Alain Bosquet, then in his late thirties. In his lifetime Bosquet won every major literary prize in France; he published twenty volumes of verse and a like number of books of fiction. He wrote for *Le Monde* and *Le Figaro*, and was compiling an anthology of new American poetry. He already had Allen's name on a list of poets he wanted to translate, but Allen thought talking to him was a waste of time because Bosquet didn't like Gregory's work or get excited about the manuscripts and magazines that Allen showed him. Nonetheless, Allen loaned him many books and wrote to Denise Levertov for poems to give him, also asking her for the addresses of Robert Creeley and Charles Olson in order to get manuscripts from them. When he saw Bosquet again he gave him poems by Levertov, a copy of Creeley's *The Whip*, and back issues of *Black Mountain Review* and *Origin*. Allen wrote Creeley, "Plus two evenings reading him poems & explaining, one free meal I got from it & lots of grief including the feeling I was a chauvinistic whore." When Gallimard published Bosquet's anthology, *Trente-Cinq Jeunes Poètes*

Américains, in February 1960, it contained Ginsberg's poem "America." That Allen should go to such lengths to get his friends published was entirely typical of his efforts at the time, and he often achieved his aims despite the uphill struggle.

Nicolas Calas, the Greek poet who changed his name from Nicolaos Calamaris when he joined the Surrealist group just before the war, visited Allen at the hotel. They had met earlier through Alan Ansen in Venice, where Calas had been staying with Peggy Guggenheim. Calas introduced Allen and Bill to the English poet David Gascoyne, who, Allen thought, "may be great." Allen particularly liked the ending to one of his poems, which read, "Christ of the Revolution and of Poetry," and was still able to quote it twenty-five years later. Gascoyne was a well-known English Surrealist but he was surprised to find that Allen knew and respected his work. Other visitors included "two leather-jacketed German writers": Walter Höllerer, whom Gregory had met in Frankfurt, and, with him, Günter Grass. Understandably Ginsberg was not yet familiar with Grass's work, whose worldwide best-seller *Die Blechtrommel* (*The Tin Drum*) was not published until the following year, in August 1959. Allen told Gordon Ball, the editor of his journals:

"He [Günter Grass] was already quite accomplished, but we didn't know that. So we told 'em all about marijuana . . . Gregory's somehow made a hit with Höllerer—his poetry was very good, see—anybody in any language could see it, especially if they knew some English."

Allen continued to see Joy, but they slept together less and less often, and most of the time they went out drinking or smoked hashish in Allen's room. By restricting Françoise to one visit a week, he had broken her obsession with him and now she just dropped by for friendly visits to say hello. Allen was meeting new people constantly. He spent all of one night talking with Baird Bryant, a filmmaker and artist. Bryant had been on the editorial team of *Merlin* magazine and, together with his wife, Denny, was responsible for the first English translation of Dominique Aury's *The Story of O*, published by Olympia Press in 1954 under the nom de plume Pauline Réage. (The translation was redone by Austryn Wainhouse when the book was issued in Olympia's Traveller's Companion series in 1957.) Bryant later wrote *Play This Love With Me* for Girodias under the name Willie Baron, and in that same year, 1955, Denny Bryant, as Winifred Drake, wrote *Tender Was My Flesh*. He had many stories about Maurice Girodias, Alexander Trocchi, and the early days of Olympia that Allen wanted to hear, fascinated by literary gossip.

The Olympia Press was an integral part of the creative momentum at the Beat Hotel and there was constant traffic between the hotel and Girodias's office on the rue Saint-Severin. Ginsberg wrote, "It was all happening about one block from the Seine River, within a few streets from each other, from rue Git-le-Coeur to rue Saint-Séverin. It was a very short walk back and forth, and everybody was seeing each other for coffee in the morning anyway."

Allen also saw the writer Herbert Gold a few times, who was a friend from their Columbia University days. Gold had always been rather skeptical of the Beats and, when they met, Allen berated him hysterically until Gold complained. He told Allen that every time they met, Allen was always very overbearing, so Allen tried to calm down. Once Allen was able to relax, they had a long talk. Allen explained all of Kerouac's work to him, reading to him from the unpublished manuscripts of *Visions of Cody* and *Dr. Sax*, which Grove was to publish in April 1959. He also read him the "County Clerk" section from the as yet unpublished *Naked Lunch*, which Gold enjoyed. Allen explained who the hipsters were and in the end he got the impression that Gold had a better understanding of what they were all trying to do, but he still couldn't really tell what he thought of it. Gold was ambivalent about the movement even though he had been there in New York at the start of it. In 1960 he wrote, "If I can ever find the main office of The Beat Generation, I plan to hand in my resignation," but in 1993 he decided he was a member after all and wrote *Bohemia: Where Art, Angst, Love and Strong Coffee Meet*, in which he gave an amusing description of a meeting with Allen and Gregory in Paris:

During one café meeting the waiter made the mistake of putting the plate with the bill near Gregory. Before I could reach for the check, Gregory slapped his hand over it. "I'm going to pay it! I'm going to pay it!" he cried.

"Don't be silly," Allen said.

"Allen! I've never paid a check before! I'm going to pay it!"

Reproachfully Allen shook his head. Firmly Allen removed Gregory's soft fingers. Generously Allen handed me the check.

Allen also took Gold to meet Bill, who had liked Gold's novel *The Man Who Was Not With It*, which described heroin addiction in a traveling carnival. Bill told him he had been a heroin addict for so long "because it was something to do." Gold was invited to dinner in Bill's room, along with Allen and Gregory, but regrettably he brought along his girlfriend, the respectable daughter of a French general, and the atmosphere at dinner was icy.

New people appeared all the time as the growing notoriety of the Beats caused like-minded people to seek them out. The poet Larry Fagin arrived in Paris and, by simply asking an American on the street where Ginsberg lived, was directed to the Beat Hotel. Allen was friendly and welcomed him in. Allen opened up a black steamer trunk and lent Fagin *Junkie*, *Howl*, and *On the Road*, plus a dozen books from the new culture, which Larry went away and read in the space of two weeks.

In March 1958, the dollar fell against the franc. Bill wrote to Jack, "The dollar is down and the WC in an unspeakable condition, that fucking South American borracho pukes and shits all over the floor and the cats are also broken [trained] to shit there. And every day the French franc more uppity." Allen ran out of money and had to live off Bill while he waited for City Lights to send him his next check. After the success of *Howl*, Ferlinghetti was after Allen to sign a contract. Allen had been avoiding it as long as possible because without a contract he kept all the rights to his work and could let anybody print it anytime. If he signed a contract, all rights would have to go through City Lights and they of course would take a cut. He wrote Eugene saying, "Ferlinghetti trying to persuade me it's for my own good in the long run. Maybe it is, I dunno."

The last gray days of winter had been grim, and for a couple of weeks Ginsberg had more or less withdrawn from everyone. He felt that he and Peter had broken up forever and was sad about this. In a manuscript from that period he wrote, "I can't write poesy no more, my glory is gone. I am hung on sitting on the bed waiting for a new thrill. Burroughs old friend, you are a drag and perpetual complaining junky—I am going to Berlin. Jack whom I dream of all the time, you are no longer a myth but a movie star without dreams." But he pulled out of it and began to stay up all night, having long, stoned conversations with B.J.

Allen realized that he was becoming too selective and negative about people, shutting them out of his life, so he made a conscious effort to soften to people more and even made friends with Graham upstairs, whom Bill liked but who was always blowing fuses. Allen had been short-tempered with Bill as well but soon got over his irritation. On March 28, they had a long talk and worked everything out. One of the main problems had been the fact that Bill did all his typing in Allen's room, "when I want to be alone to rock back and forth to sing to myself and write a Bible," Allen grumbled to Peter. "I've been serving him all along like a haggard complaining wife." Bill agreed to do his typing in his own room and also to help with the cooking.

Joy went to Amsterdam for a week. She had a new boyfriend who lived in the hotel and Allen complained to Peter that he hadn't gotten laid all month and felt bad. Gregory returned from Venice and took room 10 in the hotel, downstairs from Allen, and together they continued their exploration of Paris. By now Allen's looks were a little closer to his bohemian image: a black turtleneck, black pants, and black shoes, with hair almost to his collar—shocking at a time when American men favored the close-cropped Prussian Military Academy style.

Allen had heard that the New York writer Barbara Guest was in Paris. Guest was a frequent contributor to the Beat poetry magazines *Yugen* and *Floating Bear* and at that time her poetry was greatly influenced by both the Beats and the work of the Abstract Expressionist painters she knew in New York. She later became very interested in the Imagist poets, particularly H.D., and once said in an interview, "I drag my coattails in the dust of the Russian poets Akhmatova and Mandelstam." When Allen and Gregory visited her in her sublet apartment on the Faubourg Saint Honoré she was twenty-five years old and had moved to Paris for a nine-month stay. She showed them the secrets of her neighborhood: the rue Courcelles where Colette had lived with the dreadful Monsieur Willy and the church where Picasso married Olga. One day, while exploring the rue Pierre-Demours, she had come across a seventeenth-century chateau, seemingly untouched and unspoiled by the passage of history, which had surrounded it with shops and restaurants. She took Allen and Gregory to see the unkempt grounds and, as the great front door was open, they peeped in. At the foot of the grand stone staircase were cabin trunks, lined up against the wall, with labels and lettering identifying them as belonging to the Imperial Russian Ballet of Saint Petersburg, 1919. In the distance, someone was playing Tchaikovsky on the piano.

They went to investigate, feeling that they had stumbled upon a time bubble and been transported back forty years. In the grand salon a woman pianist sat alone. The walls were mirrored and furnished with barres for the dancers. A slender young girl, dressed in black, scurried past, as if alarmed to see them. They continued upstairs and encountered cooking smells and rooms divided into apartments. The chateau had been taken over by the Abbé of the Poor and given to Russian émigrés who were continuing their tradition of ballet in the empty salon. They were looking at the last remnants of Imperial Russia.

Barbara visited Allen and Gregory at the Beat Hotel, where Allen took her to meet Burroughs. She wrote later, "A door opened at Allen's knock and there on the bed reposed William Burroughs, his dreams interrupted by an eagerness to welcome whatever it was that Allen would deposit at his door. Burroughs was interested in me because I was Allen's find. There was a presence in that narrow room, or at least I felt it, so under the spell was I of Allen's persuasiveness, and altar of Burroughs's hypnotic speech. It was less what he said, although I recall he spoke with an edge of pragmatism, certainly not a cloud Michaux, a deliberate sort of nasal sentence in which he was cocooned purposefully, his speech alternately interpreted by Ginsberg as if it had issued from the source."

This gives a good idea of the respect, bordering upon awe, with which Allen regarded Bill, though Guest also noted that Allen seemed to enjoy taking care of his prodigy, Gregory, as much as he was proud of his elder mentor, Burroughs. She wrote, "It was Allen who truly impressed me. Returned to their meager quarters he prepared a stew for Gregory and me. There was no cult of cuisine or showmanship of the oil burner. Allen was preparing the food because it was a hospitable thing to do. No trouble. I thought he was exemplary." She and Allen met again and he showed her his favorite Arab cafés. Their last meeting in Paris was on the rue Apollinaire, at a stand-up bar with slot machines, not far from the Deux Magots.

Painter Larry Rivers, an old friend of Allen's from New York, came to Paris to spend a month playing saxophone with various jazz groups. He and Allen often spent afternoons sitting outside the sidewalk cafés in the spring sunshine. Rivers knew Paris well, having spent eight months in the city in 1950 writing poetry, though he had already had his first one-man show of his paintings in New York. One morning Allen was hailed from the tables outside the Deux Magots as he and Gregory were walking along Blvd St. Germain. It was the Indian poet Dom Moraes, whom Allen had met when he was in London two months earlier. Moraes and his girlfriend, Henrietta Abbott, were in Paris for the Easter holiday and invited them to join their table. Gregory got straight to the point and asked Henrietta, "Would you like to ball with me, baby?" She declined with a pleased smile. Gregory described how his feelings about God had been affected by watching a corpse being fished out of the Seine and they quickly found themselves in a deep discussion about God in which

Allen waxed eloquent. Allen and Gregory left, inviting them to breakfast at the hotel the next morning.

There was little sign of breakfast when Dom and Henrietta arrived and were taken up to the small attic room that Gregory had recently moved into. Bill Burroughs came up to meet them and Moraes
somehow got the impression that all three lived together there. There
were several suitcases in the room, filled with nothing but volumes of
Beat-related literature, which Allen showed and explained to Moraes
while Bill, making conversation, rolled up his trouser leg to show
Henrietta the needle tracks that covered his legs. Moraes wrote, "When
a pigeon moaned at the window, he hastily rolled his trousers down,
and said in a quiet flat voice, 'Birds, I hate birds.'

"'Cheeping beaking birds,' cried Corso, springing to the sill. 'Fly
away, bird!' The bird departed lazily into the March sunshine." Gregory rolled a joint—Moraes's first, though Henrietta seemed to know
what to do with it—and the room filled with scented smoke. In her
autobiography Henrietta wrote:

> I smoked some of it and went off to find the lavatory. It
> was tiny and the hole in the middle was blocked by the most
> enormous turd in the world. The stench of ammonia killed the
> oxygen supply and as I peed over the turd, tears poured out of
> my eyes and down my face, cascading on to my collarbones. I
> stumbled back.
>
> "It's nothing to do with any of you," I said aggressively,
> defensively and passionately.
>
> "No, it's the Turk downstairs. Same thing every morning."

Then Allen and Gregory dragged them out to meet Larry Rivers.
Bill stayed behind. Rivers was with a young American woman. In his
autobiography, Moraes reported, "They leapt at her, suggesting that
we all strip and make love on the pavement, 'Like William Blake and
the angels, man,' cried Corso. The girl became very upset and burst
into tears and the poets were much concerned, petting her with re-
pentant hands, and offering her poems and candy which Corso pulled

from his pocket." They liked Moraes and his girlfriend and saw quite a bit of them, showing them the sights. They drove around Paris in a rented convertible and made spontaneous tapes of their poetry. Moraes offered to arrange readings for them in Oxford if they visited England again while classes were in session.

Spring arrived and the Seine was heavy with mud and flowed fast and high between the quais. The first warm day came at the end of March, and Allen and Bill were able to take an afternoon walk to the post office without their overcoats; Bill dressed in a turtleneck sweater and Allen in a plaid jacket. They ran into their friend Lee, cashing a Danish money order at the international window, and marveled that he was sober. On Blvd St. Germain, at the Old Navy, they found Gregory, sitting and talking with a young French girl with red hair, a blue coat, and a large purse, which Gregory clearly had high hopes for.

A group of people stood in the street talking, most of whom they knew, including Iris Owens, an American novelist who wrote pornography for Olympia Press under the name Harriet Daimler. She was a stunningly beautiful young woman who dressed entirely in black, wore kohl around her eyes, and had moved to Paris, at age twenty, from Greenwich Village when her first marriage failed. She had been introduced to Maurice Girodias by Alexander Trocchi, with whom she was having an affair. All of Girodias's writers had fallen in love with her and she had affairs with many of them. Her books *Darling*, 1956; *The Pleasure Thieves*, 1956; *Innocence*, 1957; and *The Organisation*, 1957, made her one of Olympia's star writers. Iris was standing, wearing a raincoat, carrying the notebook in which she wrote her DBs. Each one took her a maximum of two months, giving her enough money to take off for a summer in Saint Tropez, six months in Sicily, or a winter in Hydra, where she could concentrate on her serious writing. Later she wrote under her own name and her novel *After Claude* was well received by the New York critics, but in the spring of 1958 she was working on *The Woman Thing*, the last of her DBs, which Olympia published that August. As they walked along, Allen found himself distant and worried that she misunderstood his attention for a sexual come-on—in fact, she had plenty of lovers to choose from. She read the manuscript of *Naked Lunch* and, in her capacity as another of Girodias's advisers, she suggested that Olympia should publish it. This was the third time Girodias had been approached by someone who had given the book a high recommendation and may have been the cause of the undated letter to Burroughs from Girodias, sent about this time, which reads, "Dear Mr. Burroughs. What about letting me have another look at *Naked Lunch*? I would very much like to meet you and discuss this."

They continued along St. Germain and ran into drummer Al "The Shades" Levitt and his friend Money, who was returning to New York the next day. Levitt had already recorded with Charles Mingus and was well known for his ability to get a tight rhythm section going. He was in Europe with the Barney Wilen Quintet. Years later he recorded with Chet Baker. They all decided to go to the Luxembourg Gardens, where they met Ramblin' Jack Elliott, the singing cowboy from Brooklyn, out for a spring walk with his wife. Years before, Elliott had gone off with Ginsberg's girlfriend Helen Parker. He was born Elliott Charles Adnopoz but changed his name to Buck Elliott and ran away from home to join the rodeo. He met Woody Guthrie and became a folksinger, changing his name for a final time, and spent the mid-fifties in Europe. He was a major player in the early-sixties folk revival in New York City. They also ran into John Balf from the hotel. Allen recorded in his journals, "Everybody high, nobody had nothing to say—the high trees—the sky."

Everyone they knew seemed to be out that day. They met Mason Hoffenberg carrying books and a clock. He was recovering from a junk cure and was on his way to the library to examine pictures of machines. He and Terry Southern, under the pseudonym, had, not long before, written *Candy* for Olympia, which was to become a best-seller in America. They entered the Luxembourg Gardens and walked around the Medici fountain, watched over by the bust of Henri Murger. Allen bought eight ice-cream cones and they sat in the sun at an outside table facing the gardens while Bill discussed junk with Mason and entertained them all with stories of man-eating piranha fish and sharks.

They walked back down Blvd St. Michel, past the Sorbonne bookstores, and afterward finished up at Baird Bryant's place, where Allen was attracted to a young French-speaking youth from Mauritius: "cap black hair, a boyish wisp of mustache & no hair a-chin. Soft eyes . . . a doll & Angel—I am queer." But Allen was only looking.

With the advent of spring, Bill and Allen began going out more, led by Bill, who enjoyed all the new young people and was surprisingly garrulous and friendly toward them. "Bernard the Frenchman," whom Bill knew from Tangier, passed through Paris and gave Bill and Allen a little black ball of opium. Bill also had some extremely potent marijuana, brought to him by a friend of Paul Lund's in Tangier, who was on his way to London. There were so many drugs around that, as Bill explained it to Kerouac, "The whole arrondissement is about to flip and proclaim a new religion. Play it cool myself . . ." There was also a lot of heroin about, which they all used, including Allen who fooled around with it throughout the spring but without developing a habit. From time to time Bill would cook up some majoun, or hashish candy: finely chopped kif mixed with cinnamon, ground nutmeg, caraway seeds, and honey, which he then heated until it gained the sticky consistency of runny toffee.

Allen, Bill, and Gregory spent an evening with the American jazz drummer Kenny Clarke, who had moved to Paris in 1956. They gathered in Allen's room and Bill and Kenny talked for hours about junk. Allen, Gregory, and B.J. were drunk and stood talking loudly at one another by the kitchen table. Allen made B.J. tell everyone his life story, and Gregory, the most drunk of them all, rolled on the floor, trying to get Bill and Kenny to listen. Allen explained the rhythmic structure of his poetry to Clarke and asked how it related to drumming. This led to an interesting discussion and Clarke invited Allen to come to hear him play at the Club St. Germain anytime he wanted, promising to put him on the guest list. Allen and Peter had hung around outside the Club St. Germain on their very first night in Paris, listening to the great jazz coming through the black barred windows, too broke to pay the cover charge. Even though he could now get in free, Allen still didn't go until someone took him there two months later.

Now that the weather was warmer, Allen began to explore far-ther afield, though Bill had no interest in looking at old buildings and stayed at home. Baird Bryant gave Allen a ride into the country on the back of his motorcycle, but Bryant was worried that the weight was damaging his bike so Allen declared, "I ain't tied to no bike, see you later." It was a beautiful day and he walked through the open coun-try, enjoying the wildflowers and fields. Then he hitched to the Cha-teau of Fontainebleau, about fifty kilometers from Paris, and walked through the woods and alongside green ponds watching the wakes of the swans as they sailed slowly over the placid surface. He took a guided tour of the vast chateau and was pleased to find that he understood most of the French, then took the train back to Paris and was home by six o'clock. The experience made him determined to finally visit Chartres and Versailles.

Allen had Gregory's broken radio fixed so he had some music in his room as he sat typing up his poems in final form. From these he made a selection to send to Don Allen, who was compiling the anthol-ogy *New American Poetry, 1945–1960* for Grove Press. Allen and Joy had a long talk and she told him that she couldn't make it with him anymore because she had loved *both* Allen and Peter. Allen suspected that it was in fact just Peter whom she loved. They ate dinner and took a bottle of wine up to Allen's room, where, at midnight, they decided to get drunk and write to Peter for advice. Allen's desires appeared to be simple, he said. "I want to get naked have a big happy hairy ball in bed and come but I've been locked up in this room for six weeks and now I feel like everybody hates me. Glurp." A few days later Joy gave in and climbed into bed with Allen and Gregory together, but it was not a success, "I came too fast and she never came," Allen told Peter.

Allen had better luck with his new boyfriend Billy Whitman. Allen was in the Mistral bookshop one day when a young man approached him and invited him to try some morphine he had found in his room. After this they went to Allen's room, got high, and talked for a long time. Billy asked if he could stay over and they went to bed. Allen reported back to Peter, "[he] put his hand on my shoulder in bed & pretty soon we rubbing bellies. He leaves for N.Y. in a few weeks. Bill dug him, as boy, but there's something unexplained & mysterious, like narcissistic & secretive & somewhere square, in him, I haven't been able to fathom. Meanwhile in any case he's declared himself on side of Light & so we have long talks. I tell him not to judge people, just dig them. But he has ideas about getting experience & being a distinguished man. But he's open, more than before." Allen told Whitman Zen jokes, they walked the streets of the city, and went to bed several more times.

George Whitman put a sign up in the Mistral bookshop announcing a reading by Allen, Gregory, and Bill, though he had never asked them to do one. They decided to make it a big event and crowd the place and so put up notices of their own all over town announcing the reading, which was held on Sunday, April 13. Allen and Gregory struggled all week to get Bill to read but he steadfastly refused. However, when they got there Bill saw that everybody was drunk anyway, and when Billy Whitman, whom he had just met that day, softly asked him to read, Bill agreed. He sat on the couch in his big German leather coat, sniffing, and read "I Can Feel the Heat Closing In" section from *Naked Lunch*, which had recently appeared in *Chicago Review*, and was a great success. Ginsberg read the "Mahatma" and "Yagé City" sections from *Naked Lunch*, as well as from his own work, to an audience of forty or fifty people. Allen said, "Unfortunately another poet was reciting some uncommunicative junk and we didn't like it."

Gregory added, "I protested it wasn't real poetry. Someone asked me what I meant by real poetry. So I took off all my clothes and read my poems naked. I had two big bearded friends of mine as bodyguards and they threatened they'd beat up anybody who left while I was reciting. I was a big success." It was a classic Beat reading, though, as Allen said, it was mild compared to some in San Francisco.

It was warm and sunny that April and by now they didn't even need sweaters to go walking. They visited the Japan show at the Musée d'Art Moderne, saw a Modigliani retrospective, visited the Chinese museum and the Historical museum, and Allen and Bill went to the anthropological museum, the Musée d'Homme. Madame Rachou celebrated spring by washing the bedspreads and changing the curtains in the rooms. The hotel cat fell out of a fourth-floor window and broke its leg, but it healed quickly. Balf, the hotel's informal barber, gave Allen a 200-franc haircut and Allen paid the surcharge for a bath and bought some baggy French dungarees. Graham from upstairs gave him a woollen shirt and, thus equipped, Allen was ready for the new season. He told Peter of his exploits. "Went alone (Bill uninterested) to Champs Elysees queer Turkish bath and got blowed twice in stinky steamrooms by invisible Frenchmen."

Bill was now concentrating on getting *Naked Lunch* published. Allen still believed that Ferlinghetti at City Lights would be the most likely and sympathetic publisher in the States, and he had written a number of times to Jack Kerouac—who was supposed to be trying to market the book in America—asking him to send a selection of texts to Ferlinghetti. But Jack never did. City Lights could not afford to print the whole thing because at that point their finances only ran to the publication of slim volumes of poetry. However, Ferlinghetti expressed an interest in seeing the manuscript with an eye to publishing a selection, that is, if he liked the material. Allen and Bill prepared a manuscript to send him. At this time the book was still called *Interzone* but most of the material they sent was used later in *Naked Lunch*, so City Lights essentially had the first offer on Burroughs's classic work. Unfortunately Ferlinghetti rejected it.

As Bill worked on *Naked Lunch*, Gregory was writing two of his best-known poems. He recalled, "I wrote 'Marriage' the same time I wrote 'Bomb.' That was a funny week. I did 'Bomb' in about three or four days. I had a ball with it, because to get the shape, I had to type it down on paper first, and cut it out, each line, and paste it on big construction paper. So the glue was all sticky on my fingers, and then I said the heck with it, the publisher can always line it up . . . Moralizing on things, this social shot could not be for me. I said, 'That's what it is and that's what's happening,' and let it jump."

As the Cold War raged, the threat of death by hydrogen bomb or radioactive fallout was a subject of much discussion. In Britain, the Campaign for Nuclear Disarmament was formed, which quickly grew into a nationwide organization, with a youth branch particularly active at the universities. The demonstrations and the fact that the eminent philosopher Sir Bertrand Russell was a firm opponent of nuclear weapons meant that the issue was constantly in the press. Gregory was interested in the "Ban the Bomb" demonstrations, which received wide coverage in the French press. Gregory stated, "I saw the kids Ban the Bomb, Ban the Bomb, and I said, 'It's a death shot that's laid on them, the immediacy of people being hanged in England at that time, and it's not as if the Bomb had never fallen, so how am I going to tackle this thing? Suddenly death was the big shot to handle, Gregory, not just the Bomb.' The best way to get out of it was make it lyrical, like an embracing of it, put all the energy of all the lyric that I could name. And then get to know it. But if I start with hating it, with the hate of it, I get no farther than a piece of polemic, a political poem—which I usually fall flat on. That's not a political poem exactly, that 'Bomb' poem. And you can only do it by embracing it, yes. So gee, I loved the Bomb."

The words of the poem were arranged on the page to represent the mushroom cloud of a nuclear explosion. The poem itself was very powerful, scanned well, and was accessible in a way that some of Corso's later poems are not. He used archaisms such as "Thee" in "Bomb," but as he explained, "I use it in 'Bomb' but only because it has something apocalyptic and Biblical, like 'ye BANG ye BONG ye BING.' There's a lot of interplay in that poem. When it's read, it's a sound poem. If one checks out my poems, you could really think, wow, did this guy want that big holocaust, this monstrosity, was he nationalistic? Like Ferlinghetti got screwed up about 'Power.' 'It's fascistic,' and I said, 'No, that word should be taken from that particular area. It's a great poetic word, and I want to see what I can do,' and I played all different numbers in that 'Power.' . . . Everything came after that—gay power, black power, flower power . . ."

In July, shortly after Allen returned to New York, Lawrence Ferlinghetti visited Gregory in room 41, high in the cramped roof space of the Beat Hotel. Ferlinghetti, with his big frame, found it hard to negotiate the final spiral turn of the stairs, which required going on hands and knees to get around in order to arrive at Gregory's door—

scarred with graffiti messages, from girls for the most part. Ferlinghetti decided to publish Gregory's "Bomb" as a broadside, agreeing that the type should be arranged on the page to look like the atomic cloud as the poet wanted, even though Gregory had not quite finished working on the text. Ferlinghetti remained ambivalent about the poem, in the same way he felt ambivalent about Gregory's poem "Power," and wrote to tell him so. Gregory sent the letter to Allen, who wrote Ferlinghetti saying how pleased he was that City Lights was publishing the poem. "I don't understand why you feel Gregory has ambivalence toward Bomb and Power. Because his straightforward 'position' is really the whole POINT of those poems & what makes them permanently valuable. He does love the Bomb. Why not? . . . To Hate the bomb, says the poem, is to make yourself vulnerable to it." This was Kerouac's position of detachment, an acquiescent acceptance of all the evils in the world. Ginsberg was later to change his stance and campaign strongly against nuclear weapons. City Lights printed the broadside *Bomb* in a print run of 2,000, and it sold out quickly—a perfect poem to tack on your wall.

Given Allen's success with City Lights, Gregory was upset by Ferlinghetti's reaction to his new long poems, but any feelings of rejection were soon dissolved following his acceptance by James Laughlin, the owner and chief editor of New Directions, the most prestigious avant-garde publisher in the United States. Gregory, in an interview with Robert King, said, "I didn't leave Ferlinghetti, Ferlinghetti left me. You see I wrote a poem called 'Power' that's in my *Happy Birthday of Death.* My 'Marriage' is in there, and some of the real goodies in that book. But Ferlinghetti thought it was fascistic; he didn't understand I was changing the word 'power.' I said, 'Why can't a poet handle this word, break the meaning of it?' . . . So I said, 'Well, bullshit, give me my book back,' and wrote to New Directions and said, 'Hey, you who publish Pound and Rimbaud, do you like long poems?' because these were long single-word poems: 'Army,' 'Power,' 'Police,' 'Marriage,' and Laughlin wrote back, 'Of course,' and took the book." *The Happy Birthday of Death* was published by New Directions on March 31, 1960, and is still in print.

"I remember at times when Allen read out loud the things he'd wrote that day and Gregory too," said Jean-Jacques Lebel. "We couldn't go to a damn restaurant without Gregory getting on the table, totally pissed, and start reciting 'Bomb' or 'Marriage.' I was organizing a lot of poetry readings in those days and I loved it of course but the restaurant owners would make a stink."

5 **Fellow Writers**

"Me, I've slipped the spoken word into print. In one sole shot."
Louis-Ferdinand Céline

Although many of the residents at the Beat Hotel lived in almost hermetic isolation from French society, it was impossible not to notice that there was a war on. The situation in Algeria appeared to be insoluble. After years of bombs, terrorism, and diplomacy, both Morocco and Tunisia had achieved independence from France. Naturally the Algerians wanted the same and the independence movement had wide popular support. Unfortunately there were one million French living in Algeria, known as *colons*, or colonials, whose families had lived there for many generations. They were only ten percent of the population, but they ran the country and administered the colonial government. When it seemed that France might give in to the independence movement, the Algerian *colons* threatened to declare independence from France and run the country themselves. The French military sided with the *colons* against the government, provoking a very delicate political impasse. There were huge demonstrations in the streets of Paris and terrorist bombs exploded all over the city. Police walked the streets in pairs armed with machine guns, and police and government censorship prohibited intellectual debate. France seemed poised for a right-wing military takeover, a situation not dissimilar to that of Germany in 1933. In April, Editions de Minuit published Henri Alleg's *La Question*, which described the police and army torture of Algerians in Algeria, with an introduction by Sartre. It was promptly seized by the police and banned.

Allen Ginsberg followed the situation closely and wrote long six- and seven-page single-spaced letters to his father about the situation. He told him that he'd met a French engineer "who pounded the table with a mad light in his eye and yelled 'The U.S. will never get its hands on French Sahara oil! That's what this war is about! France must have this oil or it will die as a nation!' Glaring at me—face contorted with rage—typical french bourgeois—that's what I mean by the psychosis of the bourgeoisie here. This busybody jerk screaming about oil & cursing the Arabs. That's what the Arabs have to contend with too— you know—a million of these angry colons *with pistols*." The situation changed every day; fascinating though it was, Allen and Gregory had made plans to visit London, and Gregory was keen to get on.

They arrived in London on May 6, and Allen showed Gregory the sights. They were broke, as usual, and one evening they found themselves hungry and penniless at midnight on Piccadilly. They had met the bookseller and publisher David Archer at a party and in desperation Allen telephoned him. Archer's various poetry bookshops had all folded because of his habit of giving money to destitute writers, usually in the form of a five-pound note tucked into an empty matchbox, which he would hand to them discreetly to avoid causing embarrassment. He came and found Ginsberg and Corso, bought them a meal, and gave them a little money "for poetry's sake."

Archer's Parton Press was the first to publish Dylan Thomas, George Barker, and David Gascoyne. He introduced Allen and Gregory to Barker, who took them to the French pub, the Coach & Horses, the Fitzroy Tavern, and all the Soho and Fitzrovia pubs frequented by the London literary crowd. There they were regaled by stories of Dylan Thomas, Julian Maclaran-Ross, and the hard-drinking poets and writers of the 1940s. Allen told Lucien Carr, ". . . starved most of the time, everybody fed us drinks but nobody hands out any food and we were broke, stuck on Piccadilly some midnights no money for taxi, Underground closed & bus strike, & hungry . . ."

As he had promised, Dom Moraes arranged for them to read at Oxford, starting at Jesus, his college, and going on to New College and a few others. They had tea with W. H. Auden, who showed them around

Christ Church Cathedral. They had visited it, guidebook in hand, the day before but generously described his tour as "the high point" of their visit. Gregory asked him, "Are birds spies?"

Startled, Auden responded, "No, I don't think so. Who would they report to?"

"The trees," answered Allen. On taking their leave they attempted to kiss the hem of his garment, in Auden's case the cuffs of his pants. Auden shuffled out of range, embarrassed.

They saw the effigy of Shelley in white marble at University College and Gregory wanted to kiss the statue's foot. Then he demanded to know where Shelley's rooms were. They were in fact in the southwest corner of the quad, but Moraes had no idea and vaguely indicated the nearest door. Gregory threw it open and crawled across the carpet, kissing it reverently, to the great surprise of the room's occupant, who had been making a cup of tea at the time and stared at Gregory in astonished silence.

They attended a rehearsal of *Facade*, written by Dame Edith Sitwell with music by William Walton, at the Town Hall. Sitwell intoned the words seated onstage but hidden from the audience by a screen, painted by John Piper. Unfortunately the screen was not properly attached and began to sway. Dame Edith demanded imperiously that this be put right and several people rushed forward to help hold it in place, including Allen and Gregory. However, the screen continued to sway then crashed to the stage, throwing its helpers aside, all except Allen and Gregory, who were remarkably unaffected and stood with funny little smiles on their faces. One of the organizers later told Dom Moraes, "That screen was *pushed*, you know." At the rehearsal, Allen told Dame Edith he was editing an anthology that was to feature photographs of all the poets naked and asked if she would contribute. The Dame, who was seventy, declined gracefully. Gregory offered her a joint, which she also declined, saying that marijuana made her feel ill.

Allen and Gregory's reading at the New College Henry Vaughan Society was attended by a large number of British beatniks, one of whom was barefoot and startled the audience by rolling a joint, laying on his back, placing a match between his toes, striking it on the low ceiling, and lighting up. He was soon enough not the only one to be without shoes. New College had a very strong branch of the Campaign for Nuclear Disarmament (CND), which had been formally constituted in January of that year, and the students were appalled when Gregory read his new poem "Bomb." His embrace of the subject horrified them: "O Bomb I love you / I want to kiss your clank, eat your boom . . ." Led by Steven Hugh-Jones, the editor of *Isis*, they showed their feelings by removing their shoes and throwing them at Gregory, calling him a fascist. Allen reported to Peter, "The students got mad and attacked him for being, they thought, anti-social."

"Do you know what it's like to die by an H-Bomb?" they yelled. "How do you think the people of Hiroshima would like this poem?" Gregory was offended and called them a bunch of creeps. After a brief argument, Allen then called them assholes and the reading ended in disharmony. Girls were not allowed in college after 10 P.M., so the women and a number of the men left with the poets and they finished the reading elsewhere. Then they had a party with friends of Moraes and some girls.

Allen and Gregory enjoyed their stay in Oxford. There was a poignant moment when Dom Moraes, John Howe, and other friends took the poets punting on the Isis, as the Thames is known as it passes through Oxford. Moraes recalled, "They smoked marijuana as we eddied over green scumbled water, in which trees trailed their arms. As we passed under Magdalen bridge, amidst liquid shadows, the boom of a bell came to us through the yellow stone overhead. Gregory said in a childish, wistful way, 'I wish I'd been to school here.'" Gregory, who received his education in reform school, jail, and on the street, was punting the same waters that his idol, Shelley, had sailed paper boats upon a century and half before.

Edith Sitwell had enjoyed her meeting with Allen and Gregory and invited them to dine with her at the Sesame Club in London. She wore a long satin dress and a tall conical hat, like a character in a *Book of Hours.* Allen told Lucien Carr, "Lunch with Edith Sitwell in big expensive Lady Macbeth club—potted shrimps Roastbeef & treacle tart—but that was about the only food we had there." Dame Edith discussed the work of Garcia Villa, e.e. cummings, and Marianne Moore, which she said she liked. The conversation turned to drugs, but Dame Edith disagreed with Allen and Gregory's assertion that drugs led to "heightened sensibility," saying, "No poet should need a drug to produce extreme sensibility, which must be, if he is any good, a part of his equipment." *Life* magazine reported their meeting and claimed that Allen offered her heroin, which she refused on the grounds that it brought her out in spots. Dame Edith was most offended by the account, particularly the idea that she might have spots. "I'm hardly the spot queen," she said. She told them she liked their work and that they were the hope of English-language poetry. Flattered, Allen asked, "May we own you?" and she held up her hand, palm uppermost, in a regal gesture of acquiescence.

Allen and Gregory did some recording at the BBC and they went on long walks along the bank of the Thames. Simon Watson-Taylor familiarized Allen with the arguments of the CND and together they passed out CND leaflets at the Houses of Parliament. On their last day in London, May 20, they went to find William Blake's grave in Bunhill Fields cemetery. It was a four-foot-high slab of sandstone near the graves of Bunyan and Defoe. The inscription recorded that the bones of Blake and his wife were near that spot. Outside the graveyard they saw bombed houses and a building under construction with cranes and girders. As they stood looking, they heard the voice of a bricklayer singing on the sixth-floor scaffolding, and birdsong in the trees.

While Allen and Gregory were away in Britain, on May 13, 1958, a coup d'état was engineered by the French army under the command of General Raoul Salan with the backing of the Algerian *colons*. This resulted in General Charles de Gaulle, the old wartime hero, coming into power to save France from being torn apart by opposing factions. There had already been a series of increasingly violent demonstrations, both pro and con, and there was a likelihood of a general strike. In fact de Gaulle ultimately betrayed the very men who put him in power and negotiated independence for Algeria, but had he been a Franco or a Salazar the Fifth Republic could just as easily have displayed fascistic tendencies. At the time no one knew what he would do or how he would reconcile the two sides.

There were huge pro- and anti–de Gaulle demonstrations. The political situation was changing daily. Allen, on his return from London, continued to report on developments in long letters to his father. He, Gregory, and John Balf went to a huge anti–de Gaulle march and demonstration at Place de la Republique and felt anxious, seeing the steel-helmeted riot police waiting farther down the block, but there was no violence and the police did not act. It reminded Allen of his childhood, attending political demonstrations against Mayor Hague in Paterson's Journal Square with his mother and his aunt Eleanor. He climbed a statue to watch the masses and then found a better spot on a ledge on the front of a bank, about ten feet above the crowd.

At another demonstration that summer, shortly after de Gaulle took power, Allen and Thomas Parkinson—on another visit from London—walked up through the Tuileries to Place de la Concorde. The Champs Elysée was lined with troops in full battle dress. They dodged across the traffic to the fountain in Place de la Concorde and sat looking toward the Arc de Triomphe with the Madeleine to their right and the Elysée Palace to their left. The atmosphere was tense and expectant. It was almost midday. "I wonder what is going to happen?" asked Parkinson.

"At noon, two million communists will swarm past the Madeleine and attack the Elysée Palace," said Allen. "What will you do?"

"I'll dive in this bloody fountain and stay underwater," Parkinson replied.

Allen introduced Parkinson to Burroughs. Parkinson later said, "During that period Allen was often in a manic humor, and I remember one improbable afternoon when Bill Burroughs, of all people, kept trying to calm Allen and mollify his excesses. I remember with great amusement Allen and Gregory calling from the street to our rooms at the Hotel Moderne on rue Racine at two in the morning, 'Tom Parkinson, come out and play, Tom Parkinson, come out and play,' over and over. I always regretted that I went to the window and yelled,

'Go home and let me sleep,' for who knows what foolishness we might have committed?"

Life settled into a routine at the Beat Hotel. Mirtaud the cat recovered from its fall, and the flood of summer visitors continued unabated. Gregory was usually the first to get up, rising at 10 A.M. or earlier. He ate no breakfast, just sat in his tiny green attic room and wrote or typed up poems from the night before. His room had a skylight, a cracked dormer window with a view out over the rooftops, and a bare fly-spotted 25-watt light bulb. Gregory had decorated the cramped space by covering the green walls with reproductions of old masters taken from *Life* magazine and with postcards arranged in neat rows like his beloved stamp collection. A large plaster angel was suspended from the ceiling. As a table Gregory used a framed reproduction of the Leonardo da Vinci cartoon for *The Madonna of the Rocks*, and piles of books and manuscripts were piled on its cracked glass.

Allen was usually the next to rise, getting up around noon. Bill got up at 1 P.M. and would eat a light breakfast of bread and tea, then he and Allen would usually talk until 3 P.M. In the afternoon Allen often went for a walk with Gregory. Bill would go out in the late afternoon to buy his supply of paregoric and see his analyst. Allen shopped at 5 P.M. and cooked for them all in his room, usually a pea or lentil soup with Bayonne hambone. Sometimes he made a lamb stew or spaghetti. They ate early, around 7 P.M., and after dinner they often walked over to Blvd St. Germain for coffee, accompanied by B.J. or anyone else who stopped by. Allen was usually back at his desk by 10 P.M., ready to answer letters, type manuscripts, or write in his green journal. Bill wrote or talked to visitors. Gregory disappeared into the night to look for girls. Allen kept Peter up to date with all the news and gossip. "BJ and Baird Bryant smashed up on a motorcycle the other night near Pigalle trying to score for T & Baird is in hospital . . ." Allen was thankful he wasn't on the bike this time, as he had often before gone for rides with Baird. Allen bought a new white towel, which he proudly recorded in his journal as being the size of a bathrobe.

Allen typed up a few chapters from the manuscript of *Naked Lunch* and sent them to the *Chicago Review*, whose editor, Irving Rosenthal, had written asking for more material from Bill. Allen assembled a collection of manuscripts for Nelson Aldrich at the *Paris Review*, who had asked for something representative of Beat Generation writing. *The Paris Review* had been founded five years earlier by a group of wealthy young Americans: editor-in-chief George Plimpton, editor Peter Matthiessen, and business manager John Train. Allen was anxious to penetrate this establishment stronghold even though rumors were rife that, like *Encounter* magazine in Britain, it was CIA-funded. (Plimpton later revealed that one member of the editorial team was working for the CIA at the time but said that he had resigned from the agency when asked to spy on his colleagues in the expatriate community.) Allen gave them Bill's "County Clerk" section from *Naked Lunch*, his own "The Lion for Real," Gregory's "Bomb," and typed up choruses 49, 112, 126, 226, 228, and 240 from Kerouac's manuscript of *Mexico City Blues*, which he had with him. He wrote to Kerouac telling him to send Aldrich something from *Dr. Sax* or *Visions of Cody*. Allen insisted, however, that if *Paris Review* did not take something of Bill's then they would all take back their poems. The special Beat issue was never printed, though it would have been a classic, and *Paris Review* did not publish Burroughs's work until the autumn of 1965.

A wealthy young Frenchman appeared on the scene, discovered by Gregory at the Café Monaco. William Burroughs recalled the first time they met: "I remember Gregory bringing him up to the hotel and siting him at this little bar—it had four tables, the bar in the original Beat Hotel. Now here comes Gregory and this almost transparent green demon on two crutches. It was Jacques Stern, sinister music in the background. He was very lucid, generous, he'd have some heroin, pot, he'd take you out to dinner, he'd seem very very nice and very sweet and at some point he would start to put the screws on, getting very nasty. He'd just scream at us." Stern was twenty-five years old and had been crippled by polio, which left him with braces on his thin hips and able to walk only with the aid of an aluminum crutch. He was thin and frail—he weighed only ninety-five pounds—Allen would carry him up the four flights of stairs to his room where Bill and Gregory would come to visit with him. He quickly befriended Bill and they found that they had a lot in common. Like Bill, Stern had studied anthropology at Harvard and, also like Bill, he was being psychoanalyzed. Stern was very intelligent and serious and enormously knowledgeable. Polio had kept him bedridden for many years and as he lay there he studied Roman history, anthropology, Spengler, and Indian philosophy. Bill liked him for his intellect and the factual information he had on junk or the latest experiments utilizing brainwashing.

Stern knew Salvador Dalí and Jean Cocteau and the fashionable side of Paris, but was bored by it. He had copies of *On the Road*, *Gasoline*, *Howl*, and *Junkie* but had not realized the last was by Bill because Bill had used a pseudonym. He thought that Bill was a superb teacher and frequently came over to the hotel to talk with him. Bill referred to him as "the mad baron," and told Paul Bowles that Stern was "far and away the most interesting person I have met in Paris."

Allen told Peter, "A new strange cripple boy appeared on scene, Frenchman named Jacques Stern, went to Harvard & is very intelligent & serious, is a rich Rothschild, has car & chauffeur & is a junky, he and Bill now good friends & sit and talk junk by the hour—Bill now on paregoric still trying to get off, maybe next week . . . Stern says he writes prose, he talks very beautifully in Intellectual way but seems also to have free spirit." Stern showed them a manuscript that Allen later described to Kerouac as being "very good, not totally mad, but amazing." The text Stern showed them was an attempt to "explain the soul" of his friend Peter, a fellow junkie in Nice who had died at the age of twenty.

Stern was married to a beautiful American woman with thick red hair named Dini, about whom Allen wrote Kerouac, "His tall sexy lovely wife hates us." They lived with their four-year-old son on the rue du Cirque, just around the corner from the Palais de l'Elysée, in a large duplex apartment staffed by butlers and maids. At Gregory's request Stern took them all out in his huge chauffeur-driven cream Cadillac convertible and they drove down the Champs Elysée with the top down.

One day they visited and found him in bed junk-sick because his pusher had been busted. He looked pale and thin. His butler was waiting attentively outside his bedroom door while Stern read the manuscript of *Naked Lunch*. When they arrived he rolled a joint and told them to go to the library and help themselves to drinks. Stern boasted that he had spent half a million dollars doing up the apartment and the same again on his book collection, the centerpiece of which was a set of Molière first editions. They discussed mysticism and he described the fourteen months that he had spent in India studying with his guru. He had meditated for ten hours each day and reached what he thought of as a "nirvanic void," where he remained for hours at a time. But then evil voices began penetrating the void and asking "Why? Why?" His guru told him he was not ready and sent him away. He was planning to return to India in November and invited Bill to accompany him on the trip. Anticipating the easy availability of drugs in India, Bill agreed to come along.

Stern had a friend named Harry Phipps, a twenty-four-year-old, short, blond-haired, baby-faced, narcissistic American millionaire, who had accompanied Stern on his first trip to India. According to Phipps, they had passed the time by organizing rickshaw races—a rather different story than Stern's of meditating ten hours a day. Phipps took Allen to the Club St. Germain where sax player Sonny Stitt and drummer Kenny Clarke were performing. Clarke recognized Allen from his visit to the hotel in April and waved. After so many months of counting every centime and worrying if he would be able to pay the rent, Allen found it strange to be in the position of being able to order as much Pernod as he liked and "hear driving raging drum & sax yowling back & forth in that mysterious basement." Clarke had shaved his head since Allen had last seen him.

Phipps took Allen into a bathroom cubicle where he produced a beautiful enameled box filled with heroin, which they sniffed. Drunk and high, they returned to their table. Phipps told Allen that he had made it with James Dean. Phipps had backed Dean's first play and had fallen in love with him. They blew each other and Phipps fucked Dean, though Dean did nothing in return. Allen was fascinated by the gossip and wrote Peter, "Strange to meet someone who screwed Dean. Said he fell in love with Dean, the way he lounged his body open bellied in chair, arms crossed."

Phipps brought over three of his old suits to the hotel, one for each of them. He also left a quantity of cocaine, the first Allen had had in a decade. Bill received a black worsted Avril Harriman flannel suit that fit him perfectly, making him look very distinguished along with his graying temples. Allen's suit was made of fine gray English wool. Bill and Allen sat at Allen's kitchen table, all dressed up, sniffing cocaine, pleased with this new turn of events. They walked with Phipps over the river to his house, an eighteenth-century *hôtel particulier* on the Ile St. Louis, and it was only when they saw the apartment that they realized quite how rich Phipps was. He lived in the house on the quai d'Orléans where Chopin and Voltaire once lived and Gregory sat at Chopin's piano. Gossip columnist Elsa Maxwell was giving a big party in the apartment next door; they didn't try to gatecrash but peeped through the keyhole and saw the glittering chandeliers, candelabra, red carpet, and a huge table set for a feast. A seating plan was posted near the door.

Phipps's wife decided that she needed to buy some cucumbers for a dish she was preparing and went out. Phipps immediately produced the same delicate enameled box that Allen had seen at the nightclub. Allen looked at Bill framed against the fireplace in the huge drawing room, his body thin from the paregoric, hair thinning, making stiff-armed junkie gestures, explaining a scientific theory of chess probability and horse-betting, indifferent to the roar of the party going on next door, and thought that Bill looked like "a great sober, Palm Beach chess-player private genius." That evening in Bill's room, Bill stood in his black suit looking so alone that Allen kissed him all over his cheeks when he said good night. Bill smiled impassively, a little shy, and formally bowed Allen from the room. Allen felt very fond of him and hoped vaguely that Bill would return to New York with him. He wrote his old friend Lucien Carr describing the changes that had occurred in Bill since his move to Paris: "Bill will probably stay on a while— he's in analysis here—good health except farting around with paregoric temporarily, tho he has changed a little & does finally look a little older— graying temples & face aged suddenly—illumination & analysis—"

Summer was fun with Phipps and Stern around. One evening Allen made a big pot of white beans and ham bone. Stern and Gregory arrived with 2,000 francs' worth of cheese and cold meats from the delicatessen to surround Allen's 400-franc pot of beans. Gregory asked Stern for $50 to pay his rent and Stern peeled it from a huge roll of notes in his pocket. There were enormous quantities of drugs around but Allen never took enough to get addicted, though he sometimes sat up all night grinding his teeth on Phipps's cocaine. Bill, however, had continued to experiment with his "medicaments," and was addicted again. He and Jacques sometimes went out in the Cadillac to score and began to spend a lot of time together.

Jacques was a difficult person to be around; he had screaming tantrums, and one minute he was your best friend, the next he was rude and critical. Bill spent a lot of time at his home in the rue du Cirque and became friendly with Dini to the extent that, shortly after Allen left for New York, Bill wrote him saying, "I am getting along well with Stern's wife. I think she is a really nice person and I have come to like her very much." Bill's success with Dini may have been due to his old-fashioned gentlemanly manners and natural decorum, as opposed to Gregory and Allen, who tried to impose their views and Beat lifestyle on others almost as soon as they met them. One time when Bill was dining at the rue du Cirque, Dini waited until Jacques was out of the room, then told Bill, "Jacques is a monster. Being in the same room with him is like being with death itself." Bill had his doubts about the durability of their marriage.

A few people got busted that summer, including Kenny Clarke and Stern, who was visited by the police at 8 A.M. and interviewed in his library for five hours. Given his great wealth and frail health it was unlikely that he would get anything other than a small fine and some large bills from his doctors and lawyers. He was committed to a hospital and took a Demerol cure. Fortunately the police did not normally bother foreigners, who were generally free to continue their carefree life as expatriates.

In May, Allen, Gregory, and B.J. went to a big all-night party in the studio of Sam Francis, the American Abstract Expressionist painter, where everybody had their faces painted with white greasepaint. There was a live jazz group and endless beer and salami. A few nights later, the same group of people were out again. Allen reported to Peter, "Great night yesterday, BJ and I and Gregory stayed up all night, then in the dawn BJ and I went out for coffee & went to Clochard's bums bar on rue Xavier Privas right off rue Huchette, you know street with arabs etc.—and went in to fantastical crowd of worst looking beat up hairy old creeps you ever saw—so we had some wine then BJ found he still had 500 francs—so we bought 2 bottles wine & cigarettes & got drunk with them singing & goofing all morning for about 6 hours, when we ran broke they brought out their dirty rolls of hidden thousand franc notes & bought us wine and gave us cigarettes & got us drunk, I wound up on the street near an Arab cafe singing Eli Eli to BJ with the Arabs applauding & then went home slept all afternoon and woke up it was dark. Stayed up last nite too & saw dawn."

As his thirty-second birthday approached on June 3, Allen had a brief, early midlife crisis—or it may simply have been a rush of sexual desire. His sex life during his visit to London had been unsatisfactory because he was sleeping in the same bed as Gregory, who was not into homosexual sex, so throughout their stay Allen had remained chaste. Back in Paris, Allen had sex with Billy Whitman a few more times but it felt wrong because the young man began acting strangely. Allen was thankful when Billy returned home to the States a few days afterward and told Peter that Billy was "making serious goofy faces as if sensitive & couldn't communicate in words & writing a long vague bad novel." Allen couldn't look him in the face because he seemed so weird, constantly talking about openness—which had been the theme of many conversations between Allen and Bill—but discussing it as if it were a theoretical novel. However, after sex with Billy, Allen hit the town with

B.J. and a thin young man named Jerry who lived downstairs at the hotel. They went to the *clochard* bar near the rue de la Huchette where they drank with the bums and Allen kissed B.J. and Jerry and got all excited and wanted to sleep with them. Allen continued to drink, and back at the hotel he took off his clothes but they didn't want to have sex. Allen kept this up all week, "like a fever," drinking every night.

For Allen's birthday Jacques Stern invited Allen, Bill, B.J., and Jerry over to his apartment and then took them out to get drunk in the fashionable and expensive bars on the Champs Elysée. It was then Allen realized that he was irritating everyone with his come ons. Finally he came out of it and left them alone. He told Peter he knew that B.J. was very fond of him, "But not queer, so I was just bugging him, which he took OK . . . but finally felt I acting like an old queer . . . Finally stopped trying to make them anyway—feel better, trying to make them all queer angels all involved in my hair—feel ashamed. Don't feel like laying Joy. Maybe I should see a psychiatrist in NY for some more liberation find out what's under me. Been thinking of that."

Compared to life in the Beat Hotel, the news coming in from the States was bad. Their friend Neal Cassady was arrested for selling pot to a narcotics agent; the police had also found out that he was the notorious "Dean Moriarty" in Kerouac's *On the Road*. Allen told his brother they were "apparently doing all they can to be evil about it." Allen wrote letters to everyone of influence he could think off and asked Kerouac to do the same, but though Jack had made his fame and fortune telling Neal's story, he was prepared only to send Neal a used typewriter. There was a huge police crackdown on the "beatnik" community of North Beach, San Francisco, with raids on poetry cafés. Allen told his brother, "I'm glad I'm not there and got out in time." Bill, for his part, had never been west of the Rockies and, hearing what was going on in San Francisco, he declared that he had no desire to do so now.

On June 14, they met the Dada poet Tristan Tzara in the Deux Magots. Allen had always thought that his *Dada Manifestos* were good poetry, and he particularly liked the line "Dada is a virgin microbe." Tzara invited them to visit his apartment, where he showed Allen and Gregory a long, vituperative letter of denunciation to him from Antonin Artaud accusing him of being a custodian of a museum, an archivist, and not a true Dada poet. The letter was marked with spit and cigarette burns, was stained with some of Artaud's sperm and blood, and was sent from the Rodez Hospital Asylum, where Artaud was hospitalized.

The next day they had been invited by Jean-Jacques Lebel to attend a Surrealist party at his father's house on Avenue President Wilson, near the Trocadero. His father, Robert Lebel, was then working on *Sur Marcel Duchamp*, which was to be published in Paris the next year by Trianon Press, and was a close friend of Duchamp and all of the Surrealists. Jean-Jacques remembers the occasion vividly:

> Duchamp came to Paris and my father said, "We'll have a party for him, American style, invite some friends." So we invited Duchamp, Man Ray and their wives, all the surviving Dadaists, Max Ernst and his wife, Breton and his wife, Benjamin Peret, the great Peret. All the people who were still fantastically alive. So my father said, "Of course you will come?" I said, "Listen, I would like to bring some American friends." So my father said, "Who are they?" He'd never heard of them, of course. "Well, they're great poets, very great writers and poets." And my mother said, "Not that crazy guy who vomits all over the place?" See she had come to my place to visit one day, like mothers do, and there was Gregory puking all over the place. I said, "No, no, no! Of course not!" When you're a kid you don't want to tell your parents secrets. Of course it was Gregory. William and Gregory and Allen. So I said to my mother, who is a very bourgeois lady, "Listen. You invite your friends and I'll invite mine and I'm sure they'll get along." Because I was dying for an occasion to get them together, because my obsession all my life has been to put all the people I love together. To put together these people who didn't know each other and to create a sort of hybrid mix is creating new cultures, it's actually making a dynamite event. So I knew it would be important to put those two generations together.

Allen was the only one who was really interested because he was reading Robert Motherwell's *The Dada Painters and Poets*. He had it in his room. So I said to Allen, "Hey how would you like to meet some of the guys? Do you like this guy Peret?" He said, "Peret is a great poet, I've only read one poem of his in a little literary magazine but he's great." "What about Man Ray?" "Man Ray? My dream is meeting Man Ray." "What about Duchamp?" And he said, "Duchamp? Duchamp? I tried to meet him in New York but I couldn't." So, I said, "I'll show you how much I love you man, I'm inviting you next week to my parents' house and they'll all be there." So he actually put on a tie and a white shirt. Put on his wash-and-wear things. He told Gregory, "Listen man, at least try and comb your hair and don't drink," of course, when you tell Gregory not to drink, he drinks five times as much. I went to get them because we had to cross Paris and we took two taxis. And the first thing fucking Gregory does is vomit in the staircase. I said, "One of the historical nights of my life and I'll remember it by Gregory's puking, oh Jesus Christ!" So then I had to wash this puke off the stairs because I didn't want the concierge to have to—so, stupid problems like that.

We walk in, about fifty people were there, everybody's standing. I start introducing people, and Duchamp, Man Ray and Peret were there. Breton's wife was there but Breton was not there that night because he had a flu and was in bed. André Pieyre de Mandiargues, the great writer, was there, and a few fantastic painters such as Jean-Paul Riopelle were there. Friends, friends. And I made the introductions and of course nobody had ever heard of Allen Ginsberg, or Gregory Corso or William Burroughs because their books hadn't been translated, hadn't even been published yet. So it was "How do you do?" But it wasn't "I'm glad to meet you," because they didn't know who they were. So of course what they do is all get piss drunk. And at the end, when people started going away, I see them going up to Duchamp. Gregory holding hands with Allen. Duchamp was sitting in a chair, speaking to people. The first thing goddamn Allen does, he gets down on his knees and starts kissing Duchamp's knees. Thinking he was doing something Surrealistic. And Duchamp was so embarrassed. So embarrassed! Allen being totally drunk, and he was never totally drunk. He made a mix of whiskey and red wine. He was trying to do something that he thought was Dadaistic. But the most embarrassing thing was yet to come. Gregory had found in the kitchen a pair of scissors, and he cuts Duchamp's tie. It's such a corny, childish thing. Knowing Gregory and Allen it's lovely, it's trying to be humble, it's trying to say "We're children, we're fools, we admire you." It was a loving thing.

My father comes up to me and he says, "Hah, your friends huh? Where did you pick up these *clochards*?" He didn't say it but his eyes said it. I was all upset. Here were geniuses on both sides, you know? It was very stupid to have been upset because actually Duchamp loved the guys and Man Ray loved the guys. Every time I'd see them they'd say, "Where are your American beatniks? I love these beatniks. They are completely drunk but they're childish, they're wonderful, I'm sure they're great poets." In fact Duchamp spoke excellent English, but they were too drunk to speak. How can you speak to a drunkard who's falling off on the floor everywhere?

Allen told Peter how he kissed Duchamp and made him kiss Bill; how he and Gregory fell to the floor and begged for Duchamp's blessing, as they had done with Auden, tugging on his pants leg, to which Duchamp demurred that he was only human; and how, when Duchamp tried to get away, they crawled after him on all fours between the legs of the well-dressed guests. He didn't mention that Gregory had cut off Duchamp's tie. They were fortunate that the rather formal Breton was not present.

Jean-Jacques continued, "Two days later Allen said, 'I think we fucked up a little bit,' and I said, 'Forget it, never mind.' I said I want you to meet Breton so I gave him Breton's address and Allen wrote him, saying he would like to come to visit him. I helped him translate the letter into French. Breton knew of him through me so he wrote Allen a postcard reply. Breton had an extremely fine, classical literary French handwriting, and he answered Allen saying, 'Thank you for your note, J-J told me about you, yes please do come by such and such a day, such and such a time, here's my address.' But Allen could not read the handwriting. And I had gone to Italy and he never went. And so I saw Breton when I got back and he said, 'Well, your American friend he's not very well behaved.' I said, 'What do you mean?' He said, 'Well I sent him an invitation and he never answered and he never came.' I went to Allen, I said, 'He sent you an invitation, why didn't you go?' He said, 'I got a funny-looking thing, can you translate it for me?' So he missed it. I felt so bad because I wanted those great minds to meet."

Inspired by meeting so many of the legendary figures of Surrealism and Dada, they all began reading Surrealist texts and went to see Buñuel and Dalí's famous 1928 film *Un Chien Andalou.* The scene of a girl's eye being sliced by a razor had been censored in the United States, but they found it was not as horrifying as they had been expecting.

Allen and Gregory were interviewed by Art Buchwald for his column in the *New York Herald Tribune*, Paris edition. He tried to be sympathetic, but as Allen told Kerouac, "We were drunk and cuckoo." The next night Allen wrote Buchwald what he called "a big prophetic letter" and asked him to use that instead, but of course he didn't.

Gregory recounted his version of things in a letter to poet Gary Snyder, who was now living in Japan. "Allen and me were interviewed by syndicated funny man for masses newspapers, silly jerky and drunk interview, guy named Art Buchwald who came on simpatico, but his article sounds as if he interviewed two nowhere Bohemian cats, o, well, all is forgivable, next time I know better, Allen says poetry expiates all; he's right but this 'beat generation' nonsense lessens the poetic intent, no wonder the academy poets keep aloft, poetry is not for public humor make-fun-of kicks, ridiculous, the whole thing, sardine salesmen, I've been failing my Shelley, it's so easy to jest . . . when asked to talk about poetry and life to interviewers all I can say is fried shoes or something and give them some silly experience, all very nowhere, so now I learn to keep quiet; that interview, in Herald Tribune, really got me wrong and showed me as a talkative idiot, I worry about because I, as a poet, least of all people, should not go novelty on the thing I will die for . . . I think mainly the reason for my silliness and Allen's in interview was because some girl from Frisco came to Paris and showed us articles and clippings of the SF scene that came on so nowhere and gloomy and bullshit and sad, that I felt inclined only to be silly . . . those clippings that girl brought by depressed Allen and me so much, we decided to be jerky, funny, silly, and perhaps change the clime that is threatening gloom."

Buchwald's column appeared in the *Herald Tribune* every day, so Allen and Gregory must have been familiar with it and should have known what to expect. Buchwald was not unsympathetic; he seems simply to have reported what they said, but that was enough to make them objects of ridicule to many of his readers. His column was actually quite amusing and captured some of the lightheartedness of the Beats:

> When Mr. Ginsberg met Marcel Duchamp, the French painter, he said: "I ate his shoe."
> "Why?"
> "To show him I even hated his shoe."
> At the same party Mr. Corso was talking with Man Ray, the photographer and painter.
> "Man Ray was eating a green cookie," said Mr. Corso, "and I asked him why he didn't eat the white ones. He said he only ate things the color of his tie. So I ate his tie."
> "Why?"
> "To show him I dug him. But I got sick."

Buchwald liked them and visited the hotel. He found Bill very interesting and said that he would introduce them to filmmaker John Huston, who was in Paris. Huston had just completed shooting *The*

Roots of Heaven, a film about one man's efforts to stop elephant hunting in Africa and how an American reporter championed him and made him famous. They met for coffee at the Bonaparte and Bill explained his idea for a film about Tangier: episodes seen through the eyes of a junkie looking for a drugstore, junk sick, on Ramadan when everything is closed—a street boy looking to pick up a john; an effeminate tourist sightseeing with his mother. Huston did not think it was quite his sort of movie. Despite his telling Gregory not to call him "Man," they got along well and Huston invited them all to a cast party he was giving on a houseboat on the Seine.

It was a glamorous affair with all the stars of the film present: Trevor Howard, Orson Welles, Errol Flynn, and Juliette Greco. Huston introduced them to the film's producer, Darryl Zanuck, and to the stars. They brought B.J. along with them, which turned out to be a mistake. After drinking a great deal of champagne, B.J. asked Flynn if it was true that someone had broken a popper under his nose when he was flying a plane. "Go away sonny," Flynn responded, whereupon B.J. emptied his glass of champagne over Flynn's head. Two security guards immediately seized B.J. and threw him overboard into the murky water of the Seine. Huston was probably expecting bohemian irreverence when he invited them and it did not spoil the party. The actors particularly liked Gregory, with all his energy and his "fire-engine mouth."

Gregory had a new girlfriend, a nineteen-year-old Russian girl who paid for his typewriter to be retrieved from the repair shop. She told them she had a house on the Riviera, and invited them all down, but she and Gregory broke up before the plan could materialize. As Gregory told Buchwald, "I get money from girls. Everytime I meet a girl I ask her how much money she has and then I demand half of it. I'm not doing anything wrong with money. I just use it to buy food."

One evening Harry Phipps slipped an envelope stuffed full of hundreds of dollars' worth of cocaine under Allen's door, so he and Bill spent the weekend sniffing it. Bill and Allen had a date for an interview at *Figaro Litteraire* with Michel Mohrt, an editor at *la Nouvelle Revue Française*, and one of the very few French people at that time to take the Beats seriously. Both of them kept leaving the room every ten minutes or so to go and sniff another line in the bathroom, so the interview was not a success. The most important thing to come from the interview was that Mohrt knew Louis-Ferdinand Céline and promised that he would arrange a meeting.

It was Burroughs who first introduced Ginsberg and Kerouac to Céline's work. Bill had given Allen a copy of his first novel, *Journey to the End of the Night*, in 1944 and Kerouac read it the next year when Allen, Bill, and Jack were all living together in Joan Vollmer's apartment near Columbia University. "That had a big influence on Kerouac, and Bill," said Allen. "Mentally on me, more on their prose. Kerouac's famous quote from it was, 'We are all going forward in the silence of facts to die.' Kerouac liked that. And Céline's humor is like Bill's. Bill gets a lot of that from him. That's one of the strongest influences on Bill I'm sure, literally."

Bill felt that Céline's work was episodic rather than straightforward narrative, much like his own. Burroughs stated, "I think [Céline] is in a very old tradition, and I myself am in a very old tradition, namely, that of the picaresque novel. People complain that my novels have no plot. Well, a picaresque novel has no plot. It is simply a series of incidents. And that tradition dates back to the *Satyricon* of Petronius Arbiter, and to one of the very early novels, *The Unfortunate Traveller* by Thomas Nashe. And I think Céline belongs to this same tradition. . . . Interesting about Céline, I find the same critical misconceptions put forth by critics with regard to his work are put forth to mine: they said it was a chronicle of despair, etc.; *I* thought it was very funny! I think he is primarily a humorous writer. And a picaresque novel should be very lively and very funny."

Michel Mohrt made the arrangements so that all they had to do was telephone and fix a time. Allen made the call. Céline had a shy, delicate, young-sounding voice on the telephone, which almost quavered, making Allen exclaim, "How lovely to hear your voice." Céline, speaking hesitantly, told him, "Anytime Tuesday after four." On July 8, 1958, Allen and Bill—Gregory had a new girlfriend to see—took the train to Bas Meudon, a distant suburb to the southwest of Paris, about halfway to Versailles. Here Céline and his wife, Lucette Almanzor, lived at 25 terre, route de Gardes, Meuden, in a Louis-Philippe villa owned by Lucette. It was built on the cliff where the Seine curved around to Billancourt and St. Cloud. The house overlooked the road and railway below, then the two channels of the Seine. At his gate Céline could look out over Paris in the far distance, with the Eiffel Tower on the horizon. It was a freestanding three-floor, wood-and-mortar house with a mansard roof. Bill and Allen reached the front gate and rang the bell. Big dogs ran to it, barking. Céline came to the gate to welcome them.

Céline was a large man, sixty-seven years old, tall but stooped, with gaunt features, gray skin, and burning eyes. He was wrapped in scarves, though it was summer. Despite his age he continued his practice as a family doctor—he had few patients—and his wife gave ballet lessons. As a writer he was experiencing something of a revival. He had recently completed *D'un Chateau l'autre*, which was published in June 1957, and was working on *Nord*. Earlier that year Plon had published his *Entretiens familiers* (*Casual Conversations*) with Robert Poulet. He had been interviewed in all the magazines and even had a spoken-word record released on the Festival label in their *"Leurs oeuvres et leurs voix"* series, which was recorded in October 1957. He had become a literary personality, with journalists asking his opinion about everything from the conquest of the moon to *Don Quixote*.

Not everyone was pleased with this new development. After the war Céline had been accused of collaboration and anti-Semitism, but his books had also been banned in Nazi Germany and his opinion of the Germans was no higher than his opinion of his fellow Frenchmen. During the war a Resistance raiding party had destroyed his Paris apartment and all of his papers; his neighbors shunned him. Understanding he was not welcome, he moved to Denmark, where he had a little money set aside. He returned to France in 1950 after six years in Denmark, two of which he spent in jail while the French authorities prepared a case for his extradition for collaborationist activity. The charges were dropped but the collaborationist tag and charges of anti-Semitism continued to pursue him.

Céline, Allen, and Bill sat in a little courtyard behind the house on old, rusty garden chairs, around an old, rusty table, with rusty bedsprings poking up from the overgrown garden, and Lucette brought them wine. About half a dozen dogs roamed the grounds, making Bill very paranoid, as he hated dogs. Allen asked in French if the dogs were dangerous and Céline replied in English that, no, they just made a lot of noise, in order to annoy and scare people away. "I just take them with me to the post office, to protect me from the Jews," he said, looking at Allen. He was referring to the death threats and hate mail that he still received from people who believed he had been a collaborator. He told them that his neighbors put out poisoned meat for the dogs.

Céline and Bill had a long talk about the various jails they had been in and Céline made the point that you can only know a country when you have seen its prisons. He described his incarceration in Denmark and told them, "One great brute simply butted me in the stomach without a word." His opinion of the Danes was not high: awful sniveling cowardly people. They talked about Bill's drug habits and Céline told them he had once calmed panic on a ship that was supposed to be sinking by injecting everyone with morphine, a story he had used in a book. They discussed Jean-Paul Sartre, Samuel Beckett, Henri Michaux, and Jean Genet, but Céline dismissed them all as little fish in the literary pond. They gave him copies of *Howl*, *Gasoline*, and *Junkie* and told him that they were all influenced by him. His English was no longer very good but he told them he could still read it. "I'll glance at them," he said. They conversed in a mixture of broken French and English.

Allen later described the visit. "He was friendly. And he stayed with us for a couple of hours. I don't think he had many visitors. I asked about his practice and he said, 'Ahhh, don't have much of a practice, all these young women want young doctors to look at 'em. Also . . . all the older women want to get naked in front of a young doctor. It's too filthy here to practice.' He took us in the house and showed us the room where he writes." This was a large room on the ground floor, which was a combination kitchen and dining area with piles of books and magazines and papers on the large round table. He showed them his books. "We were totally friendly, in a respectful way, we really appreciated him," Allen continued. "So we reported in as young American geniuses who were coming to salute him and I remember at the gate when we left, he and his wife had brought us to the gate, I said, 'We salute you from America to the greatest writer in France.' And she said, 'In the universe!' So they were playful, they weren't sour."

When he returned to New York, Allen described his visit to an interviewer from the *Village Voice:* "He's an old, gnarled man dressed in black, mad and beautiful, and he thought we were newspapermen— 'Ah, the press!'—until we told him we were poets."

Nine months later, on March 31, 1959, Céline gave up his medical practice, had himself taken off the roster of practicing doctors in Seine-et-Oise, and claimed his state pension. He died on July 1, 1961, of a ruptured aneurysm.

Paris had opened up for them and they were meeting interesting people, but by now Allen had been traveling abroad for eighteen months. He missed Peter and felt homesick for his family and began planning to return home. Allen asked Gregory if he felt like going back to New York, but Gregory was unsure. He still had more of Europe to explore. He had no one in the United States to return to, no money, and he was scared of the American police. Bill had no intention of returning to the States and told Allen, "I have told no one to wait." In fact, apart from a few brief visits, Bill remained abroad until 1974. For Allen, the first priority was to find the money for the passage. He considered going to Rotterdam and trying to take a boat from there as a merchant seaman. Allen had been in the merchant marine. He had his seaman's papers and had taken a number of long voyages, including one to Africa from Texas and another to the Arctic Circle from California. Allen dropped hints to Kerouac that Jack might buy him a ticket. But though Allen had housed and fed him the whole time he was in California, and Jack was making good money from the sale of *On the Road*, the idea did not enter his head. Even if he had considered the idea, his mother would not have let him do it. Allen's father offered to lend him the money but Allen felt that he should try to find the money himself, ideally through the sale of his writing.

Allen felt that he had not produced very much in Paris. "Never found the Angel of Europe, or the inspired wormy poet of France / Nor written the elegy of my Mother, nor the Fall of America . . ." he wrote in his journal. In a letter to Gary Snyder he complained of having difficulty in writing. Snyder's advice was: "The only way for you to write now is to *forget* 'Howl' and what it implies people look for from you next. I mean, drop that you wrote it and write from what you are now. That great poem ends with itself."

In fact, Allen produced many of his best-loved poems during this stay in Paris: "The Lion for Real," "At Apollinaire's Grave," "Message," "To Lindsay," and "To Aunt Rose," as well as "The Names" and the first fifty or so lines of "Kaddish." He would look back on it later as one of his most creative periods. Surprisingly, there are not that many entries in Ginsberg's journals from this period, unless some notebooks have been lost. Mostly they are filled with dreams and early drafts of poems. But sometimes they give clues to Allen's day-to-day life and thinking, e.g., "Cookstove & the great brown pot, Bill downstairs, Gregory in the attic of rue Git-le-Coeur, I must be kinder to B.J., to Françoise, to George."

Allen's efforts to get *Naked Lunch* published appeared to be going nowhere. Girodias had looked at the manuscript several times and at least half a dozen people had told him that he would be a fool not to publish it, but still he remained obdurate. Ostensibly Girodias remained Allen's only hope of getting Bill's masterpiece into print, however, because the supposed pornographic content of the book prohibited it from being published in America, where D. H. Lawrence's *Lady Chatterley's Lover* and Henry Miller's *Tropic of Cancer* and *Tropic of Capricorn* were still banned. Gregory, too, was determined that Girodias should publish it and decided that it was time to put on the pressure.

It had not escaped Girodias's attention that Kerouac had had a best-seller with *On the Road* and that each week *Time* magazine seemed to be filled with articles fulminating about beatniks. Hearing that

Kerouac had a number of unpublished manuscripts, Girodias had written to him offering to publish them, but Jack had not replied. However, Girodias had a tried-and-true beatnik right there in Paris in the shape of Gregory Corso. The fact that Gregory was a poet and not a novelist did not phase Girodias in the slightest and Gregory was soon signed up to write a "beatnik novel" for Olympia. Each month for a year, Girodias paid Gregory by check and, once the money started flowing, Gregory began to pressure him to take *Naked Lunch*. When this did not work, Gregory tried to blackmail him, telling him that if he didn't take *Naked Lunch* then he would not get Gregory's book either. There was a small element of self-interest in this because although Gregory had taken the money, he had not yet written any of his book and was therefore not in a position to deliver it. However, Girodias did not take kindly to this new development, which caused great conflict between them. Jean-Jacques Lebel recalled:

> It was very violent with a lot of screaming. I remember very well, we were at the Beat Hotel, and Gregory was the one who was most militant. And Gregory says, "Let's all go to Girodias's and piss on his carpet." So we walked up to Girodias's office on the rue Saint-Severin, near the Beat Hotel. There was Allen, Gregory, myself, and there was another person. Gregory had brought some wine and we sat on the floor, we refused to sit on the chairs. We told him, "We're not going to move from here until you sign a contract with William S. Burroughs." And Allen was giggling. Girodias was so pissed off he actually started calling the police on the phone. And I said, "Stop immediately" and spoke to him in French.
>
> And he said, "What are you doing here with these Americans?"
>
> "I'm a friend of theirs and I agree with them one hundred percent. Don't be an idiot. Read the damn book, read it."
>
> "But I can't. I hate this stuff. The drug, the drug." But finally, he was pushed shoved forced into publishing it. He didn't want to publish it, it was when the articles started com-

ing out in New York. Then he started saying, "Oh I discovered
the great William Burroughs." He didn't discover shit, you
know.

Life continued without major disturbance. Bill went to Brussels to
renew his passport, "so house quiet here," Allen wrote to Bob LaVigne.
He was away for only a few days and on his return Bill, Allen, and
Gregory stayed up all night on Phipps's cocaine. The next morning,
still high and somewhat bedraggled, they went to be interviewed and
photographed by *Arts*, the Paris literary newspaper. Media interest in
the Beats continued unabated and *Time* kept up its campaign against
them. In a review of Gene Feldman and Max Gartenberg's anthology,
The Beat Generation and the Angry Young Men, *Time*'s anonymous
reviewer voiced the usual trepidation: "The central Beat character that
unintentionally emerges is a modern psychopath. The hipster has a
horror of family life and sustained relationships . . ." and concludes,
"The future of the Beat Generation can be read in its past—The James
Deans and Dylan Thomases and Charlie 'Yardbird' Parkers—and the
morbid speed with which its romantic heroes become its martyred
legends." Allen could guess the hostility he would be up against in New
York from the clippings that had reached him in Paris, but he felt able
to deal with it and use it to publicize the writing he loved.

In the end Allen decided to accept Louis's offer and borrowed
$200 from him. He booked passage on the *Liberté*, which sailed for
New York on July 17, 1958, and paid his rent up until the day of his
departure. City Lights sent him $150 advance against royalties, and
Jacques Stern quite unexpectedly gave him a gift of 35,000 francs ($90)
for shipboard money. Allen wound up giving all Stern's money, and
some of his City Lights money, to Bill and Gregory. Bill had often
supported Allen but he was presently short of funds and Gregory was
broke as usual. Though it would have been more sensible to arrive in
New York with as much money as possible, by the time he left Allen
had only a little over a hundred dollars.

Allen said good-bye to all his friends, and rushed around trying
to see all the sights that he had missed, including Versailles. In his

journal entry for July 2, 1958, he wrote, "I looked at myself in the mirror at the Hall of Mirrors in Versailles—my face, grimacing behind the heavy glasses taped because broken—balding—black coat weighted down with 1924 red Baedecker in left hand, torn pocket, white lunchbag eggs hamburgers in right. Square blue shirt, frizzy bald hair thin, as too much cocaine & walking with dirty feet . . ." He and Joy went on a day trip to Chartres where together they wrote a postcard to Peter. Joy was very sad to see Allen go, guessing correctly that she would never see him again.

Not long before Allen's departure, they were able to contact another icon that they had long sought to meet. Early in 1957, the Belgian poet and painter Henri Michaux had published *Miserable Miracle*, a journal of many months of experimentation with mescaline. "You go from little death to little death for hours on end," he had written, "from shipwreck to rescue, succumbing every three or four minutes without the least apprehension, only to be gently, marvelously resuscitated once more." After his third experiment, he also began to make drawings under the influence of the drug. Allen and Bill both were very interested in his experiments and talked about him with Jean-Jacques Lebel, who was very close to Michaux. In fact Michaux had introduced Lebel to both psilocybin and mescaline. After the debacle of the meeting with Duchamp, Man Ray, and Peret, Jean-Jacques wondered how to bring about this meeting successfully.

Michaux lived literally around the corner, at 16 rue Seguier, the other side of the block, but Jean-Jacques was loath to bring him to the Beat Hotel. Jean-Jacques recalled, "I would often visit Michaux before going to see them at the Beat Hotel, and Michaux says, 'Where are you going?' and I would say, 'I'm going to see these crazy Americans that live here. You know, they're so wonderful. Poets and great people.' Michaux was a very reclusive monk kind of a guy. But he was very interested in these poems I was translating and I gave some of them to him including a copy of *Howl*. He was very interested in meeting them but I always thought, 'I can't take Michaux there,' because you know there were rats. It was a really terrible place, and I was afraid that he would be put off by the filth. I couldn't really bring them to Michaux's house because Gregory was pretty preposterous in those days. So I was trying to find a nice friendly way to get them together and one day it happened. We bumped into each other in the street. I said, 'Oh, Henri Michaux,' and Allen said, 'Henri Michaux. Le grand Henri Michaux?' So Allen said, in his bad French, 'Moi admirer boucoup vous,' or something, but Michaux didn't want to hear about flattery and all that but they made friends and Michaux came to see them."

Jean-Jacques gave Allen Michaux's address and Allen sent off a drunken postcard saying he had much experience in the same hallucinogenic field as Michaux and would like to exchange information with him. He asked if they could meet again. Allen received a postcard, which said that Michaux would visit on a certain afternoon. Allen was surprised because Michaux had a reputation as a recluse but Jean-Jacques had already aroused Michaux's interest in them.

One afternoon a few days later, Allen was in his room, naked, sitting and washing his feet, when there was a knock on the door. "Come in," Allen called out, as usual, and was surprised to see Michaux standing there, waving Allen's postcard in his hand. Allen later wrote a description of the occasion: "He sat on the bed, I explained to him the tradition of peyote experiment in the US of the last decade, I think he was happily surprised to find that unknown company existed in the world. I was delighted by his affection and praise of Artaud as *poet*, and his sympathetic description of the revelatory physical sound of Artaud's voice. One thing I concluded was that Michaux apparently diffident and solitary was like all geniuses, a man full of natural sympathy who could be trusted to approve enthusiasm, heart, common humor or any humane crankiness as long as it was unaffected. He had no reason to give me time and be courteous except that he was intelligent and responsive to my own intelligent curiosity . . ."

Allen asked what younger French poets Michaux recommended and he said there were not many, perhaps Bonnefoy or Joyce Mansour. They discussed the effects of mescaline and Antonin Artaud's legendary Radioffusion Française performance, recorded from November

1947 to January 1948, which the French government had banned before it was ever broadcast. Allen gave him copies of *Howl* and Gregory's *Gasoline*. They had tea with Gregory at an outdoor café on Place St. Michel and they made arrangements for Michaux to return that evening at five, as Allen was leaving the country in two days. He arrived at six and talked with Allen and Gregory about their books, which he had read in the meantime. Bill came in and he and Michaux began a long conversation about mescaline. It appeared that they had had similar experiences. Bill told him of his search for the hallucinogenic drug yagé in the South American jungle, and the more they talked the more the two men appeared to have in common. They immediately became friends. They all talked about poetry. Allen remembered, "I don't think he got much out of my English, but he certainly was sensitive to Gregory Corso's language and laughed, quoting a line he'd noticed which pleased him, 'mad children of soda caps.'" He brought a copy of *Tourbillion de l'Infini* as a farewell gift for Allen, who asked him to sign it. But Bill and Gregory wanted to read it and Allen left it with them, never to see it again.

The next night was Allen's last in Paris and Michaux said he would come over and bring a chicken for supper. He arrived with his companion, a Chinese doctor named Kim-Chi. Before they went into the building he warned her, "Be careful because there'll be rats in the hallway," and he was right. They had a very pleasant evening discussing French and American literature. Allen explained how "Howl Part II" was based upon Christopher Smart's "Jubilate Agno," and translated Gregory's "Lost Watches" into French for him. Michaux laughed aloud at the humor in it. He complained that no one in America was interested in *Miserable Miracle*, even though a number of his earlier books had been published there. Allen promised to contact City Lights about it. The evening seemed to go smoothly, but a few months later, after Allen had returned to New York, Gregory wrote to him and complained, "Did you pee in the sink when Michaux came to visit? One of us did and what's wrong with that? But rumor has it that Michaux told people about it and thought that we were trying to impress him. Really, so fucking European to even detect such an action."

On his return to New York, Allen followed up on his promise and wrote to Ferlinghetti, "Michaux said no one had translated his Miserable Miracle & his following book after that too—which was also further deathly experiences with peyote. Louise Varèse is his translator, & she has the mss complete—I mean, no one had published the translations—he was interested, & annoyed, in a nice way, that he was now having trouble in the US on the mescaline books. You could probably get the last one easily. I sent you his address. I guess Gregory's still seeing him."

Ferlinghetti liked the work and published *Miserable Miracle* five years later, at the further insistence of Anaïs Nin.

That night in his room, Allen was conscious that this would be the last time he would turn off his light and plunge the familiar room into darkness. He turned it off, but then turned it on again and sat cross-legged on the bed in his blue workshirt, knees bare, and looked around at the walls. Picking up his journal, he wrote "Last Poem There," in which he describes all that he saw: his chair, where he had written "The Lion for Real" and "To Aunt Rose," his American knapsack, already packed, leaning against the wall next to a box of books marked "Europe." A rose stood in a beer bottle, and cigarettes, an ashtray, and a handkerchief were laid out by the bed. On the table stood a shiny brown teapot next to a silver can of sugar, which had once contained peas. The curtains, newly cleaned after six months, rustled as a breeze came in through the dark window from the Seine, five doors away. On the whitewashed wall hung an old photograph of Theodore Roosevelt, one of Jean Genet, and a calendar that had been kept by Peter but neglected by Allen. The cupboard was filled with olive oil, vinegar, and a year's worth of accumulated spices and cooking equipment. It was a sad, fond moment realized. He put out the light and thought of New York City, which he had not seen for eighteen months.

The next day Bill was in tears as he and Gregory saw Allen off on the Boat Train. Allen was sad too, knowing there was a chance that he'd never again have such close relationships with his two friends. Bill had been talking of visiting India with Jacques Stern and Allen wondered if he was doing the right thing in leaving him.

As soon as he arrived in New York, Allen took a bus to Paterson to see his parents for the first time in over a year. On the way he scribbled in his journal, "Bill downstairs, Gregory in the attic. Will I ever see Bill again? Alas to leave him in tears—distinguished sanctity." Back in New York, where interest in the Beat Generation was still running high, Allen was interviewed by Marc D. Schleifer for the *Village Voice*. When he was asked why he'd come back, Allen replied, "To save America. I don't know what from." As usual he devoted much of his time to promoting his friends, though they were as yet virtually unknown, even to the hip Greenwich Village readership. "Eight months in Paris living with Burroughs and Gregory Corso. Corso's poetry is really flowing now, he and Burroughs are still living there, he's writing great perfect rich poems. Corso has extended the area poetry covers since *Gasoline*. I'm too literary, you know, but Corso can write about moth balls or atom bombs . . ." The same page featured a small ad from City Lights Books advertising Gregory's broadside *Bomb*, which had just been published.

Allen Ginsberg's period as an American in Paris was over. He had been influenced by its respect and acceptance of artists and writers and had written some fine poems in its supportive atmosphere. Though he visited many times in the future, he was never again able to consider himself a resident there. The Beat Hotel, however, was to continue through several more phases yet.

6 **Ports of Entry**

"Now, I regard you, Brion, as being in my own line of work. Being strictly an experimenter, I say: 'Science, pure Science!' All of us are pure scientists, exploring different levels of fact, and if we turn up something nasty, we're not to blame."

William Burroughs, "Ports of Entry"

When Bill Burroughs first moved into the hotel he lived in room 15—one of the "cells." These were tiny rooms leading off the landings, each with a small window looking out on to the stairwell, which could be opened but had bars for security. Some people painted them over, some hung curtains, and others didn't mind if fellow residents looked in on their way up the stairs. The only light that reached the "cells" was from the stairwell and the stair windows themselves had not been cleaned since long before Monsieur Rachou had died. Bill: "Here I am on the first floor. My room 15 looked on the stairwell and there was no light at all. Then there was T, the incestuous Tony in there. There was a whole room between me and the street which was occupied by this Sicilian called Tony and his wife and daughter and they'd come in and start screaming at each other; it would go on for hours. I think he was a gangster on the skids and on the run but he had no money. He was always screaming at this woman and she was screaming back. Skinny guy looked a typical gangster, you know, sunken cheeks, high cheekbones. He had his daughter living in the room and she was accusing him of fucking his daughter probably, I don't know.

"There was one they called 'The Old One,' heh heh, the old one, this old woman, but by and large it just wasn't the kind of hotel that depended on normal sort of people. She didn't have any. It was almost entirely writers and painters." Also on the first floor were a trumpeter who played all night at the Moulin Rouge and practiced all day in his room; an American guitarist who lived with her Greek lover; a photographer; a painter who liked to play the tuba; and La Patronne herself, as Bill sometimes called Madame Rachou.

Throughout the period that Bill lived at the Beat Hotel—on and off from 1958 to 1963—he was still receiving a steady allowance from his parents, who ran a garden supply and gift shop in Florida called Cobblestone Gardens. They had a reasonable income and lived a comfortable middle-class life and would probably have sent him more were they not also looking after his eleven-year-old son, William III. As it was, there was a very favorable exchange rate and Bill was able to live quite comfortably on the money, perhaps running a little short toward the end of the month. When Ginsberg was living in the hotel, Allen usually cooked and they ate in his room, but when Allen returned to the States, Bill reverted to his old habit of eating his main meal in a restaurant every day and only occasionally cooking in his room.

"At that time in Paris," Bill remembered, "they had these great little alcohol stoves, and they had no odor like kerosene does, you just get this industrial alcohol and it made a beautiful hot blue flame and you could cook over it and make tea and coffee. They cost very little, say twelve dollars. Everything was so cheap. I often went to the restaurant St. Andre Des Arts. It was so so good and cheap we didn't have to cook in to save money. Now that wasn't more than 1,000 francs, two or three dollars, and you got an excellent meal. There were long tables where people sat, with a paper covering, and they just had a very simple menu, and it was always good, a half carafe of good vin ordinaire, all for about three dollars. Then there was the Balkans, on the other side of St. Michel. They had couscous, all sort of semi-Eastern stuff and Italian lasagne, a good good place, about the same price. There was another one on the rue Dragon that just had a prix fixe, just one dish every day. We had a lot of choice, four or five restaurants that didn't cost more than two or three dollars. But I was doing well then, I had two hundred dollars a month! Everything was cheap."

* * *

With Allen gone Bill spent a lot more time with Gregory, though Gregory was not always in town—he loved traveling and exploring Europe and took any trips that were offered. On July 31 Gregory flew to Stockholm, intending to visit Lapland to see the sun at midnight. It was a typical trip for him, his partner on the expedition being an explorer he had met only the day before they set off. Gael Turnbull, the poet whom Allen had visited in England, arrived at the hotel just before Gregory left and recorded his impressions in his journal. "Gregory came in, small, a monkey grin of an Italian face," he wrote, "restless almost aggressive at times, under pressure, dynamic, black curly hair and burning black eyes, a face of a faun, something elemental and Mediterranean, in a miniature bouncing sort of way—not really Puck nor really Pan, neither comparison fits . . . in some excitement partly repressed over the trip to Sweden, apologetic to me for leaving as I came, but it was quite obvious to me that he had to go as he had to breathe—every now and then, grinning in spontaneous friendship like a street urchin—then intent again, off to the North Pole to write a poem that would melt all the icebergs." Turnbull described Gregory's conversation, his dislike of Kerouac's *The Subterraneans* and its "aesthetic wonder-working vision of America," which Gregory believed to be false and wrong, and his obvious pride in being praised by Henri Michaux. Gregory tried to rent his room to Turnbull while he was away, but when they approached Madame Rachou she was adamant in her refusal.

After Allen left, Bill allowed his paregoric habit to increase, even though the business of extracting the opium from it was slow and time-consuming labor. Bill claimed to have been to virtually every pharmacy in Paris in order to buy it. Eventually he turned to the much simpler expedient of using heroin. Bill: "There was a guy called Hadj and he had good, good inexpensive H. So many of Maurice's authors were among his clients. They were all heroin addicts, they were always pawning their typewriters, borrowing twenty dollars. By the time they got their book finished they were in hock deeper than when they started."

Gregory's trip to Sweden lasted for only one week because he was unable to hire a horse in order to join his host and ten others on the trek to Lapland. He attempted to go north by train but gave up ninety miles out of Stockholm and returned to watch the life there instead. When he got back to Paris he found Bill in bad shape. He reported to Allen, "When I came back Bill was about to leave for Spain and then Tangier. He looked ill and seemed determined to kick, never saw him so set on what he was going to do, anyway I saw him off and Jerry downstairs will meet him in Tangier, not all alone. I guess I should have gone with him . . . surely he needed help and I should have gone for that."

Bill's analyst had left for his August vacation and Bill thought a trip to Tangier would enable him to both kick his habit and escape the endless interruptions from summer visitors to Paris. He told Allen, "I am going to ruthlessly eliminate, or at least trim, the ranks of visitors on my return." When he reached Tangier, he was horrified to find how much the scene had changed. There had been a police crackdown on homosexuals—"Many a queen has been dragged shrieking from the Parade . . ."—and the police were blackmailing known drug users. He realized that Morocco was no longer an option; he was stuck in Paris.

There were still lots of visitors around the hotel, most of them looking for Allen, who had managed to set up an enormous network of contacts. Turnbull had visited the various bookshops and hangouts of the Left Bank and wrote in his journal, "I note what an impact Gregory and Allen have made, their names are common currency." Not everyone knew that Allen had returned to the States, and when they were unable to find him they made for Burroughs's room, causing Bill to write Allen that he was "going to put up a sign on the door: *Ginsberg Doesn't Live Here Anymore.* That fucking Arab woke me up at three A.M., and at eight A.M. somebody came around looking for 'friends from Oxford' . . ." The "fucking Arab" was Bouraba, an Algerian who had written seven novels and who wandered around Paris, staying wherever he could, often sleeping rough. Allen had sometimes let him stay on the floor of his room if the weather was bad.

Life for the Beat Hotel residents was still restricted to the small area of the Left Bank described by the Seine to the north, the English

Bookshop on the rue de Seine to the west, the cafés and bars of St. Germain to the south, and the Mistral Bookshop to the east. That July, George Whitman had expanded the Mistral's premises, opening a new reading room in the apartment above the shop, giving it three rooms of books. Sylvia Beach attended the party given to inaugurate the new space, and six years later Whitman changed the name of the shop to Shakespeare and Co. in her honor; it was also a way of attracting American tourists, many of whom, to this day, believe that George's shop on the rue de la Boucherie was where Beach first published Joyce's *Ulysses*.

With Allen not there for companionship, Gregory naturally began to see more of Bill. Gregory had of course tried all the coke and heroin that was around when Stern and Phipps visited, but like Allen he had not taken enough, nor taken it regularly enough, to become addicted. Bill, on the other hand, now had a habit and so had heroin around all the time. Given the situation, it didn't take long for Gregory to get hooked. When Gregory asked Bill if he could have some, Bill said, "Yeah, but it's poison, Gregory."

Back in Paris, Gregory and Bill developed an idea for a magazine called *Interpol:* "the poet is becoming a policeman." Gregory told Allen the contents would be "of the most sordid, vile, vulgar, oozing, seeping slime imaginable. We only want the most disgusting far-outness." They intended to include international heroin news, especially changes in the law: for instance, that a prescription for the opiate Diosan was now needed in Spain, or that certain drugs were available across the counter in France under new brand names. It was to be a forerunner of the underground press, but not surprisingly it never saw the light of day. It would surely have caused a sensation, particularly with its stated intent to review "books written by junkies, fiends, cross-eyed imbeciles, huge-footed oafs, etc. We will praise and hail and laud all kinds of bile, and put down, pan, condemn all kinds of respectability and whiteness."

Gregory had a tempestuous summer and managed to fall out with many of the hotel residents, including Guy Harloff, who told him he was no longer to speak to himself or his girlfriend. Gregory even got into a fistfight. He reported the details to Allen: "Dave McAdams gets me one night for not realizing how negroes suffer or something when I was drunk, on and on. So I told him I hate inferior races, Jews negroes Italians and then some creep came up to me and spilled beer on my head sarcastically thinking me real Jew hater. I get up and for first time in long long time I got to violence and punch him and punch him again, and he was big and he didn't hit me, and they took me away and I felt good, because they are all here now picking on me with questions Beat and so on, so I just don't go out." Gregory holed up in room 41 and finally bought himself a little kerosene stove so that he could fix meals in his room instead of having to eat every meal out.

Gregory spent the middle weeks of August working on "Bomb" and on August 23 told Allen, "Yes, I've finished the Bomb poem and *Paris Review* is almost certain to take it . . . I had much pain trouble with ending, whether to end in joy or light or bitterness, I ended in bitterness . . ." Gregory sent copies to *Isis*, the Oxford University magazine *Poetry London*, and to *Evergreen Review*, but none of them were interested. George Whitman was considering doing it as a broadside from the Mistral bookshop but nothing came of the idea. Lawrence Ferlinghetti's mushroom-cloud-shaped broadside turned out to be the poem's first publication. Gregory sent it to Allen asking him to try and get it published, telling him, "I need it published in New York . . . it is poem worthy of anyone, really labored over it."

On his return to Paris, Bill contacted Jacques Stern. Stern's wife, Dini, had thrown him out and Stern asked Bill if he would go to the rue du Cirque and visit her on the pretext of commiserating over the breakup of their marriage or possibly as an emissary to mend the relationship. The idea was for Bill to somehow gain access to the library, and once there, to pocket some of the small Molière first editions, which were tremendously valuable. This was not the sort of thing that Bill was at all comfortable with, but Jacques had been very generous toward him and he felt obliged. He went to see Dini, who by this time knew him quite well, but she was immediately wise to the plan and cut his conversation short, telling him she knew he was there only to try and take the Molières. Jacques was beside himself with rage when

Bill reported back, and called him every name he could think of. Bill received the abuse with equanimity and did not break off the friendship; he was used to Jacques's violent mood swings, tantrums, and petulant rages. In fact, shortly afterward, Jacques invited Bill to accompany him on a trip he intended to make to London to take an apomorphine cure for his heroin addiction.

That October, Stern had rented an apartment at 2 Mansfield Street, just off Harley Street in London, and wrote from there asking Bill to join him. Bill had allowed his addiction to escalate and knew that he should take a cure, though as usual he felt that he could handle it himself. He claimed to have devised a new system that enabled him simply to pass through the depression associated with kicking and come out the other side.

To Bill the distinction between waking and dreaming consciousness was obscure, particularly as his waking hours were much altered by narcotics of one sort or another. Bill's psychoanalysis combined with his heroin addiction had made him very introspective and given him a very rich dream life. He began to think all life was a dream and that nothing could stop a really powerful dream. He saw the two states as separate but overlapping realities that could and did affect each other. His proof was that one night he dreamed he had money in his pocket and conjured a supply of heroin and opium. Sure enough, the next day he awoke junk sick and flat broke, then Bernard Frechtman showed up and gave him a big ball of opium, another friend insisted that he borrow ten thousand francs, and a long-lost heroin connection put in an appearance, no doubt smelling the money. Bill wrote Allen, "I have visions now practically constant."

Nevertheless, his addiction had reached the point that it was clearly time for a cure. Bill swore by the apomorphine treatment but Dr. Dent, in London, was the only person who offered it (he had cured Bill once before in 1955). Bill began packing his bags.

Stern told him to go to the rue du Cirque and collect $200 from Dini, and then to join him in London to take the cure. Dr. Dent saw only two patients at a time so, as Bill wrote his old friend Paul Bowles in Tangier, "there were no alcoholics about to lower the tone of the establishment." Bill and Stern intended to remain in London until they were both completely clean, but Stern had such a need for heroin that it was not long before Bill found himself in a red London telephone booth collecting the stash that a pusher had hidden there for him. But when Bill returned with the drugs, Stern went through one of his mood swings. William remembered the incident: "He accused me of being a con man, he suddenly said, 'You son of a bitch, you're conning me! You sneaked around to Dini and got two hundred dollars off her.' He accused me of all this and said I should get out. And he walked out. I packed up my stuff and sat down to write him a note of farewell. I said, 'Classifying me as a conniving con man is one of the most grotesque pieces of miscasting since Tyrone Power played Jesse James.' I walked out on to the street and there is the *Evening Standard:* 'Tyrone Power Dead in Madrid.' I remember seeing a picture of him later in a magazine shortly before his death and boy you could see the death in his face."

The extraordinary thing was that Burroughs always continued to write, though he was growing more and more dissatisfied with what he was getting down on paper. He told Allen, "Unless I can reach a point where my writing has the danger and immediate urgency of bullfighting it is nowhere, and I must look for another way."

In September 1958, a few weeks before his trip to London with Jacques Stern, Burroughs was crossing Place St. Michel when he saw Brion Gysin. They knew each other from Tangier but had never been friends. Their first meeting was around Christmas 1954, at an exhibition of Brion's paintings in the Rembrandt Hotel in Tangier organized by Brion and Hamri, the manager of Brion's restaurant, the 1001 Nights. According to Brion, Burroughs "wheeled into our exhibition, arms and legs flailing, talking a mile a minute . . . he trailed long vines of *Bannisteria Caapi* from the upper Amazon after him and old Mexican bullfight posters fluttered out from under his long trench coat instead of a shirt. An odd blue light often flashed around under the brim of his hat."

Bill soon became a fairly regular client at the 1001 Nights, showing up once a month when he received his check from his parents to watch the dancing boys and fire eaters, but the men were suspicious of each other. Brion: "Hamri and I decided, rather smugly, that we could not afford to know him because he was too Spanish," referring to the fact that Bill had Spanish boyfriends and not Arab boys—the two scenes did not mix in Tangier. Burroughs for his part reported to Ginsberg several instances of catty behavior on Brion's part, referring to him on one occasion as that "paranoid bitch on wheels Brion Gysin," and in June 1954 telling Allen, "We had just been in Dean's Bar, where I encountered a barrage of hostility. Brion Gysin was there and wanted to cut me, but I am learning the practices of this dreary tribe."

However, on this autumn day in Paris, four years later, Bill greeted Brion and muttered "Wanna score?" Brion was in need of a place to live and Bill suggested he try to get a room at the Beat Hotel. Bill introduced him to Madame Rachou, whom Brion quickly charmed. So began a new creative phase in the hotel. Brion later stated: "The years at the Beat Hotel were full of experiments . . . it was the right time, the right place, and the right people meeting there together, there were lots of experimental things going on . . ."

Brion had the physique of a Swiss mountain man. He was six feet tall and big-featured, with a mottled complexion, sandy hair, and blue-green eyes. He was born John Clifford Brian Gysin on January 19, 1916, in Taplow, Buckinghamshire, not far from Windsor Castle, of a Swiss father, who died in the war when Brion was eight months old, and a Canadian mother. In typical tall-tale fashion, he claims upon birth to have hollered, "There's been a mistake in the mail! I've been delivered to the wrong address. I never asked to be born. Don't you know there's a war going on? Send me back. There must be a return address on me somewhere."

Brion lived in Canada with his mother until he was fifteen, when he left to attend Downside, an English public (which is to say "private," in American terms) school. He trained as an historian, both at Downside and, later, at the Sorbonne in Paris. He hung out at Sylvia Beach's bookshop and met everybody in the Paris literary and artistic worlds. His evenings were spent at the Café Select: "A literary café by day, the Select turned into a sick *Cage aux Folles* by night. Queers

Peter Orlovsky and Allen Ginsberg on rue St.-Germain-des-Près,
1957. *Photo by Harold Chapman.*

Peter Orlovsky and Allen Ginsberg in rue St.-André-des-Arts, 1957.
Photo by Harold Chapman.

Madame Rachou, la patronne de l'Hotel. *Photo by Harold Chapman.*

Allen Ginsberg in his room at the Beat Hotel. His portrait of Rimbaud hangs on the wall behind him. *Photo by Harold Chapman.*

Guy Harloff, Dutch painter. *Photo by Harold Chapman.*

Gregory Corso his attic room of Rue Git-le-Coeur, wooden angel kid hung on
wall right, window on courtyard half block from Seine. Burroughs came to
live a flight below, Peter Orlovsky & I had windowed street two floors
down, room with two burner gas stove where we all ate often. Gregory
had "Marriage", "Power", "Army", "Police", "Hair" and "Bomb" poems ready
I began Kaddish, Peter "First Poem", Burroughs was shaping Naked Lunch.
Paris 1957.
                                              Allen Ginsberg

Photo by Allen Ginsberg.

Gregory
Corso
eating
grapes in
his attic
room.
*Photo by
Allen
Ginsberg.*

Christmas 1957: Peter Orlovsky and Allen Ginsberg. *Photo by Harold Chapman.*

William Burroughs at the door of the Beat Hotel. *Photo by Brion Gysin, collection of Barry Miles.*

William Burroughs with Brion Gysin in Moroccan costume. *Photo by Ian Sommerville, collection of Barry Miles.*

William Burroughs and Brion Gysin interviewed by the "*Time Police.*" *Photo by Loomis Dean/*Life *Magazine © Time Inc.*

Ports of Entry: William
Burroughs with one of of
Brion Gysin's paintings. *Photo
by Loomis Dean/*Life *Magazine ©
Time Inc.*

L to R: Jean Noire-Jean, Swiss comedian; Jean Oartle, painter; William Burroughs; and American writer Kenneth Tindall and his wife; in the bar of the Beat Hotel. *Photo by Loomis Dean/Life Magazine © Time Inc.*

Ian Sommerville in Room 18 of the Beat Hotel. *Photo by Harold Chapman.*

Gregory Corso at the Mistral Bookshop, with Mistral proprietor George Whitman in the background. *Photo by Harold Chapman.*

The South African poet Sinclair Beiles. *Photo by Harold Chapman.*

Brion Gysin with his creation, the Dreamachine. *Photo by Harold Chapman.*

Brion Gysin at the Domaine Poetique multimedia show. *Photos courtesy of Special Collections Library of Arizona State University, Tempe.*

The end of an era: Madame Rachou with American poet Harold Norse, one of the last to leave the Beat Hotel. *Photo by Harold Chapman.*

and mad queens from all over Europe poured in, making entrances,
throwing fits, making scenes . . . Once caught up in this sordid scene,
I came out." Brion later described himself as a "Butch queen"; he didn't
much like effeminate men.

Brion was working on poetry and, increasingly, paintings. At
nineteen, he had his first showing at a Surrealist exhibition at the
Galerie aux Quatre Chemins on Blvd Raspail alongside Picasso, Dalí,
Max Ernst, Magritte, and Man Ray. But Brion's work offended André
Breton, so he arrived at the vernissage to see it being removed by Paul
Eluard on Breton's orders. Brion would reencounter many of the Sur-
realists, including the painter Matta Echaurren as well as the austere
Breton, in New York during the war.

Brion went to New York in 1940, where he would remain until
1949, working mostly on Broadway, designing costumes for musicals.
He spent much of his time in Harlem where, though he was often the
only white in the room, he was generally accepted as somebody's pale
cousin. His intimate friend throughout the period was the librettist John
LaTouche, whose biggest hit was "Taking a Chance on Love" from
Cabin in the Sky. He was a colorful character who loved to announce,
"I'm making more money than the President of the United States!" or
"If you don't throw your money out the window, it won't come in the
door anymore."

Unfortunately for Brion, he missed the beginnings of bebop in
the clubs of the period: "In those great 52nd Street days I was always
on the wrong side of the street. I was always at the Cloop or Tony's or
whatever, which was just exactly opposite. I'd just go dashing over
like that to ask Billie Holiday where to score and I remember John
LaTouche and me, she gave us the key to her flat, and we took a cab
wa-ay uptown, you let yourself in, and on the piano there's this great
big lamp and you unscrew the lamp and you reach in and you find a
couple of joints. And instead of sitting at her number, 'Touche would
drag me back to listen to something he had written for a Broadway
show that he was going to be doing."

Very many of Brion's friends were homosexual and the flavor of
his life at the time is caught in a letter that the writer and photogra-

pher Carl van Vechten wrote to John Breon in September 1949: "Brion Gysin gave a wonderful party for me at John LaTouche's that lasted all night. Meg Munday was there and Beatrice Pearson and Nora Kaye (of the Ballet Theater) and Rosella Hightower who is dancing next week in Paris with the Cuevas Ballet and Gore Vidal, and the Perpers, and Donald Angus (whom Alice will remember) and dozens of others, white and Negro, and Juanita Hall (*South Pacific*) sang at 2.30 and two of the Negro boys took off their clothes and danced marvelously."

William Burroughs and Brion Gysin almost met during this period because William's first wife, Ilse Klapper, was John LaTouche's secretary. Brion remembered her well, a "German lady with a monocle and sort of mannish tweeds . . . One day I was in 'Touche's house and the telephone rang, and she goes to answer the telephone. And 'Touche says, 'If that is your husband William Burroughs, don't let him up here because he's got a gun!' and I thought, 'Who—who's this William Burroughs? I mean, she's married to the man. Come on, he must be kidding.' And he says, 'Yeah, yeah, she's married to this dangerous lunatic and I don't want him up here.' I said, 'Ooh.' First time I'd heard of him."

In March 1944, Brion joined the U.S. Army as a parachutist. There he befriended Tex Henson, the great-grandson of Josiah Henson, who had inspired the celebrated book *Uncle Tom's Cabin*. Brion wrote a book on Henson, *To Master, A Long Goodnight*, which was published in 1946. It contained an appendix on slavery in Canada and slaves who, like Henson, had fled there; it won him a Fulbright three years later. The other outcome of Brion's military service occurred after he was transferred to the Canadian military in November 1944, where he trained as a Japanese translator. Though the war ended before Brion and his colleagues could use their skill, this exposure to Japanese calligraphy had a profound effect on Brion's painting.

In 1949 Brion returned to France on a Fulbright to research the history of the slave trade. Unfortunately, wartime bombardment had destroyed many of the relevant documents, which were held at the University of Bordeaux. He returned to Paris, where he met up with Paul Bowles. He had known Bowles since the 1930s in Paris, and

Bowles was also a friend of John LaTouche's. In the summer of 1950, Bowles took Brion to Tangier.

Brion recalled the impact that Arab culture had upon him: "It was not until I got to Morocco in 1950 that I became really aware of Arab calligraphy, which rushes across the picture space from right to left like an army with banners. When I wrote my own sign repeatedly linking it across the picture space, I discovered dense Moroccan crowds dancing across my pictures. For me, they danced to the music of Jajouka, the hill village of the Master Musicians who still celebrated the Rites of Pan under Moslem disguise. Their magical music held me spellbound in Morocco for what is still a third of my lifetime, from 1950 to 1973." Brion's love for the music of Jajouka inspired him to open a restaurant, which he called Les 1001 Nuits de Tangiers (the 1001 Nights), at which a five-man troupe of master musicians provided music whenever the restaurant was open. Paul Bowles introduced Brion to Burroughs at Brion's desert paintings show in the Rembrandt Hotel, thinking they would get on as they had similar interests, but this would not be the case.

The International Zone of Tangier existed on its own almost as a small country, independent of the rest of Morocco and characterized by a medieval native culture and a large, decadent expatriate population. But the old, easygoing, openly colonial life in Morocco changed dramatically when Morocco gained independence from France, and Tangier was folded back into its government. Business fell off at the restaurant. Brion met John and Mary Cooke, a wealthy hippie couple on the hash trail. The Cookes were also practicing Scientologists, and when Brion stayed with them in Algiers during the war for Moroccan independence they gave him a full audit. He returned to Tangier and reopened the restaurant, but things never went right again. Burroughs wrote to Allen, "Brion Gysin has opened the Thousand and One Nights with troop of sorry dancing boys, all with ferret faces and narrow shoulders and bad teeth, looking rather like a bowling team from Newark." The end came in January 1958.

Because of a legal problem with a chef, Brion had signed ownership over to the Cookes, trusting that they would return it once things were sorted out. But the Cookes took over the restaurant and kicked him out. Shortly before, Brion had found on top of a ceiling fan a magic talisman—a small package of seven seeds, seven pebbles, seven shards of mirror, a likeness of him, and a calligraphy scroll, held together with a mixture he described as "chewing gum and menstrual blood." The scroll was inscribed with an invocation to the Demon of Smoke, one set of lines written over with another perpendicular one, which read, "May Ibrahim [Brion] leave this building as smoke leaves this chimney."

However, Brion gained much from the restaurant days: his boyfriend Salah, referred to by Brion's friend Felicity Mason as "once the most beautiful and blackest boy on the beach," remained with him until his death, as did Targuisti, his "gentlemen's gentleman" and cook for more than thirty years. He was also able to transform the magic spell from a portent of disaster into something positive, taking its grid of right-to-left Arabic calligraphy and combining it with the vertical script of the Japanese he'd already learned, coming up with a grid of glyphs or *ecritures* that was the signature for all of his post-1958 work. On the strength of his very first painting in the new style, he was offered a one-man show at the Arthur Jeffress Gallery in London in 1959 and commissioned to do a lithograph for the Museum of Modern Art in New York.

After the London show, Brion went to Paris for a group show at the Galerie a la Cour d'Ingres with Matta, among others. After three months in Paris, supported in luxury by Princess Raspoli at her town house, he felt he had overstayed his welcome and jumped at Burroughs's suggestion that he get a room in the Beat Hotel.

William took him to the hotel and showed him his tiny cell-like room 15. There was a young American living upstairs in Allen's old room 25, which was rather bigger than Bill's room. The American said that he was leaving but that he wanted key money. Brion remembered, "I said, 'Don't be silly, it doesn't exist in a situation like this.' He said, 'Oh yes yes yes, or I'll give it to somebody else.' So I went home and did a Moroccan magic that I had learned in my days of interest in magic. The way you do it, if you want to get into a place, is you do these magic preparations and you set yourself in a certain sort of state—a lot of hash or grass will help you get into that state of mind—and then you get that room into your head, and you start moving the furniture around like you would like to have it. And you do this several times like that until you've got the room utterly changed and then you go back and say to the cat, 'Give me the place' and he hands it over to you. Because you've already moved in, apparently. He certainly found the place very uncomfortable."

Room 25 had not changed much since Allen had left. Brion unpacked his paintings and arranged them so that they covered most of the wall space, hanging several above one another, rather like Gertrude Stein and Alice B. Toklas's famous parlor. Brion knew Alice and often went to visit her on the rue Christine. She probably visited him at the Beat Hotel, as she certainly saw the paintings he was doing then. "You ask after Brion Gysin," Alice wrote Ned Rorem, "he is here and painting beautifully—working hard. Do you know everyone works in Paris—except the workingmen."

Away from the gossip of Tangier, Bill and Brion rapidly became close friends—but never lovers—and Bill began to spend most of his free time in Brion's room, watching him paint or else just talking and smoking kif together. Brion was clearly fascinated by Bill. "Burroughs was in room 25 as much or perhaps more than he was in whatever room he was living in," he said in an interview over twenty years later, "William often sat in on painting sessions, following big oils on canvas from inception to completion. Here I was teaching myself to do something bigger and a lot different from what I had ever attempted and I let him sit in on it. There he was and I just had to get on with it. I never let anyone do that before nor would I again in my right mind. The process is more solitary than masturbation, or should be."

The first works Brion did after establishing himself in the hotel were his *ecritures*—the calligraphic white writing paintings based upon the black magic spell. "I'd actually had the kabbalistic square of paper where you write across this way and then you turn the paper and you write across the other way, and then you've got the thing locked in and it *happens.* I thought, yeah, how about using Japanese calligraphy in this direction, which is without changing, and then just running an Arab line across it and so I had a grid. And so that's how it all came into being for me."

You can't read the writing on Brion's *ecritures* but they have many of the forms of writing. Brion: "It has most of the sort of magic things of writing in it. The attack of the brush to the paper, or the pen to the surface." These paintings have often been compared to the work of Mark Tobey, but Brion had not seen a Tobey work at that time. As Brion said, "It was in the air, somehow" and both painters had reached a similar conclusion independently and from disparate directions; Tobey (born 1890) first encountered Chinese calligraphy in the mid-'20s in Seattle and then studied Japanese brushwork in a Zen Monastery in Kyoto. In fact Brion's biggest influence was undoubtedly Matta.

Bill was astonished by the paintings and was fascinated watching Brion execute them. He told Allen that Gysin was doing "GREAT painting. I mean great in the old sense, not jive-talk great. I know great work when I see it in any medium. I see in his painting the psychic landscape of my own work. He is doing in painting what I try to do in writing. He regards his painting as a hole in the texture of so-called 'reality' through which he is exploring an actual place in outer space. That is, he moves into the painting and through it, his life and sanity at stake when he paints. Needless to say no dealer will touch his work. It is unlike anything I ever saw. When you see it your thought process stops dead and *satori* opens up in front of you."

Fortunately, there is a transcript of a tape-recorded conversation between Bill and Brion made in 1959 in room 25 while Bill was looking at a four-panel painting consisting of very dense calligraphy. It tells us as much about Bill's own approach to painting as it does about Brion's paintings:

> *Brion:* "How do you get in . . . get into these paintings?"
> *Bill:* "Usually I get in by a port of entry, as I call it. It is often
>   a face, through whose eyes the picture opens into a land-
>   scape, and I go literally right through that eye into that

landscape. Sometimes it is rather like an archway . . . any number of little details, or a special spot of color, makes the port of entry and then the entire picture will become a three-dimensional frieze in plaster or jade or some other precious material.

"The picture in front of me is in four sections. The remarkable thing is the way in which the sections—when hung a few inches apart—seem literally to pull together. The substance of the paintings seems to bridge the gap. Something is going streaming right across the void. Surely this is the first painting ever to be painted on the void itself. You can literally see the pull of one canvas on the other.

"Now you suddenly see all sorts of things here. Beautiful landscape. And then always bicycles. The whole bicycle world . . . scooters. All sorts of faces . . . monkey faces . . . typical withered monkey faces. Very archetypical in this world. And you do get whole worlds. Suddenly you get a whole violet world, or a whole gray world, which flashes all over the picture. The worlds are, as it were, illuminated by each individual color . . . worlds made of that color. You think of them as the red world, and then the blue world, for example.

"I was taking a color walk around Paris the other day . . . doing something I picked up from your pictures, in which the colors shoot out all through the canvas, as they do on the street. I was walking down the boulevard when I suddenly felt this cool wind on a warm day, and when I looked out I was seeing all the blues in the street in front of me . . . blue on a foulard . . . blue on a young workman's ass, his blue jeans . . . a girl's blue sweater . . . blue neon . . . the sky . . . all the blues. When I looked again, I saw nothing but all the reds . . . of traffic lights . . . car lights . . . a café sign . . . a man's nose. Your paintings make me see the streets of Paris in a different way.

And then there are all the deserts, and the Mayan masks, and the fantastic aerial architecture of your bridges and catwalks and ferris wheels."

Brion: "You mentioned once that you can't see all of these at the same time."

Bill: "No. This is the first real space-time painting in which there's a presentation of what is actually going on in front of the painter and the viewer in a space-time sense, both through the forms and through the color, because the color makes the shifting forms. And then this is related to actual time-sequences. I know of no other example of the way in which time is represented here . . .

"When you see one layer of the picture, then you suddenly see it all. The eye which I am using as a port of entry jerks me abruptly into a landscape I never saw before. It is a sort of toy world, and one that is somehow alarming, populated with mechanical insects attacking each other, and men in armor from other planets. Or they may be simply modern welders with bridges in the background . . .

"Very strange! Just for a moment there I caught an absolutely clear photographic picture of Gregory Corso. It has gone now, but I feel sure it really is in there and will come back again. It is queer how these photographic shocks of yours flash in and out. It is one of the most remarkable phenomena I have ever witnessed in all my practice. Their strangely familiar faces are all growing together, bound up by vines and tendrils . . . monkeys' faces. At one point a very mean, ravished seventeenth-century face with a ruff around his neck, standing outside some sort of native hut.

Brion: "Doesn't that look like some kind of writing?"

Bill: "It does. I can read it: 'Wings tack quietly . . . vines crying . . . not crying . . . kiss . . . noisy pissing Tex . . . Gysin not sin was not crying . . . fix Gysin . . . Brion . . .'

"Looking at these paintings of yours is often like focusing an optical instrument. I find that it takes about
twenty seconds to focus at all. The viewer has to learn
how to flicker back and forth between a telescopic and a
microscopic point of view, while his attention is centered
on some small beautiful scene which may be no bigger
than your index fingernail at one moment, and then your
attention is suddenly jerked back to a clear, long-range
view of the picture or its all-over pattern . . . a series of
neural patterns which already exist in the human brain."

7 Through the Magic Mirror

"It was the biggest adventure when Girodias published Naked Lunch. *We all took it for granted it would never be published anywhere else—which just shows how it changed the whole world scene."*

Brion Gysin

Allen Ginsberg and Bill Burroughs had very different experiences of Paris and the Beat Hotel. Whereas Allen assiduously visited all the sites and museums, reading up on their history and studying the guidebooks, Bill had no interest in old buildings and only visited museums to check on certain subjects that he was investigating. In this way Bill's experience was much more internal; his was more a landscape of ideas, and in many ways he could have been living anywhere. Once Burroughs joined forces with Brion Gysin, the Beat Generation presence in the hotel became a very different one than that propagated by Ginsberg. Allen's approach was all-embracing—he was happy to spread the good word to anyone—whereas Bill preferred an anonymous, invisible presence. Bill's life happened mostly in his room, or in Brion's room. People were welcome to visit, but only *certain* people.

There were many reasons why Bill and Brion were not part of the everyday life of the hotel: they were a bit older than most of people there and they were homosexual. Gregory moved more freely among the other guests and also ranged far and wide across Paris in his quest for women and beauty. With about seventy people living in the hotel at any given time, there were many distinct groups of friends. Tom Neurath, who later would become publisher of Thames and Hudson art books, was living at the hotel then, sent to Paris by his father to learn the book business. Neurath's group included Cyclops Lester, who wore a patch over his left eye and sometimes sported a black beard, mustache, and full-length leather coat. Cyclops worked as the circulation manager for the Paris-based *New York Herald Tribune*. There was also twenty-two-year-old Kenneth Tindall, a novelist and poet from Los Angeles, who looked the beatnik part with a full beard and wispy mustache. He wore a huge, chunky sweater and went barefoot in sandals. He lived in the hotel with his Danish wife, Tove. Living there as well were the American writer Jonathan Kozol, who before his famous works on children and poverty was published extensively in *Olympia* and other little literary magazines; the English painters Bob Grosvenor and Pip Rau; Dixie Nimmo, the West Indian poet and novelist; and Kay Johnson, known as "Kaja," the painter and poet whose book of poetry *Human Songs* was later published by City Lights Books. There was even a Portuguese political-dissident contingent who were less given to partying than the young Englishmen and Americans. As to the rest of the hotel's residents, many were students and a lot were painters—though few became well known. Others were writers, poets, artist's models, and photographers, like Harold Chapman, who carefully documented the hotel and its inhabitants, from the hotel cat and the bar tariff to the hole-in-the-floor toilets. His 1984 book of photographs, *The Beat Hotel*, is a precious record of the period. They were primarily young, almost all English-speaking, enjoying their freedom at a time when freedom for young people was much frowned upon back home in Britain or America. Gregory is the one who came up with a name for Madame Rachou's establishment: he called it the Beat Hotel.

Brion remembered, "Just about everybody and anybody passed through the Beat Hotel but some of us got to be more or less fixtures, fiercely protected by Madame Rachou who ran her hotel by radar . . . I built myself into room 25 on the third floor front for years while Burroughs ran in and out grabbing this room or that one for a few months and then splitting, abandoning manuscripts that I stashed away in my padlocked footlocker I liberated from the U.S. Air Force in Morocco and had painted blue, decorated in Tetouan. Burroughs and I saw each other more than a lot. No, not twenty-four hours a day. No matter what people may say, we were never lovers. Allen Ginsberg writes that he has one set of ideas about making it sexually with friends and I have another. Not a matter of principle. Friends just don't turn me on, I guess.

"Anyway, William and I lived through some very thin, slippery times together, doing our psychic symbiosis numbers. It was often downright scary and positively dangerous but all a barrel of fun at the same time, if you can hear me. William could be so scary he was positively hysterical. It was all a Psychedelic-Psyche-Sick joke. What were we up to? We were whipping up the 'complete derangement of the senses' as preached almost a century earlier in the self-same Parisian circles known to those earlier hashishins like Baudelaire and Co. and then young Rimbaud. Burroughs used to be able to just sit there in my room and simmer in a cloud of smoke through which he would turn into all the great literary junkies one after another, De Quincey, Coleridge and Co., or the Old Man of the Sea from Sinbad's story. Oh he could sit there staring into my canvases and simply melting into them to move around in there, disappearing . . .

"If I formulated a question such as: 'What is time?' I would propose it to William who would stand there looking rather strange, as if he were swallowing his Adam's apple. It would move up and down for quite a few minutes, and, um, he seemed to be making this sort of humming, like he has a machine in there that he set to work . . . as though he had submitted this question to a computer and he would come up with a convincing answer, like: 'Time is that which ends . . .' It was like having one's own oracle at home at all hours. So, in that way, a good many amusing and instructive things were . . . discovered or rediscovered. . . ."

In October 1958, William bought a stainless-steel dowsing ball from a magic shop called La Table d'Emeraude and hung it up in his room for decoration. Brion looked at it and saw something in its shining surface. "Bill looked over his shoulder and said, 'Why, yeah. It's your restaurant in Tangier, but where are those people going and where are they coming from?' The musicians were there in their usual place and people came down from the staircase carrying a cadaver, like a

Moslem funeral, and passed through the doors and went out. We realized we were both seeing exactly the same thing. It therefore wasn't based on suggestion." Bill told Allen, "I know I am in a very dangerous place but the point of no return is way back yonder." Bill and Brion both had read about scrying. Using the polished surface of the ball they learned how to do it and the results were so interesting that they rapidly moved on to a mirror.

Scrying is a *magick* technique, the ancient act of divination for the purpose of clairvoyance, and is achieved by focusing attention on an object having a shiny surface until a vision appears. Scrying is best known to the general public by the stereotype of a Gypsy fortune-teller looking into her crystal ball. The word *descry* means "to discern" or "to reveal," and in the Middle Ages the art was used to see into the future and to find lost objects or people. It is usually accompanied by traditional ritual: witches usually scry in a magic circle to prevent outside influences from distorting their visions, which is also why most scrying is done at night; the area is protected by a circle, either drawn in chalk or imagined; guardians are summoned—if you have any. The room is very dimly lit, preferably by moonlight, and a candle is placed behind the viewer in order not to cause reflections; or, alternatively, the space is illuminated by a candle at either side of the mirror, set back to give no reflection. As scrying takes some time—twenty minutes for a beginner and longer as you become more experienced and see more—the physical height of the mirror or crystal ball is important, as is the comfort of the seating arrangements.

After a few deep breaths the viewer looks intently into the mirror. Staring causes the eyes to produce tears, which make the viewer blink, so the correct scrying technique is to relax the focus of your eyes but remain alert. The viewer gazes lightly at the mirror or crystal, not hesitating to blink when necessary. At this stage, the eyelids are allowed to close halfway. After a while, the surface of the mirror will begin to change and fade; a dark mist will appear. Some people experience a tightness in the forehead but this is no cause for alarm. The viewer should remain relaxed. Next a small light appears, and from the light point, clouds form and spread to fill the mirror. Sometimes people even see a small light show within the clouds. The viewer's inner eyes are now said to be open, and the journey into the mirror begins. Eventually the clouds clear and pictures begin to emerge. Frequently the visions are symbolic and, in theory, the scryer must be trained in order to interpret their meanings. Brion recalled, "We did a great deal of lengthy mirror-gazing at that time. We felt that we had all the time in the world to give to such explorations and we did see some strange stuff, just like 'they' always said we would."

Brion had two armoires with two very heavy plate-glass mirrors in each that enabled him to open the doors in such a way that he was surrounded by mirrors. He recalled, "I sat once for thirty-six hours looking directly at the mirror; I was sitting lotus position on the bed, the mirror was face to me, and anybody could hand me things around the corner of the mirror, like food or cigarettes or joints or whatever, to keep me there for that length of time, and I sat and kept awake for thirty-six hours, just staring into this big mirror . . . saw all sorts of things . . . you see great galleries of characters, running through."

He saw nineteenth-century scientists in their laboratories, whole scenes acted out before him, Oriental faces frozen in time: great chieftains of unknown races, going back further and further in time and history, wearing amazing headdresses with deeply scarred and tatooed faces. "I got to a point where all images disappeared, eventually . . . and certainly after more than twenty-four hours of staring . . . where there seemed it was a limited area that one could see only a certain distance into, uh, where everything was covered with a gently palpitating cloud of smoke which would be about waist-high . . . that was the end, there was nothing beyond that." In his novel *The Last Museum* Brion wrote, "Enough is enough! Let's have no more retreads, no more images of images of images. It's all done with mirrors. We want the real thing now and nothing but."

December 1958 was an extraordinary month for Burroughs and Gysin and to Bill it seemed as if the events of ten crowded years had been compressed into thirty days of discovery. He had wanted to experience danger and, through Brion, he was getting it, with paranormal occurrences coming thick and fast. Bill wrote a text called "Fats Ter-minal," which became the "Algebra of Need" section of *Naked Lunch*, and later that day Brion showed Bill a magic Arab necklace. In an amber bead, Bill saw Fats's face, like a monster virus, frozen in the precious stone, looking for a way out: "a lamprey disk mouth of cold, gray gristle lined with hollow, black, erectile teeth, feeling for the scar patterns of junk." Another time Bill distinctly felt Jacques Stern touch his arm, even though he was seated across the room. He looked in the mirror to shave his face and saw someone else there.

Bill watched Stern loose seven pounds in ten minutes when he took a shot of heroin for the first time in a week. According to Burroughs the flesh that the body gains back when coming off junk is initially soft and ectoplasmic and literally melts away at the first touch of junk. As usual, Bill used his experiences as raw material for his writing. The incident appeared in *Naked Lunch*, albeit slightly exaggerated: "I saw it happen. Ten pounds lost in ten minutes standing with the syringe in one hand holding his pants up with the other, his abdicated flesh burn-ing in a cold yellow halo."

One day, in the course of a mirror-gazing session, Bill saw him-self in the mirror with completely inhuman hands: thick black-pink, fibrous, long white tendrils grew from curiously abbreviated finger-tips as if the tips had been cut off to make room for the tendrils. Jerry Wallace, a twenty-year-old boy from Kansas who was sitting across the room, exclaimed, "My God, Bill! What's wrong with your hands?"

"My hands?" asked Bill.

"They are all thick and pink and something white growing out of the fingers . . ."

Several people commented on Bill's growing invisibility, some-thing the Spanish boys in Tangier had noticed, which gave him the epithet El Hombre Invisible.

The psychic transformations seemed to be infectious. Brion re-membered other people in the hotel getting in on the act: "Well they'd come, stand in front of the door and go through incredible changes . . . rather a dark hallway, they'd stand there glimmering, showing off their psychic aptitudes."

Bill's friend Shell Thomas joined in the experiments and confirmed Bill and Brion's findings. To Bill's dismay, Shell decided to return to the United States, and he left Paris for Spain on February 9 after an altercation with Gregory over money. Bill wrote Allen, "Sheldon took off for Spain yesterday . . . I really dug him. Wonder what story Gregory will tell about keeping that money instead of taking it to Sheldon?? I trust Sheldon's version over Gregory's, and in fact, I think a lot more of Sheldon than Gregory." Bill was sorry to see him go because he already regarded him as part of a triumvirate of mystical experimenters: "the three mystics I had hoped to form nucleus and get something definite and usable via cross-fertilization—Shell, Gysin and Stern."

Bill warned him not to go. "He came to me and said he was going to buy an ounce of heroin and take it back and I said, 'Man, I don't even want to hear about this.' Well the wind up is he got it back in and tried to sell it in Houston, Texas. He made contact with a guy he knew who turned out to be a stoolie and he got some twenty years in the pen. In Houseville penitentiary, a penitentiary I know because my friend Kells Elvins used to work there as a psychologist, so I know something about it. Well anyway he sort of wrote his way out of there with a novel called *Gumbo*, which was published eventually by Grove Press."

Shell was busted in San Francisco with two bags of heroin. He was given a twenty-two-year sentence and went to jail in November 1958. He became eligible for parole in September 1962. He was unanimously recommended by the Texas Board of Pardons and Parole, but former Governor Price Daniel rejected the request by executive action. Daniel's reason given was that while he was a U.S. Senator, he had served as chairman of a special Senate Committee investigating nationwide narcotics traffic. In his term as governor he felt compelled to observe a strict policy of never knowingly approving parole for narcotics offenders. When John B. Connolly became governor of Texas in January 1963, he too rejected all appeals on Shell's behalf.

Shell had three poems in a bilingual anthology of new American poetry coedited by Gregory Corso that was published in Germany, but it was his "Toby" stories, appearing in four different issues of *Ever-green Review* from 1961 to 1963, that drew attention to him as a literary talent. His first piece was accompanied by a poem: "Do not these iron bars / Long to be guns in future wars? / I think they must! / It comforts me, somehow / To know, a thousand years from now, / They will be dust."

Bill felt that Shell had drawn attention to himself when he returned to the States carrying the heroin and wrote to Allen, "Imagine that idiot going back with a saxophone and loud clothes . . . a *saxophone!!!* My God, how fucking stupid can a man get . . . ?"

Bill thought that Shell's literary activities helped reduce his sentence. "They put a word about here and they got him out after about four years, five years. I saw him again in New York. He lived for a while in Puerto Rico but he didn't like it. Then he went to New Mexico and he's still there. He's got a nice place there with a trout stream that runs through it. He's diverted some of it into a pond so I can go out and catch my breakfast sometimes."

Brion went to spend the Christmas and New Year holiday with friends in La Ciotat, an artists' colony on the Mediterranean between Marseilles and Toulon. On his way to Marseilles, sitting in the back of the bus, he had yet another extraordinary experience. He recorded it in his journal for December 21, 1958: "Had a transcendental storm of color visions today in the bus going to Marseilles. We ran through a long avenue of trees and I closed my eyes against the setting sun. An overwhelming flood of intensely bright patterns in supernatural colors exploded behind my eyelids: a dimensional kaleidoscope whirling out through space. I was swept out of time. I was out in a world of infinite number. The vision stopped abruptly when we left the trees. Was that a vision? What happened to me?"

He wrote to Bill, telling him of his experience. Bill replied, "We must storm the citadels of enlightenment. The means are at hand." In fact, it was a year before Brion understood what had happened to him, but it was to become the basis for one of his most interesting inventions: the Dreamachine.

During all his mirror-gazing, Bill was tossing back whole boxes of Eubispasmes, which kept his habit in check but meant that he was clean in the event of a police raid. Eubispasmes were small black opiate pills laced with codeine, sold as a cure for the grippe and available at any pharmacy in France without a prescription. Bill spent his time in Room 25—wrapped against the winter drafts in an old gray sweater, which had been given to Brion by Mary Cooke in Algiers in 1955—watching Brion paint. He began to do a little painting himself, and at the beginning of January 1959, he sent Allen some examples of his work, consisting of a series of Gysin-style calligraphic gestures. Despite Brion's huge influence, they were nonetheless distinctly Burroughs's marks, not Brion's.

Felicity Mason, an aristocratic Englishwoman, often visited Brion in Paris. A former spy who was related by marriage to the Queen Mother, Felicity went to Marrakech in 1952 after her second divorce, where she met Brion in the café of her hotel. As it transpired, they were from neighboring villages on the Thames, and each had a sibling who had died. They rapidly evolved a fantasy of being related, so that when a friend of Brion's joined the table he casually announced, "This is my sister. She's just arrived."

Brion admired her quest for adventure and showed her the sights. She began by having an affair with two Arab boys "of good family"— one for her afternoon siesta and one for the nighttime. "They were both neatly circumcised, well hung, and I could not tell their penises apart. Thus they became known as the Heavenly Twins."

Felicity did not much like the Beat Hotel. In her book *The Love Quest*, where Brion is called Max—a name he chose for himself—she wrote:

> I did not spend much time with Max in his cheap hotel; the stinking Turkish lavatories, one to a floor, with the threat of rats on the worn wood stairway spiralling up to Max's room were enough to put me off. The Beat Boys were interesting once you got there, and the tiny room had an intense social life of

junky expatriates from an intellectual world, but I was used
to the previous generation of Hemingways and Gertrude Steins,
where food and drink and the glamorous life went with intellectual pursuits. Here drugs had reduced everyone to poverty.
The Beat writers at that time were still all relatively unknown,
and were struggling and living in the unprecedented squalor
of this Left Bank hotel. I was younger than most of them, but I
felt from another generation, from another country. I loved them
and admired them just the same, and somehow I hung in there
from time to time and fitted myself to their strange world.

Felicity preferred the luxurious life, to which she was accustomed:

Brion, as usual, flitted in and out of many different
worlds. He could leave the Beat Hotel in old blue jeans, which
were not yet fashionable, and look like a prince and mingle
with the highest. I can remember on occasion when we were
invited by rich friends to "a little bistro down the road" which
turned out to be the Tour d'Argent, where they swirled ice
around in the glasses to make sure they were cool enough for
the vintage white wine, and pressed a whole duck just to make
gravy for another duck. Brion put on his habitual air of arro-
gance as we entered, and I trained behind him in bare legs and
sandals carrying a string bag of groceries, trying to look as if I
had on a feather hat, diamonds and a little black dress. Together we pulled it off and were shown to the best table, that
big round one in the bay window overlooking Notre Dame.
Everything went beautifully until Brion had an attack of asthma
and I had to hurry him back to the Beat Hotel. Nevertheless we
made a grand exit with everyone bowing. From the sublime to
the seedy, it didn't matter, he was always the king.

Bill liked Felicity, who became one of his few lifelong female
friends. He once made a pass at her at dinner on the quai de la Tournelle
with some other expatriate Americans. Brion had passed out drunk

on the floor and Bill asked her to come back to the hotel with him but she declined, saying later, "He was not my type."

Bill was always amused by Brion's bourgeois pretensions and the way he would introduce his various aristocratic friends—"Some of Brion's well-to-do friends came in from time to time. 'The princess'!" This was one aspect of life at the Beat Hotel where Brion felt inconvenienced. As there were no telephones in the rooms, Brion's society friends had to either leave messages or persuade Madame Rachou to fetch him to the phone. Jean-Jacques Lebel recalled, "When somebody would call for Brion or Allen or Gregory, it was very rare but it did happen, she would go out into the street and call the rooms that were on the street, 'Hey, M'sieur Brion! Telephone! C'est Madame Rachou!' The whole city knew who had a phone call. It was like a village, you know."

Meanwhile, in response to Ginsberg's tireless efforts, *Chicago Review*, the literary magazine of the University of Chicago, had published a section from *Naked Lunch* in their Spring 1958 issue, which also contained three pieces by Kerouac and three poems by Allen. Editors Irving Rosenthal and Paul Carroll followed this with more Kerouac in their Summer issue, and the Fall issue contained a further excerpt from *Naked Lunch* and two letters from Allen. But this was 1958 in the Midwest and the Fall issue attracted the attention of Jack Mabley, a muckraking gossip columnist for the *Chicago Daily News*, who fulminated against the contents of the magazine. He headed his column "Filthy Writing on the Midway," and ended his piece by saying, "But the University of Chicago publishes the magazine. The trustees should take a long hard look at what is being circulated under their sponsorship." Naturally, the trustees did as he asked and Dean Wilt summoned Rosenthal to his office, asking him to bring with him the material he intended to run in the Winter 1958–59 issue of the magazine. The dean did not want anyone rocking the boat and offending the local community. Rosenthal was told that the Winter issue had to be "completely innocuous." Ten chapters from *Naked Lunch*, Kerouac's "Old Angel Midnight," and a prose piece by Edward Dahlberg would all have to be dropped, and even an article on German Expressionism was thought to be too racy for the impressionable minds of Illinois.

Both Rosenthal and Carroll resigned and formed a nonprofit trust to publish the suppressed issue as it was originally intended. They asked Kerouac if he could think of a name for their new magazine. He looked at a note to himself on his desk that read "Buy big table." The new magazine was called *Big Table*. Allen and Peter, both back in the States by then, and Gregory, who was in New York on a visit, all flew to Chicago to take part in a benefit reading to pay the printer.

Because anything to do with the Beat Generation was now newsworthy, the arrival in Chicago of Allen, Gregory, and Peter on January 28, 1959, merited a front-page news story in the *Chicago Sun-Times*, complete with photographs, and a fashionable party hosted by socialite couple Mr. and Mrs. Albert A. Newman in their Lake Shore apartment, attended by local reporters and photographers. A *Time-Life* team photographed them in front of works by Picasso, Jackson Pollock, and Monet. Each day the citizens of Chicago followed their movements in the newspaper gossip columns.

At the reading, held in the Sherman Hotel, Allen read from "Kaddish" and delivered a powerful rendition of "Howl," a recording of which Fantasy Records finally released on an album, as Allen had been unable to record well in Paris. The first issue of *Big Table* was published in March and contained ten chapters from *Naked Lunch*. But Rosenthal and Carroll's troubles were not yet over; the publicity surrounding the suppression of the magazine had attracted the attention of the Chicago postal authorities, who promptly seized issues on the grounds of obscenity. It was a repeat run of Ginsberg's *Howl* trial and caused yet another flurry of interest in the new writing.

The appearance of such a large section of *Naked Lunch* in America resulted in a great deal of interest in Burroughs, whose work was then virtually unknown. Norman Mailer's assessment of Burroughs led the way: "The ten episodes from *Naked Lunch*, which were printed in *Big Table* 1, were more arresting, I thought, than anything I've read by an American for years. If the rest of William Burroughs's book is equal to what was shown, and if the novel proves to be a novel and not a collage of extraordinary fragments, then Burroughs will deserve rank as one of the most important novelists in America, and may prove comparable in his impact to Jean Genet."

Back in Paris, Brion had an attack of appendicitis in February and had to undergo an operation. Afterward he went to Marrakech to recuperate in the warmth. In April, Bill followed him to Morocco, flying to Tangier for a winter break, but his arrival was poorly timed as he found himself wanted for questioning by the police.

About six months previously, Bill had considered the possibility of improving his financial situation by pushing a little Moroccan marijuana in Paris. He had a friend in Tangier named Paul Lund, an English thief who had retired to Tangier and opened a bar in November 1957 called the Novara. Bill wrote asking if he could sell him any "Moroccan leather goods." Nothing ever came of the idea, but for some reason Lund gave Bill's letter to one Captain Clive Stevenson, the owner of a three-masted topsail schooner named *Amphitrite*. Stevenson was busted trying to buy a half-kilo of opium from "The Old Black Connection" in the Socco Chico. Lund and The Old Black Connection were held incommunicado and the latter gave the police a story involving both Lund and "an American with glasses." On the evidence of Bill's letter, which they found in Stevenson's pocket, they concluded that Bill was the Paris connection. The police searched Lund's place and found a suitcase of manuscripts that Bill had left there. Bill told Allen, "[they] wade through a suitcase of my vilest pornography looking for 'evidence.' (They must figure hanging has a code significance.)"

To further complicate matters, the police also had a letter that Bill had sent to Mack Shell Thomas, saying something to the effect that "Pooling our knowledge could be of great benefit to both parties," which again suggested Bill as the mastermind behind a narcotic ring though it probably referred to psychic matters. The police now had his address in Paris but were not aware that he was just then there in Tangier. One day Bill was visiting Paul Lund when the police made another search of Lund's premises. Miraculously they did not ask to see Bill's passport, nor did they search him, which was fortunate because he had five grams of opium in his pocket at the time.

Bill had his scrying ball with him but found it painful to use. He seemed to feel a physical pressure on his body, pushing him away from the ball, which made him so uneasy that he had to sleep with the light on. However, he told Allen, "Well, I will not turn back (even if I could)." He also revealed the state of his psychoanalysis, telling Allen, "Seems I never think about sex—so don't know if I'm interested in man or woman or both or neither. I think neither. Just can't dig the natives on this planet—certainly the analysis has, with a slow scalpel of fact, cancelled my sado-masochist visa to Sodom. I wonder if any but the completely innocent can enter without a S-M Visa?" Bill's lack of sexual drive may also, of course, have been attributable to his drug addiction, which was severe at this point. His discovery that Diosan was freely available in France, under a different brand name, had not improved his health.

Bill returned to Paris via the packet boat to Gibraltar with Alan Ansen, who had also been visiting Tangier at the time. Bill demonstrated to Alan his latest psychic discoveries, one of which was a magnetic attraction between Bill's silver scrying ball and a magnifying mirror that he'd bought. According to Bill, the ball moved every time the mirror was placed near it, no matter what the circumstances, and Ansen confirmed that this was the case. Back at the hotel, Bill now prudently kept his stash of kif out of his room in case the police came to visit.

When Ansen returned to Venice, Bill found himself suddenly alone on the rue Git-le-Coeur. Jacques Stern was in complete self-imposed isolation and refused to answer letters. Shell was in jail in America, and Brion was still in Tangier. In any case, Bill regarded Brion as more of a "catalyst or medium in strict sense" for his psychic experiments, though this was probably because Brion did not use hard drugs. Bill continued to be buffeted by psychic forces; he saw visions and experienced strange currents of energy. He was also growing painfully thin and by mid-May he weighed only 120 pounds.

Bill planned to return to the United States and was about to write to his parents for the ticket money when Jacques Stern reappeared on the scene and invited him to spend a month with him on his yacht in Monte Carlo. Bill was anxious to let people know that it was not his taste for luxury that made him accept, rather that Stern had discovered an abbreviated form of psychotherapy that lasted only two weeks and had promised to show Bill how it worked. Stern told him that he had been in London, where he had fallen and broken his leg—an easy thing for him to do in his leg braces. With his leg in plaster, he decided to combine the healing process with a detoxification and once more checked into Dr. Dent's London clinic to kick junk at the same time.

The first week went well, but then he came down with a severe sinus pain, which spread down his spine until his whole body was wracked with pain and he was screaming in agony. Dent was nonplussed, and Stern said later it was the first time he had seen him at a loss as to what to do. Then Dent began shooting Stern with heroin, a grain at a time, twelve grains in two hours, but even then the pain did not let up. In Bill's opinion, no other doctor in the world would inject that amount of heroin, and he told Allen, "There is no question that he saved Jack's life." Two nurses had to hold him down; he was in such agony that he bit a piece of wood in half, then went into a catatonic state. The coma lasted for two days. Dent called in a shock specialist who said that the catatonia was a psychological escape from the pain that would otherwise have killed him. They gave him electroshock; he came out of the coma and immediately began writing. He wrote solidly for nine days, at the end of which he had a novel that he called *Fluke*. He told Bill that Faber and Faber in London was going to publish it. Bill read a part of the manuscript and pronounced it great. Bill told Allen, "I think it is better by far than mine or Kerouac's or yours or Gregory's or anyone I can think of. There is no doubt about it, he is a great writer. I think the greatest writer of our time."

Jacques remained accident-prone. He invited Bill on a trip out of town but Bill was tired and declined. Afterward Jacques told Bill that he had run his Bentley into a concrete traffic island at 130 mph, turned the car over twice, and ended right side up without a scratch on the car or injury to himself. That same week he took an overdose of sleeping pills from which he nearly died, fell down a marble staircase and chipped a tooth, then almost poisoned himself with heroin laced with scopolamine, which Bill had to confiscate for Jacques's own safety. "Never a dull moment around Jack," said Bill.

Bill later found out that the entire story concerning Dr. Dent and the heroin injections, the catatonia, and the electroshock was pure fiction. He also found that there was no evidence the Bentley had ever been rolled (or could even attain such a speed), and to cap it all, there was no yacht; not in Monte Carlo or anywhere else. Stern saved face by claiming that he had accepted a cash offer for the boat that he could not refuse. This was of course also fictitious, and Stern's "alleged yacht" became a favorite jumping-off point for many of the routines that Bill wrote around this period. As to Faber and Faber's publishing the novel, that was also not true, but the book did exist. Stern eventually published it himself, but no one else appeared to share Bill's high opinion of it.

One of the more eccentric young men in the hotel was Sinclair Beiles, whom Bill had known previously from Tangier. Beiles was a South African Jew who lived with a German girlfriend whom he used to chase on the roof with a sword as payback for what the Germans did to the Jews. As she was built like an Olympic wrestler and whereas Sinclair was skinny and out of shape, it was a contest that she could end any time she chose. Sinclair suffered extreme mood changes. He would see a van in the street and become convinced that it was filled with electronic surveillance equipment, spying on his every move. He had episodes of terror where he would refuse to leave someone's room in case he was murdered by his persecutors. Other times he would act goofy, smoking four cigarettes at once while walking down the street. On one occasion Bill, Gregory, and Sinclair were walking down by the Seine. When the sight-seeing boat *Bateau Mouche* passed them, Sinclair pulled down his pants and stuck his finger up his ass in front of the tourists. William was shocked. "That is deplorable behavior," he told Sinclair. Another time, filled with the joys of spring, Sinclair threw his shoes into the Seine in exhilaration.

Sinclair was fascinated by Bill and Brion and had quickly become involved with their mysterious psychic activities. Brion remembered how Sinclair would present himself at the door of room 25: "[He] used to stand there with a kind of . . . bluish glow around him in the dark, and turn into a rather fierce Chinaman, and I'd say, 'No, no, Sinclair, you can't come in' and I'd send him away." Sinclair had written a DB for Maurice Girodias called *Houses of Joy*, a tale of a geisha girl written under the nom de plume Wu Wu Meng, and had stayed on afterward at the Olympia Press working as one of Girodias's assistants.

One morning in early June 1959, Bill received a visit in his room from Sinclair, who told him that Girodias wanted to publish *Naked Lunch* and that he needed a complete manuscript in two weeks. Girodias had seen the flurry of interest caused by the suppression of the Winter issue of the *Chicago Review*, and the subsequent seizure of copies of *Big Table* for obscenity, and realized that *Naked Lunch* was just what he was looking for: a banned pornographic book, the subject of ongoing controversy, which had already been written about in *Time* and *Life*. If he could get it out quickly enough, he could sell it on the existing publicity.

Back in January, Bill had told Paul Bowles that *Naked Lunch* was finished but that he had no idea if it would ever be published in its complete form. Now that Girodias wanted to publish the book, Bill looked at the manuscript again. So many sections in so many different arrangements and versions had been circulated—mostly by Allen—that Bill no longer had a final form in his head. He had also continued to write, and there were a number of new sections that needed to be fed in as well as new, improved versions of existing routines. However, Girodias believed it was imperative to get the book out quickly.

Bill's room became a hive of activity. Most of the typing was done by Brion or Sinclair. Bill was not a good typist so once he decided which sections he wanted to use, and had marked them up to show where inserts belonged, or annotated them with new text, he devoted most of his time to sticking photographs onto the wall of his room with Scotch tape. Brion Gysin wrote in "Cut-ups: A Project for Disastrous Success": "Showers of fading snapshots fell through the air: Old Bull's Texas farm, the Upper Reaches of the Amazon ('Yagé country, man. See the old *brujo.*'); Tangier and the Mayan Codices ('Ain't it almost too horrible. Dig what they really up to and you wig.'); shots of boys from every time and place. Burroughs was more intent on Scotch-taping his photos together into one great continuum on the wall, where scenes faded and slipped into one another, than occupied with editing the monster manuscript. ('Am I the Collier brothers?') When he found himself in front of the wrecked typewriter, he hammered out new stuff . . ." Many of the snapshots were later to appear in the collages Burroughs would create in the 1960s, often with remnants of sticky tape still attached.

Bill remembered assembling the book: "We made the selections from about a thousand pages of material, which overflowed into *The Soft Machine*, into *Ticket That Exploded*, and into *Nova Express* as well." All the available sections, or "routines," were read, and those that Bill chose to include were retyped, incorporating any changes or additional material that he now had. Bill recalled reading through the pages: "It's funny, some sections worked, some were very dislocated, and others had to be mapped out, so on and so forth. A great deal of editing and a great deal of typing was needed to put this manuscript together." Bill was heavily addicted to codeine at this time and that, combined with the speed with which the book was being assembled, resulted in some material's appearing twice. For instance, the ten-line section at the end of the first chapter beginning "I was traveling with Irene Kelly . . ." was repeated, inadvertently, and without change, 170 pages later in the "Coke Bugs" section. As each section was completed, it was taken to Girodias, who marked it up for the printer to typeset.

Somehow, though, the book came together. Bill remembered, "Much of what went into the book had been previously retyped by Alan

Ansen and Allen Ginsberg in Tangier. The sections were sent along to the printer as fast as they were typed, and I had planned to decide the final order of chapters when the galley proofs came back. Sinclair took one look at the galleys and said: 'I think this order is the best.' By some magic the chapters had fallen into place, and the only change was to shift the 'Hauser and O'Brien' section from the beginning to the end." With this one exception, the book was printed in the random order that the sections had been typeset. By moving that section, Bill opened the book with "I can feel the heat closing in . . ." and ended up with "the heat was off me from here on out," framing the book with police. Bill was pleased with the result. "That's the thing, we didn't order it, it just had come out right. That was purely random. How random is random? Exactly, that's the whole question that everybody asks, how random is random? Well, how much more do you know than you know that you know?"

Though Bill tells the reader that the book can be read in any order, some critics have imposed what they see as an intended structure upon the book. Jennie Skerl in her Twayne's United States Authors Series volume on Burroughs develops an elegant argument, stating, "Although the routines can stand alone and the form is a montage, the order is not random. There is an overall psychological pattern, an order of increasing complexity in the use of experimental technique, and a didactic frame." This passage amused Burroughs greatly when it was shown to him.

Bill also developed the jacket design, giving Girodias a series of Gysin-like calligraphic glyphs to use. Bill described the painting: "It is influenced by Brion, that's the whole idea, but it still is my version of the idea." The book came out in July, two weeks after the printers had provided proofs. Bill did mark up the galley proofs and a set of final proofs, though the latter was not used and the published book had many typographical errors in it. Nonetheless William was proud of their achievement: "One month after Sinclair's visit, *Naked Lunch* was out on the stands, setting a record for prompt publication."

Girodias gave Bill an $800 advance against royalties and took a third of all foreign-edition income. Allen, writing from New York, was concerned that Girodias was ripping him off—which of course he was. Bill replied, "I am sure that the deal I made with Olympia was the best deal I could have made. I saw Jack fucking around five years with American book publishers. . . . Of course the two pornographic sections—'Hassan's Rumpus Room' and 'A.J.'s Annual Party' are in, and very important part of the whole structure."

Though *Naked Lunch* was composed essentially from the routines that Bill enclosed in his letters to Allen from Tangier, written during the period 1954–57, the version that was finally printed was considerably different from that typed in Tangier by Kerouac, Ginsberg, and Ansen. Unfortunately no complete copy of that version of the text exists, but Burroughs was always clear that the book, as we know it, was composed at the Beat Hotel; as he told Maurice Girodias in an interview, "The point is that the manuscript which you saw in 1958 was not even approximately similar to the manuscript published in 1959."

Thus, by the end of the 1950s, all four key members of the Beat Generation now had their most important texts in print: *On the Road; Howl and Other Poems; Bomb;* and *Naked Lunch.* Other works of theirs might be argued to have greater literary significance, but these were the texts on which each of their reputations was made.

Publication of *Naked Lunch* did not change Bill's routine significantly, though he was pleased to see it in the bookstores. Gaït Frogé gave him a window display at the English Bookshop, but there were no reviews and life went on as usual. The psychic experiments continued and he found that he was now able to turn himself into other people: "not a human creature but man-like: He wears some sort of green uniform. The face is full of black boiling fuzz and what most people would call evil—silly word . . ." he told Allen. Both Brion and Stern claimed to have seen this and Bill found that people were staring at him in restaurants.

In late July, Bill was arrested in connection with the Paul Lund affair in Tangier. The police came tapping on his door at 8 A.M. with a warrant dated April 9, more than three months old. He spent twelve hours at police headquarters, becoming progressively more junk sick while they typed out forms. They attempted to take his picture but there was nothing on the plate when they developed it. It took three tries and two hours before they managed to get an image. "Not for nothing am I known as 'The Invisible Man,'" Bill commented. They found a small amount of hash between the floorboards in his room, but it was questionable whether it was even his, and they found nothing harder.

Initially Girodias seemed to be working out well as a publisher. He had moved very quickly to get the book out and had arranged for his brother, Eric Kahane, to translate it into French, though *Le Festin Nu* was not published by Gallimard until 1964. Flush with cash from the sale of Nabokov's *Lolita* in America, Girodias had opened a nightclub called Le Grand Severin where he and Bill discussed business over blackbird pâté. Bill decided to let Maurice handle all the contracts for foreign editions, including the negotiations for a contract with Barney Rosset of Grove Press for an American edition. Maurice told Bill, "This is a complicated business full of angles. I know them—you don't. Let me handle it. You will have to trust me." Bill did. The book sold to Grove Press for $5,000 but Bill did not see one penny of it. Charming as he was, Girodias was a crook. It was not until 1967 that Burroughs, after a bitter struggle, finally regained the copyright to *Naked Lunch*.

Bill's legal difficulties regarding the Tangier drug affair had begun to worry him. His lawyer, Maître Bumsell, introduced to him by Girodias, told him, "It is only a mistake that you are not inside now." To shift the blame away from himself, Paul Lund had produced the letter written by Bill sounding out the possibility of Lund's sending some hash to him in Paris. "I have no words to waste on Lund," Bill told Allen, "Wouldn't you? Yes, in his position I would do the same. Anything to salvage the old skin, what? No, I blame myself for knowing Lund in the first place." Lund was a professional thief who had done considerable time in prison. He had already run up against the authorities in Tangier in the incident involving the good ship *Amphitrite*, a complicated story told at length in his biography, *Smiling Damned Villain*, and he had no intention of seeing the inside of a Moroccan jail if he could avoid it.

In order to cover himself, Bill decided to write an apologia for *Naked Lunch.* He told Allen, "I am writing a short deposition with regard to Naked Lunch. This is essential for my own safety at this point; Naked Lunch is written to reveal the junk virus, the manner in which it operates, and the manner in which it can be brought under control. This is not an act. I mean it all the way. Get off that junk wagon, boys . . ."

Allen did not like "Deposition Concerning a Sickness," which he thought was contrary to the central message of the book. He thought that by claiming he had "no precise memory of writing the notes which have now been published under the title *Naked Lunch*," Bill was over-reacting to the very slight possibility that the book might be used as evidence against him in a drug case. Bill replied, "The article is intentionally humorless and moralistic . . . I said the junkies were to be pensioned off with junk if they need or want it—what more do they want from me yet, cold and junkless charity." Bill said he regarded junk as "one of the most potent instruments of Evil Law." He did not see junkies as revolutionaries, rather he saw junk as one of the many ways society has of controlling people.

In the same letter he suggested that Allen read L. Ron Hubbard's *Dianetics*, and then check out his local Scientology Center, something that both Brion and Jacques Stern had recommended Bill do. "Don't forget to give Hubbard a run for his money." As with everything he became interested in, Bill delved deeply into Scientology. He was intrigued because neither hypnosis nor drugs was used and problems were solved by deenergizing them. The method of constantly bringing unpleasant events to mind and working through them was similar to his own self-analysis in Tangier before he had moved to Paris: "simply run the tape back and forth until the trauma is wiped off." He was well aware of Scientology's origins in Russian brainwashing techniques and had few illusions about it. He told Allen that it was "used more for manipulation than therapy." As usual with his interest in fringe science, pseudo-science, and alternative medicines, Bill was able to use parts of Scientology's techniques to his own advantage. He remained interested in Scientology until the early '70s, when he was drummed out of the organization in what they termed a "condition of treason."

Back in 1959, however, he immersed himself in it and found many of its techniques useful. By the end of October he was recalling his manuscripts in order to subject them to his Scientology-enhanced scrutiny. He told Allen, "I have a new method of writing and I do not want to publish anything that has not been inspected and processed. I can not explain this method to you until you have the necessary training. So once again and most urgently (believe me there is not much time), I tell you: 'Find yourself a Scientology Auditor and have yourself run.'" Scientology may have been the abbreviated form of psychotherapy that Stern was going to explain to Bill while they were on the "alleged yacht."

The combination of Stern's unpredictable mood swings, his lies, and the business of the yacht had changed Bill's assessment of the man and they were no longer close. Bill told Allen he doubted that Stern wanted to see him anymore and said, "The end of Naked Lunch is addressed to Jack, as he must know. I don't think we were ever friends, but he acted like a friend. I really learned about Europeans from him. In fact, I learned more from Jack than from anyone else I ever knew, except Brion." The passage Bill was referring to is the description of Stern's losing ten pounds in ten minutes after injecting junk, which occurs in both the first and last sections of *Naked Lunch*, the latter a somewhat unflattering description. Bill also thanked Stern for some of the ideas in the book, saying, "Note: The Heavy Fluid concept I owe to Jacques Stern." This acknowledgment, on page 55 of the Olympia Press edition, was dropped from all subsequent editions, presumably at Stern's request.

In late June 1959, the gay American poet Harold Norse called on Bill in room 15 at the suggestion of Gregory Corso. He had moved in New York literary circles since before the war and had met Dylan Thomas,

Christopher Isherwood, Gore Vidal, and Paul Bowles. Like Alan Ansen, he was for a time Auden's secretary. In 1953 Norse sold a Picasso print given to him by a millionaire boyfriend and left for Europe on the proceeds, living in Italy, Greece, France, and Morocco until 1968. His first book of poems, *The Undersea Mountain*, was published in 1953. In Paris he got to know the Trianon Café crowd of *Paris Review* and ex-*Merlin* writers: Nelson Aldrich, Austryn Wainhouse, and George Plimpton. It was there that he met Corso, who then introduced him to the people at the hotel.

Norse has provided some of the most evocative descriptions of life at the Beat Hotel, beginning with an account of his first visit to Burroughs. He described room 15 as tiny, with a cot, a naked lightbulb, two chairs, a table, and a well-worn typewriter. Bill attempted only the bare minimum of conversation, leaving it to Norse to ramble on and fill the embarrassing silences. "[He] proceeded to ream his fingernails with the end of a match," Norse wrote, "the classic stereotype of the 'drug fiend' in the silent movies: taut parchment skin, pale impassive features, bladelike lips, expressionless eyes . . . he looked as if he had driven himself insane."

Norse was living nearby on the Ile de la Cité and, despite his inauspicious introduction to Burroughs, he continued to visit the hotel and to see Gregory, Bill, and Brion. Norse spent much of his time at George Whitman's Mistral bookshop, which was just across the Seine from his hotel, on the rue de la Boucherie. Whitman ran the place in a very easygoing manner and had rooms upstairs where "book people" could stay for up to a week at a time. That summer a highly strung young Englishman named Ian Sommerville, from Darlington, County Durham, was staying there in exchange for doing odd jobs around the shop. He was studying mathematics at Corpus Christi College of Cambridge University, but was spending the summer in Paris in order to learn French. Norse invited him to dinner at his apartment and found him a very entertaining companion, but Ian was not his type. Not long after, Norse was visiting Bill at the hotel and Bill asked him where he went in order to meet people. Norse mentioned the Mistral but Bill told him that he had never been able to pick up anyone there. Norse described Ian and told him that Ian liked older men, and Bill seemed interested.

Acting on Norse's tip, Bill set out to visit the Mistral and found Ian perched precariously on a ladder, arranging books. Ian must have liked the look of him because he accidentally dropped a book, hitting Bill on the shoulder, then proceeded to apologize profusely. Ian was thin, with intense eyes and sallow, yellowish skin pulled taut across his high cheekbones. He was very soft-spoken, so that you had to lean forward to hear what he was saying, and had a nervous gesture of running his fingers through his reddish-blond hair, making it stand on end. He was well read but the only member of the Beat Generation that he'd heard of was Kerouac; however, he proved to be a fast learner and quickly read his way through the available books. Aside from Bill, Ian decided that Paul Bowles was the author whose books most appealed to him.

Bill had obtained some apomorphine from Dr. Dent and was determined to kick his codeine habit by himself. He had taken careful notes during his previous cure (as well as he was able), and he had a little copybook that had been given to him by Dr. Dent's assistant, the celebrated Nurse Smitty, in which she had listed the exact sequence of the treatment. He just needed someone to act as his attendant and nurse during the period of withdrawal. Gysin had refused to help, afraid of the psychic changes that Bill would be going through, but eighteen-year-old Ian innocently accepted the challenge, unaware of the dramatic scenario about to be enacted.

Burroughs has stated, "The thing about apomorphine is that it requires pretty constant attendance. In other words, you've got to really have a day and a night nurse, and those injections have to be given every four hours. And it isn't everybody that's in a position to do that. But at least for the first four days, it requires rather intensive care. And it is quite unpleasant."

In his delirium Bill reran all of the hideous personages he had uncovered in the course of his scrying activities and during his experiments with the hallucinogenic yagé: he became the invisible man, his face boiled with black fuzz, he transformed himself into a prissy English nanny, an old Southern nigger-killin' sheriff, a giant centipede, Hassan-i-Sabbah, and the Ugly Spirit, changing his voice and visage to assume each persona in rapid succession. Sweat poured from him, soaking his shirt. He thrashed in fits and convulsions, he retched and raved, vomited, and scared the neighbors with his terrible groans. For an entire week Ian fed him tea and toast and each day doled out the apomorphine and an ever-diminishing dose of codeine until Bill was clean. A codeine habit is far more difficult and painful to kick than heroin and Bill swore he would never touch it again.

On August 24, Norse dropped by with a friend who wanted to meet Bill. The door was opened by a slim figure stripped to the waist and in the feeble light Norse mistook him for Bill. It was Ian. He explained that Bill was kicking and he was taking care of him. Norse gasped and told Ian that he had thought he was Bill. "Everybody does," Ian replied. "I'm a replica."

Ian would not let them in, but confided, "It's been fuckin' unbelievable. I never want to go through this again. Hallucinations, convulsions, freakouts, the edge of insanity. But it's been worth it; he's getting well." Shortly after that, Bill went to London to finish his apomorphine cure with Dr. Dent. While he was away Ian told Norse, "I had to hang on to my sanity by my fingernails and they're bitten down to the moons." This was the beginning of the longest and probably most intimate love affair that Burroughs ever had. Ian became Bill's lover, companion, collaborator, and protector. He was Bill's fiercest critic in private and his staunchest defender in public. He regarded Bill as the greatest writer alive and Bill, for his part, deferred to Ian on all things practical and scientific.

According to Brion, "Ian Sommerville was skinny and quick as an alleycat with bristly red hair that stuck up all over in pre-punk style. He was crisper than cornflakes and sharp as a tack. He crackled and snapped with static electricity, often giving a strong shock with an icy handshake. He was not fond of water and panicked at the idea of rain on his hair. He was an expert model-maker, handy with tools. We made the first Dreamachines together. He was as fascinated by tape recorders as I was."

Ian worked with Bill and Brion on the technical side of tape recorder cut-ups, on photographic collages—instructing the pharmacy on how to reverse the negatives and superimpose them—and coinvented, with Brion, the Dreamachine. His relationship with Bill was a meeting of equals and Ian's healthy English skepticism tempered Bill's forays into Scientology and the like, making them more like anthropological expeditions than the unplanned investigations they'd been previously. Ian did not tolerate fools easily and could be offhand and rude with people who bored him, but he was loyal and steadfast with his friends.

Ian was often moody and difficult, criticizing Bill for his sloppy ways. His own behavior was a model of scientific procedure: pencils in a row, surfaces clean before work, books carefully arranged, clothes carefully brushed. He was a brilliant mathematician and could make Einstein's theory of relativity or the principles of free-floating equations sound so simple that his listeners often wondered why they had never been able to grasp it before. He had another, giggly, campy side but he rarely revealed that in public. Bill was forty-five and Ian was only eighteen, but they were a well-matched couple. Ian announced that he intended to remain in Paris but Bill, sensibly, insisted that he return to Cambridge at the end of the summer and complete his studies. He would arrange to visit England and travel to Cambridge from London on the weekends.

Bill: "He wasn't through with Cambridge, he didn't have his degree yet, and I told him, and Brion told him, we both told him, we urged him very strongly to go back. It's very much worth having for practical purposes, so he did go back and he did get his degree. He was a very talented young man. I mean he understood things that I could just grasp, like probability theory and floating equations, physics. It all came naturally. It just doesn't for me; I don't know what they're talking about. It's too bad he wasn't able to follow that up. Then he got into computer programming. Well he could have possibly added a new dimension but he didn't."

Many of Bill's friends could not understand the relationship because Ian did not seem like Bill's type at all. Bill was normally very secretive about his sex life. He received regular visits at the hotel from an Arab boy from the rue de la Huchette but made sure that none of his friends met him. Felicity Mason was curious and asked Ian what Bill was like as a lover. "I once said to Ian, 'I simply cannot imagine William in bed in a sexual situation . . . what have you got to say about that Ian?' and Ian said, 'Creepy kicks, man, creepy kicks . . .' and then laughed. Ian would laugh about the relationship and say, 'Well, he's a creepy man, but . . .' Ian could quite easily have been straight, he wasn't at all queeny. Ian was super-intelligent but very much on self-destruct. He didn't quite have the aggressive push to know how to market his extraordinary brain . . . maybe he should have stayed in an academic career . . . but he got into the wrong set and into drugs. He was a sensitive and neurotic young man in a Rupert Brooke way."

Some idea of the complicated dynamic of their relationship was revealed in an interview by Ted Morgan for his biography of Burroughs called *Literary Outlaw* in which William said, "When I first met Ian I was definitely the master. I was in charge. I'd had all this experience with Spanish boys and I was the one in charge. I had been used to being in charge. The shift came much much later when he managed to gain the upper hand. That was many years later. Ian's upper hand was in 1965. You don't gain the upper hand, you just have it. I had it, have it, lost it."

That summer, Gregory rented a house in Venice, which he shared with Jean-Jacques Lebel; it was where Modigliani had lived in 1903. They each had a large room and there was a palm tree in the garden. Jean-Jacques shared his room with his girlfriend, the American poet Sandra Hochman, who later won the Yale Younger Poets Award for her 1963 collection *Manhattan Pastures*. Jean-Jacques said, "She was a very charming lovely American sexual hysteric. And Gregory asked me to share this house with him and we had a wonderful summer. Alan Ansen was there and Harold Acton, an English lord, a friend of the Queen, multimillionaire with this fantastic art collection in Florence. He was gay and he liked the beatniks, he liked us a lot. I wasn't gay and Greg-

ory wasn't gay but he liked Alan Ansen and they used to go out looking for boys together."

Gregory enjoyed dining with Acton and Ansen and moving in their
upper-class circles. He bought himself a dinner jacket and went to the
Casino, where he naturally lost what little money he had brought with
him. Then his luck changed. Jean-Jacques remembered, "I remember
Gregory getting money for *Gasoline* from Ferlinghetti. It was a $1,000
check. It was the first $1,000 check he ever had. He didn't know what
to do with it. He didn't have a bank account, neither here nor in
America. It took two weeks to find a way to translate it into Italian
lira. And he went into the choicest tailor, on St. Marks Square, where
Harold Acton got his suits. So Gregory got this suit made out of white
alpaca. He was so proud. I think he spent half of his check on that
suit. It was a suit for a prince. He came to the restaurant and said,
'Look at my suit man, no more of this Lower East Side shit for me,
man! I'm a prince!' and everybody applauded, everybody was so
happy. And after a week he had never taken it off, he slept in it, he
spilled wine on it, vomit on it. And from white it had become a sleazy
disgusting grayish color, and it was full of spots. But he still wouldn't
take it off, 'Look at my suit man! Look!'

"I remember very well, one evening we were leaving Montin's on
the Dorsoduro, that fantastic restaurant where we all paid for our din-
ners with our paintings. It's a traditional artists' place where we all
used to eat, on a small canal. Everybody had lots to drink. There was
Alan Ansen and Gregory. And Sandra had this big enormous New York
Jewish ass. That's what I liked about her, and everybody liked. It's
disgustingly chauvinistic but it's the way we felt. And Gregory was
not a sexual person at all, but that evening, I don't know what happened, he felt that he was allowed to be a little bit of a rascal and he
did something very New York Italianish. He went 'Ugh!' and he
grabbed her ass. And Sandra, remember she's trying to behave like
a lady, she turned around and said, 'Oh! Gregory, man, stop it!' and
he says, 'Wassa matter Hochman?' He called her Hochman. 'Why is
it this Frenchie can see your ass, and I can't see it? That's discrimina-
tion, man! I wanta see it too!' You know what she did? She just shoved

him. Right into the canal. It was one of the small canals, the Rio delle Eremite, and immediately all the Italians start screaming, 'Man in the canal!' And it was filthy. They dragged him out from a gondola and there was the $500 alpaca suit and it was just like an old Kleenex out of the gutter. And he says, 'Hochman, what did you do to me? I'm a poet. You don't throw poets in canals, Hochman!' He started raging. It was wonderful and horrible at the same time. She shouldn't have done it but Christ, it's her ass, you know? These things happen. Oh God, his poor suit was all fucked up."

Gregory, broke as usual, returned to the Beat Hotel from Venice. The Casino had taken the remainder of his royalties. Bill regarded the situation with equanimity: "Of course Gregory was always in and out. I remember someone saying, 'Gregory is difficult.' Well he's a poor Italian thief. He went to reform school. He was brought up in that whole atmosphere of being a thief. He had sense enough to get out. See there's not so very many ways out from that; one of course is the Mafia, but not anybody can get into that. They all want to but they don't want so many of them. Gregory decided he was a poet and he just stuck with it. He called up Auden in the middle of the night. 'This is Gregory here!' 'Gregory who?' 'Gregory the POET!'

"Gregory had no visible means of support and managed to live in Paris on his wits, able to cadge a drink here, a meal there, to sell something or be given gifts, usually by women. My dear he always had girls. Always had girls. He had one there called April, or was she November or September or something? Yes he did. He always wanted his rocks off. He always came up with something. He was always writing big manuscripts and annotating them and selling them as first drafts. Somebody else would find they had one too. He wrote a great deal when he was there."

His Beat Hotel period in Paris was of the greatest significance for Gregory. His work underwent a sea change; he discovered his mature style. Gregory himself saw the change in his Paris-period work from that in his first book, *The Vestal Lady on Brattle:* "The first book, it's very awkward, a green book, just ideas trying to come out. Lots of imagery, conglommed together; and I cut out lots of fat. I thought in those days that poetry is a concise form, built like a brick Acropolis; but in 1957–58 in Paris things burst and opened, and I said, 'I will just let the lines go and not care about fat.' I figured if I could go with the rhythm I have within me, my own sound, that that would work, and it worked. In 'Marriage' there was hardly any change—there are long lines, but they just flow, like a musical thing within me."

Bill came before the *juge d'instruction* on September 25, 1959, on his drugs charge. On Brion's advice, Bill had decided to admit to writing the incriminating letter to Paul Lund, and his lawyer, Maître Bumsell, had managed to get Bill before a judge whose own wife had once been a drug addict, hoping he would be more understanding. Fortunately, Bill's "Deposition Concerning a Sickness" was due to be published in the January 1960 issue of the prestigious literary journal *Nouvelle Revue Française* and Bumsell was able to read sections of it aloud in court, proving that Bill was indeed a man of letters. Their defense was that Bill was a writer, always looking for new experience, but that he had fallen in with a bad crowd who had led him astray. The judge told him he did not think this was a serious crime, particularly as the plan had been canceled before any drug shipments had been made, but warned Bill not to treat him like a fool. Bill told the truth: he was not engaged in trafficking and he was not about to, nor did he want to see Paul Lund or his cohorts again. He was given a suspended sentence and fined $80 and he gasped audibly with relief.

That autumn Bill asked Allen to send him some mescaline, available legally by mail order in the States, which he did. It was also legal in France so there was no danger. He split it with Brion "for a short trip home." Bill continued to see Henri Michaux in order to discuss the effects of mescaline and other hallucinogenic drugs, and that October he wrote Allen a story:

> It seems that M. was hurrying home after swallowing his
> mescaline tablet with hot tea in a cafe—too cheap to support
> a hot plate you dig—and he met B in the market and he had

met B before but never seen him as hardly anyone does see him which is why he is known as *El Hombre Invisible*—So B said "Ah Monsieur M. Sit down and have a coffee and watch the passing parade." And M shook him off saying: "No! No! I must go home and see my visions," and he rushed home and closed the door and bolted it and drew the curtains and turned out the lights and got into bed and closed his eyes and there was Mr B and Mr M said: "What are you doing here in my vision?"

And B replied: "Oh I live here."

8 Cut-ups

Money is what words are.
Words are what money is.
Is money what words are.
Are words what money is.
Gertrude Stein, *The Geographical History of America*

After the publication of *Naked Lunch*, *Time-Life*, pursuing its love/
hate relationship with the Beats, tracked Bill down to the Beat Hotel
and sent a reporter-photographer team to see him. Bill was in London, getting yet another apomorphine cure from Dr. Dent and visiting Ian in Cambridge, but met the reporters for lunch on October 1,
1959, the day he returned to Paris. They spent several days feting Bill,
who was prepared to go along with it to get publicity for the book. He
wrote Allen, "LIFE was around the other day several days in fact
took pictures and concocting a story. Brilliant photography. Two very
amusing and knowledgeable characters. Names: Snell and Loomis."
Reporter David Snell set the tone after introducing himself by saying
"Have an Old Gold Mister Burroughs," a reference to the Hauser and
O'Brien section that ends *Naked Lunch:* "A vaudeville team. Hauser
had a way of hitting you before he said anything just to break the ice.
Then O'Brien gives you an Old Gold—just like a cop to smoke Old
Golds somehow . . ." It showed not only that Snell had read the book,
but that he knew Burroughs regarded anyone from *Time-Life* as a cop.
     Bill remembered that Snell even used that same brand of ciga-
rette. "He did smoke, he had an Old Gold. He knew he was a cop. He
had been a bouncer at one time and he was allergic to penicillin. He

had one of those allergies where he thought by talking about penicillin it wouldn't hurt him. Of course it didn't work. Fortunately he'd been over this with his doctor and the ambulance was there in just minutes and he just made it. She's just waiting there with the syringe and gave him a shot. He reported all the symptoms of death that are in the *Egyptian Book of the Dead:* Blazing heat, freezing cold and then a feeling of exploding in all your parts. He wrote about it in *Reader's Digest.* The other guy's name was Loomis Dean. He really got some weird shots of the Rothschilds at a party. He was a very great photographer.

"See here's Snell talking to me, David Snell was his name, he's dead now, and he's hearing my reactions to what he is saying. See in photography it's the same as in boxing, when you see an opening, it's gone. In other words, he has to take it a fraction of a second before this guy to get the reaction. There was old Burns on the floor, he'd been skinned on the tree, he'd been skinned alive, ho ho ho! They spent several days taking me out to lunch, all kinds of things. Apparently Mr. Luce was interested in me."

The piece, by staff writer Paul O'Neil, appeared in the November 30, 1959, issue of *Life.* Called "The Only Rebellion Around," it predictably put the Beats down. Presumably Snell's report was favorable, however, because it devoted only one or two largely uncritical paragraphs to Burroughs and said, "For all his hideous preoccupation with man's lowest appetites, William Burroughs has a terrible and sardonic eye and a vengeful sense of drama." Bill had been expecting something like that. He had told Allen, "The Life interviewers here are two far out cats with real appreciation for my work that can't be faked. Of course, they have nothing to do with the final form of the story."

Dean and Snell accompanied Bill back to the hotel after lunch and were consequently present when Brion Gysin showed Bill his new discovery: Cut-ups. Bill confirmed that they were there: "When they came back they saw it all. They saw the first Cut-ups." Bill recorded the incident in *The Third Mind:* ". . . fade out to #9 rue Git-le-Coeur, Paris, room #25; September, 1959 . . . I had just returned from a long lunch with the *Time* police, putting down a con, old and tired as their namesake: 'Mr. Burroughs, I have an intuition about you . . . I see you a few years from now on Madison Avenue . . . $20,000 per year . . . life in all its rich variety . . . Have an Old Gold.' Returning to room #25, I found Brion Gysin holding a scissors, bits of newspaper, *Life*, *Time*, spread out on a table; he read me the Cut-ups that later appeared in *Minutes To Go*."

Brion described making his discovery. "While cutting a mount for a drawing in room 25, I sliced through a pile of newspapers with my Stanley blade and thought of what I had said to Burroughs some six months earlier about the necessity for turning painters' techniques directly into writing. I picked up the raw words and began to piece together texts which appeared as 'First Cut Ups' in *Minutes To Go*."

On the table were the Paris *New York Herald Tribune*, the *Observer* (London, Sunday), the *Daily Mail* (London), and advertisements torn from *Life* magazine. The Cut-ups made a weird sense and seemed to be messages that were somehow appropriate to the situation: "Her father, a well-known Artist until a bundle of his accented brush-work blew up in the sky, said 'We can't do that yet . . .'" (from "First Cut Ups"). Lines such as "It is impossible to estimate the damage," which now sound distinctly Burroughsian, came from everyday sources like the *Observer* or *Time* magazine. Brion: "It was a readymade phrase that simply dropped onto the table; several layers of printed material were laid one on top of the other and cut through with the Stanley blade and one simply chose the morsels and put them together, and that was one of the particular phrases that has amused me—this was before I had shown them to William . . . my first games by myself, like that which set me laughing so loud, because the answers were so apt and so extraordinary."

Bill was in London when Brion made his original discovery and they had not had time to see each other before Snell and Dean, who had been waiting for Bill in Paris, dragged Bill out to interview him. Brion remembered Bill's reaction. "When he came from lunch I showed him these things, saying that it had happened during the last two or three weeks, during his absence at any rate. And that I found them very amusing. Bill takes off his glasses in order to read. I remember him whipping off his glasses and plunging right into the page and he realized immediately that this was a tool of enormous importance to him, and said, rather diffidently: 'Do you mind if I try some of these?' I said: 'No, go right ahead. That's what it's for.'"

Bill shared Brion's amusement at the aptness of the random juxtapositions and laughed aloud. "We both were [amused] for a while. It was very funny at first. It was quite exhilarating, like pot you know. Yes certainly, indeed." Bill set to work cutting up newspapers and magazines. One article, "New Clues in the Search for Cancer" in *Saturday Evening Post* of October 31, 1959, gave rise to literally dozens of Cut-ups, as did an article on viruses in the *New York Herald Tribune*.

The actual method used was simple. A page of typewriting, or a printed page, was cut vertically and then horizontally, giving four small rectangles of text. These were rearranged in a different order to give a new page. Often it read much like the original but Bill and Brion soon found that by cutting up political texts they seemed to be reading between the lines, cutting through the words to find out what the politicians were really saying. They found that by typing out familiar sections from great poets such as Shakespeare or Rimbaud, whose words had lost their meaning through repetition, they could create refreshing new poems from the same words. As Bill said, "Cut up Rimbaud and you are in Rimbaud's place . . . Shakespeare, Rimbaud live in their words. Cut the word lines and you will hear their voices. Cut-ups often come through as code messages with special meaning for the cutter. Table tapping? Perhaps. Certainly an improvement on the usual deplorable performances of contacted poets through a medium. Rimbaud announces himself, to be followed by some excruciatingly bad poetry. Cut Rimbaud's words and you are assured of good poetry at least if not personal appearance."

Cut-ups became their new and all-consuming interest. Brion explained, "We began to find out a whole lot of things about the real nature of words and writing. What are words and what are they doing? The cut-up method treats words as the painter treats his paint, raw material with rules and reasons of its own . . . Painters and writers of the kind I respect want to be heroes, challenging fate in their lives and in their art. What is fate? Fate is written: *Mektoub*, in the Arab world, where art has always been nothing but abstract. *Mektoub* means 'It is written.' So . . . if you want to challenge and change fate . . . cut up words, make them a new world."

It was the facility to use words in the same way that an artist uses paint that was of the greatest interest to Gysin. "There's an actual treatment of the material as if it were a piece of cloth. The sentence even, the word, becomes a real piece of plastic material that you can cut into. You're not just juggling them around, or putting them into . . . Tzara's words out of a hat were simply aleatory, chance . . ." Cut-ups are often compared with Tristan Tzara's famous Dada game of pulling words from a hat, but the circumstances were entirely different. Section eight of Tzara's *Dada Manifesto on Feeble Love and Bitter Love* reads:

> To make a dadaist poem. Take a newspaper. Take a pair of scissors. Choose an article as long as you are planning to make your poem. Cut out the article. Then cut out each of the words that make up this article and put them in a bag. Shake it gently. Then take out the scraps one after the other in the order in which they left the bag. Copy conscientiously. The poem will be like you. And here you are a writer, indefinitely original and endowed with a sensibility that is charming though beyond the understanding of the vulgar.

This was followed by an example. The manifesto was first read at the opening of an exhibition of paintings by Francis Picabia at a small art gallery owned by Jacques Povolozky on rue Bonaparte on December 9, 1920. Almost forty years later, the discovery was made again. "It was an accident," Brion said, "but one which I recognized immediately as it happened, because of knowing of all the other past things—I knew about the history of the arts, let's say." Cut-ups were different because, although the cut itself is random, the selection of what to cut is a determined choice, and the choice of words used from the juxtaposition are very much an artistic decision.

Bill and Brion did not restrict themselves by imposing rules on Cut-ups: the words were not individually cut out, and only a few words or phrases were chosen from each page—there was no requirement to use them all. It immediately became apparent that the quality of the original words counted a great deal. The fragments from news clippings and magazines were not good enough. Brion suggested that they should use only the best, only the highest-quality material in their Cut-ups: the King James translation of the *Song of Songs* of Solomon, T. S. Eliot's translation of *Anabasis* by St.-John Perse, Shakespeare's *Sonnets*, Aldous Huxley's *The Doors of Perception*, Rimbaud, Ezra Pound. One of Burroughs's earliest Cut-ups used a section from Pound's *Cantos:*

Cut/up of Ezra Pound made in 1959 using only the very own words of Ezra Pound.
Keep off impetuous down the longer ladder
Fool of recent narrow sword
Impotent unguarded
Usures squeezing the air
Solid the silence of black beetles.

It was still Pound, but it was also Burroughs. As far as Bill was concerned, he was taking on the spirit of the person whose words he handled. He became a Rimbaud, or a Shakespeare. As Gysin commented, "Obviously those are roles which are given to the writer. He has all the rights to those roles after all." Early Cut-ups, those done in 1959, concentrated almost entirely upon cutting up the words of others. Bill did not restrict himself to printed words; many of the Cut-ups from this period have titles like "Cut-Up With Jacques Stern's Telegram to the Captain Barrie of His Alleged Yacht" and "Cut-Up With Jacques Stern's Telegrams & Letters," illustrating as well that he had not forgotten Stern's offer of a Mediterranean cruise on his fictitious yacht.

Though Cut-ups were Brion's invention, it was Burroughs who realized their potential; Cut-ups, fold-ins (where the manuscript is folded rather than actually cut), and their application to tape, film, and photography, were to preoccupy Bill for the next decade until he had finally exhausted every area of investigation. Brion was happy for him to take it over. "It seemed like a marvelous thing to give to William, who had a huge body of work to which it could immediately be applied. It wasn't applicable to my condition because I didn't have that body of work just to take and cut up and produce something new with. I would have to produce new work which then I would cut up—it seemed like a contradiction in terms—and William was doing so well with the marvelous subjects that he had."

Bill, in his important essay on the subject, "The Cut-Up Method of Brion Gysin," wrote:

> The cut-up method brings to writers the collage, which has been used by painters for fifty years. And used by the moving and still camera. In fact all street shots from movie or still cameras are by the unpredictable factors of passers-by and juxtaposition Cut-ups. And photographers will tell you that often their best shots are accidents . . . writers will tell you the same. The best writings seems to be done almost by accident but writers until the cut-up method was made explicit—all writing is in fact Cut-ups; I will return to this point—had no way to produce the accident of spontaneity. You cannot will spontaneity. But you can introduce the unpredictable spontaneous factor with a pair of scissors . . .

> All writing is in fact Cut-ups. A collage of words read heard overheard. What else? Use of scissors renders the process explicit and subject to extension and variation. Clear classical prose can be composed entirely of rearranged Cut-ups. Cutting and rearranging a page of written words introduces a new dimension into writing enabling the writer to turn images in cinematic variation. Images shift sense under the scissors smell images to sound sight to sound sound to kinaesthetic.

This is where Rimbaud was going with his color of vowels. And his "systematic derangement of the senses." The place of mescaline hallucination: seeing colors tasting sounds smelling forms.

The Cut-ups can be applied to other fields than writing. Dr. Neumann in his *Theory of Games and Economic Behavior* introduces the cut-up method of random action into game and military strategy: assume that the worst has happened and act accordingly. If your strategy is at some point determined . . . by random factor your opponent will gain no advantage from knowing your strategy since he cannot predict the move. The cut-up method could be used to advantage in processing scientific data. How many discoveries have been made by accident? We cannot produce accidents to order. The Cut-ups could add new dimension to films. Cut gambling scene in with a thousand gambling scenes all times and places. Cut back. Cut streets of the world. Cut and rearrange the word and image in films. There is no reason to accept a second rate product when you can have the best. And the best is there for all. "Poetry is for everyone."

Bill was remarkably prescient in his observations. Cut-ups were rapidly assimilated into films, recorded music, and advertising so that today's swift jump-cuts within rock videos and ads are not the least bit unusual to viewers.

Some people objected to their words being used, particularly Gregory Corso. When another of the hotel residents, Patrick Bowles, Samuel Beckett's translator, objected to Bill's appropriation of other people's words, Bill wrote an amusing routine around the idea:

As you cut up and fold in the texts of other writers, they become inextricably mixed with yours. So, who owns words?
. . . fade-out to room #30, 9 rue Git le Coeur, Paris, France . . .

"Yes, boys, that's me there," Patrick Bowles sits opposite.

"Something on your mind, P.B.?"

"Well, yes, you might say so . . . thought some of my words might have strayed up here . . ."

"Free range country, feller say."

"Maybe a little too free, Martin."

"Don't know as I rightly understand you, P.B."—cold, distant point—

"Well, you might put it this way, Martin . . . words have brands just like cattle. You got no call to be changing those brands, Martin . . . When you use my words, they carry my brand."

"Sorry, P.B. . . . I been running brands for years . . . never could account for it. See on back what I mean; each time, place dim jerky faraway across the wounded galaxies a distant hand lifted the phrase from your sonnets . . . You see, I prefer not to use my own words."

Brion loved that routine. "As he wrote in that piece in *The Third Mind*, he branded them like cattle he rustled out there on the free ranges of literature. I realized right away that Cut-ups would never serve or suit anyone quite like they fitted William and served him. Not even me, even though I had first evoked them." Gysin perhaps best summed up the technique when he said, "The idea is to put the material into a certain risk situation and give it a creative push. Then the thing makes itself. That's always been my principle."

Though Burroughs appropriated other people's material, in the majority of his Cut-ups he employed his own work. There was a huge amount of material left over from *Naked Lunch*, which he soon set to work on. Brion: "Then William had used his own highly volatile material, his own inimitable texts which he submitted to cuts, unkind cuts, of the sort that Gregory Corso felt unacceptable to his own delicate 'poesy.' William was always the toughest of the lot. Nothing ever fazed him."

Gregory was very disturbed by the Cut-ups, which he thought would destroy the idea of the poetic muse. He was very much in favor of a strong division between poets and their audience, the poet and his sponsors. It was, after all, his livelihood. He did not want people to think that anyone could be a poet. Not for him Lautréamont's statement: "Poetry should be made by all, not by one." Gregory had also reacted angrily when Bill took a group of his poems and cut them up without asking.

Bill remembered with some amusement, "Gregory had a very stormy connection with the Cut-ups. He said, 'I don't want people to cut up my poetry!' I said, 'I don't know how you're going to prevent them.' He said, 'You shouldn't tell 'em how to do it.' He was very upset about the whole Cut-up thing. He told me it was distracting from his muse. 'Oh,' I said, 'Gregory, these days nobody cares about poetry. Too much colic in your ego like that.' 'Oh,' he said."

At the root of the problem was Burroughs's belief in the importance of random factors, that ultimately writing decays into stale repetition, whereas with Cut-ups the introduction of unpredictable factors brings in something new and fresh. Brion and Bill held out for randomness and chance, whereas Gregory and also Sinclair Beiles, who, after the publication of *Naked Lunch* had become part of the original group experimenting with the technique, felt that imagination and poetic inspiration were of the greatest importance. The arguments were caustic, loud, and acrimonious, and the tension was so great at times that Sinclair sometimes had to go outside and vomit. Nevertheless, Beiles produced a lot of Cut-ups, some of which were published later, such as a collaboration with Stuart Gordon called "Metabolic C Movies," which appeared in the first issue of *Outsider* magazine in New Orleans in the fall of 1961.

Despite the altercations, the four original participants decided that the experiment was of sufficient importance to merit a book and late in January 1960 they prepared the best of the early Cut-ups for publication. Fortunately they already had a publisher, a young doctor from Mauritius named Jean Fanchette who published a bilingual Left Bank literary magazine called *Two Cities.* The first issue had appeared in April 1959, with about half of its contents in English and the rest in French. It featured work by Henry Miller, Alfred Perles, Richard Aldington, and Anaïs Nin—who was the American correspondent— as well as reports on the London art and theater scenes. Sinclair Beiles was on the staff, such as it was, which provided the Beats' introduction. Fanchette's relationship with Beiles was one of tolerance: when Beiles threw food from the window and poured champagne over the breasts of an eminent lady barrister, Fanchette merely called him a "beatnik and guttersnipe." Fanchette enjoyed the company of bohemians, whose lives were in such contrast to his own respectable one as a physician.

The book was called *Minutes To Go,* a phrase described by Gysin as coming from Beiles: "I chose the title by words said by Beiles, 'You've got to get this going, there are only minutes to go.' He provided that rush of enthusiasm." Bill, however, remembered it as coming from an overheard conversation, as a fellow resident of the hotel yelled up the stairway for his companion to hurry up because they were late. Beiles himself attributes the title to Bill: "Burroughs named it *Minutes To Go* after pulling out a pocket watch and looking at it."

The work of these collaborators belies the idea that Cut-ups do not reflect the identities of their authors. It is immediately obvious as to who wrote each of the poems even if they were not captioned. Bill's work selects words and phrases that have a literary ring to them. Brion used the space to publish his original Cut-ups, but also to print his experiments with permutations of phrases. Beiles cut up the sentences so completely that his work made little sense, whereas Gregory's poems do not appear to have been cut up at all. Gregory's contribution was grudging, to say the least, and at the end of the book, he included a postscript disassociating himself from the experiment. He wrote:

> Note for my contribution to the Cut-Up System.
> Poetry that can be destroyed should be destroyed, even if it means destroying one's own poetry—if it be destroyed. I join this venture unwillingly *and* willingly. Unwillingly because

the poetry I have written was from the soul and not from the dictionary; willingly because if it can be destroyed or bettered by the "cut-up" method, then it is poetry I care not for, and so should be cut-up. Word poetry is for every-man, but soul poetry—alas is not heavily distributed.

Unwillingly because Tzara did it all before; willingly because Mr. Burroughs is a knowing man, and I am in soul to abide by him his "unlock your word horde" is good charity.

Unwillingly because my poetry is a natural cut-up, and need not be created by a pair of scissors; willingly because I have no other choice. I have agreed to join Mr. Gysin, Mr. Beiles, and Mr. Burroughs in this venture and so to the muse I say, "Thank you for the poesy that cannot be destroyed that is in me"—for this I have learned after such a short venture in uninspired machine-poetry.

For many years Gregory refused to sign copies of the book; however, he was able to use the method for his own purposes and, twelve years later, in an interview about his work, he said, " 'Death of 1959' was a cut-up poem. I had maybe three of four pages and I cut it up. I like working with Burroughs. Say: 'Here is a book of Rimbaud, cut it up and make your own, make a million Rimbauds.' You have to see what you've got when you pick up the thing, you have to see if, wow, does it look great, by that accident of cutting, and *then* put it down. There was a lot that I didn't put in. I wasn't able to put the whole shot in. I picked out what was good. It sounded very much like the poem it was anyway . . . as I wrote the poem itself without being cut up; I just shortened the sentences, that's all, and it gave it a different kind of sound, it gave it like a very far-out spatial sound."

Some of the most vociferous arguments against the muse came not from Burroughs but from Gysin, who remained unrepentant: "I've been quoted as being absolutely down on poetry—well, I'm against what I call *poesy*, poesy gives me a pain in the ass . . ." Understandably, this viewpoint was the cause of some disagreement between Gregory and Brion.

To Bill, the poetry created by the Cut-up System was like a doorway into the unconscious, a way of accessing things that you already know but that are buried. He saw it as a means to an end similar to that of scrying or the ports of entry he found in Brion's paintings. To him, the choice of what would be appropriate to cut up was in itself a very personal thing, "so on some level you knew exactly what that was. That is the level that knows, and perceives and remembers everything. And this helps to expand your awareness into these areas of the things that you know and don't know that you know. There is a tremendous amount of data that you have, a pool of knowledge, that you don't know that you have because it's not immediately available to you."

Minutes To Go contained several quotes from Hassan-i-Sabbah, the Old Man of the Mountain; it opens with an epigram attributed to him on its title page: "Not knowing what is and is not knowing *I knew not*," but this, like everything else in the book, is a Cut-up—in this case of something that came to Brion in a dream. There is also a Cut-up incorporating passages from the January 29, and January 30, 1960, issues of the Paris edition of the *New York Herald Tribune*, which ends with the line: "'Nothing is true—everything is permitted.' Last words of Hassan Sabbah. The Old Man of the Mountain quoted from *The Master of the Assassins* by Betty Bouthoul." Bouthoul does quote Hassan's last words in her book but these are not the words. The phrase: "Nothing is true—everything is permitted" is the title of Chapter 13 of her book. The suggestion that these were his last words comes from the fact that the line itself is a Cut-up from her book. It was a new meaning discovered using the technique.

Hassan-i-Sabbah was introduced to Bill by Brion and quickly became part of the Burroughs cosmology. Bouthoul's book had a tremendous impact on Burroughs, who featured Hassan-i-Sabbah as a character in many of his own books. The first use was in *Naked Lunch* in the section called "Hassan's Rumpus Room"—one of the chapters that the censors found objectionable. Over the years, Bill evolved an elaborate cosmology around Hassan, which bore little relationship to historical fact.

Betty Bouthoul was a society portrait painter whom Brion Gysin had met at a dinner party. She was the wife of a distinguished French polemologist and her study of the Assassins, *Grand Maître des Assassins*, published in 1936, is approached from this discipline—the philosophical study of the art of war. Hassan-i-Sabbah invented a new kind of warfare. While he remained secluded in his fortress castle of Alamout, in northern Iran, north of Tehran, his followers obeyed his every command and spread out across the Middle East, infiltrating courts and castles, ready to do his bidding. Legend has it that they were adepts, whose reward for a successful mission was to spend time in the beautiful gardens of Alamout, where they were given large quantities of powerful hashish and passed their time in a dreamlike state, with unlimited food, dancing girls, and courtesans. When they awoke, they thought they had been to heaven. The word *assassin* is thought to have its root in *hashishin*.

Bouthoul asks many questions: How did Hassan train his adepts? Did they smoke cannabis or eat it? Was there in fact a garden? The ruins of Alamout on its rocky perch do not provide any evidence and there certainly seems to be little space for a garden. She also dealt with the problem of legitimate descent, which claims that Hassan founded the Ishmaili imams' line of succession, the latest incumbent being the present Agha Khan, who is still weighed in diamonds by his followers on his birthday.

It is easy to see why Bill was attracted to Hassan-i-Sabbah. For Bill he was someone who had had complete control over his own life; and he was apparently someone who had mastered the Ugly Spirit. Bill adopted "Nothing is true—everything is permitted" as his personal maxim. For Bill there was no individual censorship; no thoughts were too personal, embarrassing, or obscene to write down, no idea too crazy not to be considered. Bill's crackpot biography of the man is almost idolatrous:

Hassan i Sabbah The Old Man of The Mountain Master of The Assassins lived in the year One Thousand. From a remote mountain fortress called Alamout he could reach a knife to Paris. There were not more than several hundred trainees in any one Alamout shift. Hassan i Sabbah made no attempt to increase numbers or extend political power. He took no prisoners. There were no torture chambers in Alamout. He was strictly a counter puncher. When a move was made against Alamout by the multiple enemies of Hassan i Sabbah he reached out with his phantom knife and a general a prime minister a sultan died. Hassan i Sabbah Master of the Jinn. Assassin of Ugly Spirits.

There was much of Hassan-i-Sabbah in the character of Inspector Lee of the Nova Police, whom Bill created in 1961 (at first Burroughs referred to them as "novia" criminals but then quickly switched to "nova," possibly because he suddenly realized that *novia* means "girl-friend" in Spanish):

> The purpose of my writing is to expose and arrest Novia Criminals. In *Naked Lunch The Soft Machine* and *Novia Express* I show who they are and what they are doing and what they will do if they are not arrested. Minutes to go. Souls rotten from their orgasm drugs, flesh shuddering from their novia ovens, prisoners of the earth come out. With your help we can occupy The Reality Studio and retake their universe of fear death and monopoly.
>
> signed Inspector J. Lee Novia Police

Minutes To Go was designed by Fanchette to look exactly like *Two Cities* magazine, with the same light-blue paper wrappers, in this instance drawn by Gysin. The book was proofed and 1,000 copies were printed, but then Fanchette ran out of money. Gaït Frogé came to the rescue and paid the printer and so became the de facto publisher. The book was issued first with a wraparound band in the French manner but, unusually, this band read *"Un reglement de comptes avec la litterature"* ("To settle a score with literature").

The Cut-up group was quite taken by Jean Fanchette and his stories of bad behavior with Lawrence Durrell and Henry Miller. Brion was of two minds about Fanchette, whom he once described as being "small enough and black enough for me to be afraid to hit him." Brion's paranoia was tempered by a respect for the man's obvious abilities in the medical field and his ensured success in life. Fanchette later became the director of a mental hospital, causing Burroughs to develop a humorous routine in which Fanchette would declare his enemies insane and incarcerate them in his institute, where he lobotomized them and performed other unspeakable operations. Fanchette was the subject of a conversation in room 25 of the hotel, which, fortuitously, was recorded on Brion's Revere. The tape captures a moment in time when all four of the original collaborators on *Minutes To Go* were together, and dates from late April 1960, a few days after the publication of the book. Brion, as usual, dominates the conversation but Bill feels able to interrupt at will and insists on reading aloud from a letter that he cuts up in their presence. Gregory laughs a lot but says little and Sinclair, for the most part, remains silent except to laugh. Clearly, they are all smoking pot.

> *Brion:* "You see Fanchette has been a part of this. He was saying the other day he watched the lobotomies being done. You see this is somebody we're going to see for a long time, I'm sure. I'm sure we're going to see around for the next twenty years."
>
> *William:* "Well, I wouldn't go as far as to say that!"
>
> *Brion:* "When he says, 'After all I could make a lot of money as a doctor,' well I'm sure he could. He could make big money, big houses, big cars within five or so years, maybe less. Within his specialty, you know how fashionable it is, with the talent that he has and all his connections."
>
> *Gregory:* "He has performed a lobotomy?"
>
> *Brion:* "He's assisted at the performance of a lobotomy."
>
> *William:* "He has actually performed a lobotomy. Are you sure?"

Gregory: "Assisted."

William: "It's a specialized job."

Brion: "That's what he's specializing in."

William: "Exactly, brain surgery."

Gregory: "He must be a very strong-minded individual."

Brion: "Very strong-minded. Very special. It must take a very special kind of mind to be a surgeon."

William: "I think so."

Brion: "So is a diamond cutter. What kind of man would be a diamond cutter?"

[Sinclair Beiles discusses a brain-tumor operation at some length.]

William [bored]: "Look at this creepy letter. I'm gonna cut it up right now!"

Sinclair: "Why don't you read it before you cut it up?"

William: "I've read it." [snipping sounds] "You wanna hear what he's *really* saying?"

Brion: "I'm afraid. I'm afraid."

William: "We've got something really creepy now. Prepare yourselves. [William hums as he slices the letter to pieces] Listen to this!

"'R, William Burroughs help. In one of the PR hotel X. I wrote tell credit to thank you for the tie absent. I would be on my brief pass on an evenings out so would interesting indications my funds are very thoughts during sometimes voosh and wondering how recent events indicating something which you quote Paris during the anti intellect I thank you in it advance carrying over at all profitably.'

"That's what it says.

"'Word of poet is that you allotted me.'"

Brion: "Ahah!"

William: "'Through Paris. Well that was a man, the one I, yes. Through upon which I hope to . . .'"

Brion: "No doubt."

William: "'. . . see before drawing any issue of les arts. I came to the realization you all please help instantly after all of earnings one's spread and certain traits somewhat of dual purpose lies attitude. [much laughter] Secondly I would like tea.'"

Brion: "He would like tea, no doubt." [laughing]

William: "'Now that I have a friend, is now shacking of you obligations to him, I the possibilities of using he rooms some of who all of my time is needed, overly.'"

Brion: "I think the key word is the 'he rooms,' he wants to move into your pad with you, man. He doesn't want the pad when you're away. He wants to slip in there, cold and chilly, and . . ."

William: "'If you could be along this line. He of the second of April seventeenth of me, any help you mall sincerely. Charles E. Butterworth.'"

Brion: "Butterworth? Is that what he uses."

William: "Yesss!'

"'It is supposed pleasing leaving by one. Thank you for the tie. Interesting indications during sometime and recently very rich for you quote tend to be anti intellect carry over in all only a job and another way damn sight more simpler, this letter, sir, if you wish to communicate, you, you permitted me.'"

Brion: "That's it. You did, you must have. By the way you brought him in."

[Brion tells an involved story about a man with a patch over his eye who tried to move into someone's room.]

William: [returning to his cut-up letter] "'A room is tempo-rarily library ax, BJ ays to be to come on, able . . .'"

Brion: "He lays it on that you invited him in."

William: "'Last fort gave me some, conclusions, let me in. Be your judges and at first, I. Interzero ask bordo . . .'"

Brion: "The man from Interzero, that's who he is!"

William: "The man from Interzero."

Brion: "It sounds a great place."
Gregory: "He'll be coming back here, because I remember you
　　asking me did I know him."
William: "That's the whole point."
Brion: "We should ask John Balf, but he claims he doesn't know
　　John Balf."
William: "I'm just saying . . . [lots of stoned laughter] 'the pos-
　　sibility of using spectacles.'"

This could be the source of the dream that Burroughs had the
night of June 26, 1972:

> I wake up and hear breathing from the front room . . .
> *The Book Of Breethings* . . . and a young man is sleeping in
> there. I wake him up and ask him to leave. He refuses. I say I
> will call the police and go in the other room and dial 999 . . .
>
> "A burglar, having broken into my apartment now re-
> fuses to leave . . ."
>
> "Refuses to leave, sir?"
>
> "That's right. I'd be willing to forget his breaking in if
> he'd run along like a good bloke."
>
> "I quite understand, sir . . . Now, what is the address?"
>
> "8 Duke Street St. James's."
>
> However, I am actually in Pasadena and have I done the
> wrong thing in sending cops around to 8 Duke Street in
> London?
>
> Back in the front room, the young man who is in his early
> or middle 20s does not seem to be much worried. He is thinnish,
> sandy-haired with a clinging blackmailing invertebrate some-
> thing about him, at once helpless and brutal, unable to ini-
> tiate action but infinitely capable of taking advantage of any
> weakness in another.

Minutes To Go was launched with a party at the English Bookshop
on April 13, 1960, and though it was hardly a best-seller, it did re-

ceive at least one review. John Raymond in the London *Sunday Times* said, "*Minutes To Go* includes some of the best (and funniest) beatnik *vers libre* that I have yet encountered." The book is like a time capsule, preserving the preoccupations and interests of the Cut-up group at that minute. Burroughs's interests are all here: viruses, cancer cures, and control systems, including Scientology. (Brion later commented, "Ian says Bill is only interested in Scientology because he wants to have power over people.") The book even includes Joan Vollmer's favorite line, which she used to quote all the time: "But an emergency, a shocking emergency has arisen since then." The Cut-up went on to encompass an avant-garde genre of its own, with magazines such as *Fruit Cup, Rhinozeros, Insect Trust Gazette,* and *Bulletin From Nothing,* devoted to publishing the work of its adherents: Claude Pélieu, Mary Beach, Jeff Nuttall, Harold Norse, Jürgen Ploog, Carl Weissner, Udo Breger, Jörg Fauser, and a number of others, most of them Germans. Burroughs himself continued to use Cut-ups for the rest of his life, usually as a way of seeing if he could move a text in a new direction after he had exhausted its other possibilities.

Looking back a quarter century, Brion wrote amusingly about Cut-ups in *The Last Museum,* parodying the tremendous importance that they had assumed in their lives:

> "Your old broken black suitcase stuffed with papers was taken up one flight to Room Fifteen directly above you on the stairs."
>
> "I never had a black suitcase. What do you mean? Who broke it?"
>
> "They had orders to bundle up all the loose papers they found and put them in Room Fifteen."
>
> "Loose papers?" I screech. "They must be all mixed up by now and my pages were not even numbered. I've got a real story to tell, the real lowdown on that little chauvinist pig, PG Six, and by now my report must have lost all its narrative flow."
>
> "Oh, dear," murmured Madame Rachou. "That's what comes of all these new-fangled shuffle-ups and cut-ins."

"What do you *mean*?" I scream.
"Oh, people changing sex in midstream and all that . . .
Go on upstairs to retrieve your manuscript . . ."

Even before *Minutes To Go* was ready for publication, Bill had produced enough new Cut-ups to fill a second volume, most of them done in December 1959. This time Gregory and Sinclair were no longer participating. Gregory by now thoroughly disapproved of the whole idea and, according to Burroughs, Cut-ups had driven Sinclair mad, though he would not be hospitalized until January 1961. Sinclair flipped out, breaking windows and throwing his bed out of the window of the Beat Hotel. Gaït Frogé took him to the British hospital, and then his mother arrived and checked him into a private clinic, the Chateau de Suresnes, outside Paris, where he spent the time working on a book of poems that he hoped would be published by John Calder in London. The tensions and arguments surrounding Cut-ups had been too much for Sinclair's sometimes tenuous hold on reality. Bill said that Sinclair's mother came to the hotel to berate him: "His mother said I'd driven him crazy."

Brion's contribution to the next volume, called *The Exterminator*, consisted of a number of permutated poems: one short line with its words reworked in as many different arrangements as possible. A line like "Junk is no good baby" came out as a poem with thirty-four permutations. Brion also added some of his calligraphic drawings but the book was mostly a vehicle for Bill's new work and was copyrighted to him. Dave Hazelwood's Auerhahn Press in San Francisco published it later in 1960 in a beautiful hand-printed edition with a drawing by Brion on the paper cover. One of the early poems in it was a newspaper Cut-up taken from a group of stories found in the *New York Herald Tribune:* "Queen Gives Birth to Second Son," "After Pleas By Uruguay . . . ," "Fifth Bomb in Madrid," and "Chessman Reprieved for Sixty Days by Brown." This text not only existed on the page but was the subject of one of Bill's earliest tape recorder Cut-ups.

The Cut-ups on tape began almost immediately after the Cut-ups on paper. Bill credited this development to Brion: "It was Brion's suggestion. It was the same thing. You can put something on the tape recorder. Say you take something from the newspapers. Go over that at random, cut in just a short piece or whatever you want to cut in, and you'll see how. And it was amazingly appropriate, it was just like the completion of a sentence. Amazing, and that was the point of it. The point that exploded the myth of the omniscient author in a vacuum. When someone walks out that door and he sees something, little did he know that I'm waiting. It gets you down to what actually happens, that life is a Cut-up. Every time you look out the window or walk out the door or answer, you're consciously being cut by supposedly random factors."

Brion had been interested in tape recorders ever since they were invented at the end of World War II, but though he recorded a lot of the music at 1001 Nights, his Tangier restaurant, to his everlasting regret he had never been able to get his hands on a professional machine. As the power supply to each room in the hotel was only 40 watts, residents were restricted in the amount of technology they could use, in any case. Brion had an old Revere tape recorder that was not working but Ian Sommerville knew all about tape recorders and soon fixed it. It was used to record the first "Cut-ins," or aural Cut-ups. These were readings from texts that they rewound and recorded over at random intervals with new sections of texts, creating an aural palimpsest. Brion told his biographer Terry Wilson, "There is something to be said for poverty, it makes you more inventive, it's more fun and you get more mileage out of what you've got plus your own ingenuity. When you handle the stuff yourself, you get the feel of it. William loved the idea of getting his hands on his own words, branding them and rustling anyone else's he wanted. It's a real treat for the ears, too, the first time you hear it."

At this time Bill did not yet have his own tape recorder and the first recording was made by Brion, called "Poem of Poems," using texts by Shakespeare and the *Song of Songs* to demonstrate to Bill what could be done. Bill caught on right away and went out and bought a cheap Japanese recorder. Tape recorders were all reel-to-reel then; the Phillips cassette machine was not invented until 1965. The cumbersome reel-to-reels had to have the tape threaded on and were operated by punching big buttons. Bill punched with such tremendous force that he could destroy a machine within a matter of weeks; Cut-ins required a lot of stopping and starting.

At the end of the school term Ian returned from England and took a tiny room on a lower floor, which he decorated with a chromium-plated bicycle wheel, without its tire. Years later he described it as a tribute to Marcel Duchamp's 1913 *Bicycle Wheel.* Tom Neurath was skeptical that Ian was familiar with Duchamp's readymades: "I wonder, do you think he would have known about Duchamp? I think he was just a great bicycler. I'm sure when he was a kid he bicycled a lot." Neurath helped Ian a great deal, financially and otherwise, in later years, and was in a good position to know the depth of Ian's knowledge of art, especially as an art-book publisher. The first time someone mentioned Duchamp's bicycle wheel to him, Ian must have decided to call it his own Duchampian readymade. The wheel is featured in many photographs from the period, as it dominated his small room.

Ian brought his own tape recorder with him from Cambridge, which was a far better machine than Brion's Revere. Bill, Brion, and Ian then began an extended series of tape recorder experiments that dominated their lives the entire spring of 1960 and, like the Cut-up texts, were to continue for some time, in Burroughs's case until 1966. Brion recalled, "Ian was an extraordinary technician, had obviously ever since childhood been the sort of boy who can fix things, or make things, or mend things, or invent things. . . . Life begins with two tape recorders, because with two you can make copies. Experiment begins with three tape recorders, where you can really get things going back and forth, and at that time we had three, until somebody came and stole Ian's, I'm afraid, out of his room."

Power lines were strung from room to room, to enable more than one tape recorder to be used simultaneously. Brion: "So when Ian came back the next holidays to the Beat Hotel where we were staying, we didn't have enough watts. We had three rooms, Burroughs in one room, Ian in another, and me in a third, and we sort of ran wires loose out the windows and everything so we could get enough." One tape, from April 1960, consisted of Bill's "Klinker Is Dead" text cut in with a terrible New Orleans–style banjo version of "Brother Can You Spare a Dime" and Jajouka music, while in the background can be heard, on the other tape recorder, voices being played at different speeds in front of the playback head. As usual, Bill was inexhaustible and produced hour after hour of cut-up tapes, which, like everything else he did, are immediately recognizable as his despite the increase in random factors when dealing with aural material. Bill wrote in *The Third Mind*, "Record a few minutes of news broadcast. Now rewind and cut in at random short bursts from other news broadcasts. Do this four or five times over. Of course, where you cut in words are wiped off the tape and new juxtapositions are created by cutting in at random. How random is random? You know more than you think. You know where you cut in."

Toward the end of 1959, around the time Bill and Brion were engaged in their first experiments with Cut-ups, they got to know the American writer James Jones, author of the 1951 best-seller *From Here to Eternity*. He had arrived in Paris in the summer of 1958 with his new wife, Gloria, and took an apartment on the Ile St. Louis. He came to Paris originally intending to write a novel based around the life of jazz guitarist Django Reinhardt but claimed that he was unable to find enough material and gave it up. By the fall of 1959 he and Gloria had bought a place of their own on the Ile St. Louis and Jones was hard at work on another novel about World War II, eventually published as *The Thin Red Line*. The Joneses had an open house every Sunday evening and Bill and Gregory and Brion would often go along, sometimes taking other residents from the hotel, but always telephoning first.

One of the people taken by Bill to a James Jones cocktail party was Bill Belli, a young Italian American from New Jersey who looked like someone out of *West Side Story*. He'd graduated from Rutgers in the spring of 1959 and the next day set off to hitchhike to San Francisco with a copy of *On the Road* in his pocket. Belli knocked around the States, hitchhiking across the country four times, then arranged to meet his girlfriend, Jane, in Paris. She told him she would be staying with George Whitman at the Mistral. Belli arrived in Paris on Christmas Eve, penniless and without a change of clothes, and found Jane at the bookshop. They spent the night on the sofa and on Christmas morning he was awakened by the loud voice of Gregory Corso. They got to talking and Gregory invited them over to the Beat Hotel. Later that day the couple made their way over to the rue Git-le-Coeur, but Gregory was out. Jane knocked on a door and it opened a crack to reveal Bill Burroughs, dressed formally as ever in his suit and tie. He invited them into his room and asked what was happening in New York. Belli told him all about juvenile delinquency, which was one of the big media scares at the time. Bill seemed interested.

A week later they ran into Harold Norse at the Mistral and Belli told him how he had hitched across the States and now planned to travel all over Europe and North Africa. When he said he wanted to visit Tangier, Norse told him that both Gysin and Burroughs had lived there for many years and said he would take them over and introduce them. They walked over to the Beat Hotel and found Bill, Brion, and Gregory sitting in the ground-floor café. They were introduced once again and Bill invited the couple to join them for dinner at a little restaurtant on the rue de l'ancienne Comedie. The conversation was about agents—who was a spy and for whom—a theme that Bill would develop into a full-blown conspiracy theory in the coming years. Gregory claimed that the Beats were all under surveillance because the American government thought they were a potential force for revolution. Gregory thought that there were already agents among them, reporting back. This was not far from the truth; in 1961 J. Edgar Hoover declared beatniks one of the three greatest threats to American security. As far as Bill was concerned, proof that he was under surveillance came that April when he was summoned to the American

Embassy, where a tough-looking narcotics agent advised him that, as he had been convicted of a narcotics offense in a French court, they were entitled to confiscate his American passport. They said that they did not wish to do that, but advised Bill to return to the United States because the French were preparing to deport him, and it would be better for everyone if he left of his own volition. Bill was told to stay clean until he did so and to make sure there were no drugs in his room.

Bill contacted Maître Bumsell, who looked into the matter. It turned out to be a bluff on the part of the embassy; there were no moves being made to deport him. The only heat on him was from his own embassy, probably alerted to his presence in Paris by the article in *Life* magazine about the Beats, reported and photographed by Dean and Snell. It had attracted rather more attention than Bill would have liked.

Tom Neurath remembers, "Burroughs and Brion had their own scene. I think actually Burroughs and Gysin really kept themselves to themselves; they weren't very standoffish but I think everyone was in awe of them. Nick Smart, a wonderful American football-playing character, was a go-between. I think he was accepted by them and gravitated between the two groups. Burroughs was plagued by people wanting to meet him after the *Life* article. As a result of that he got pestered by a lot of people but he was always very polite when one met him on the staircase, in his three-piece suit. Brion was quite friendly toward me but I was really in awe of Burroughs. However there certainly were occasions when I can remember ending up in his room with Brion and five or six people. He always gave the impression he had a lot of work to do."

Though Bill complained about the interuptions, he told Gregory that he had a foolproof method of getting rid of unwanted visitors. Gregory remembered in an interview, "People would come to his door and bring him big pieces of opium . . . I said, 'Bill with all those people coming and buggin' ya, how can you work?' He said, 'Well Gregory, I send their spirits out and they have to leave with their spirits. When someone comes in and I want to get rid of them, I look at them and repeat inwardly, "I love you I hate you I love you I hate you . . ." They get the feeling and say, "I gotta go, see ya Bill."' After that I was always wondering if he was doin' it to me."

Cut-ups had been accidentally discovered while Brion was preparing artwork but they had inspired him to return to writing as an art form. Although he worked on Cut-ups and permutated texts, he realized that these were strictly noncommercial literary experiments. Seeing how everyone else in the hotel was being published by Girodias, Brion decided that he would also write a book for him. Naturally Brion did not consider cranking out a DB, which he would have seen as beneath his dignity. Instead he did a rewrite of *Le Rouge et le Noir*, the story of a gigolo who married the daughter of his keeper and then murdered her. He based the novel, called *I Am Out*, on the notorious Lonergan case.

Wayne Lonergan was convicted in 1944 of murdering his wife, Patricia Burton Lonergan, the heiress to the Burton-Burnheimer beer fortune, by beating her over the head with a silver candelabra shortly after she had filed for separation and cut him out of her will. His defense was that while she was sucking his cock she bit it, "inflicting great physical pain" on him, and that he seized the nearest weapon to fend her off. However, when the candelabra broke, he went and found another one and continued to beat her brains out. It was this search for a second weapon that the prosecutor used in a bid for a first-degree murder verdict; Lonergan had time to premeditate as he walked back across the huge living room looking for another weapon. He was found guilty of second-degree murder and served fifteen years in Sing Sing. Lonergan had previously been supported by a series of male patrons and had been the "protégé" and lover of Patricia's father, William Burton, a notorious old homosexual whom Burroughs had known in New York. It was a lurid case that Brion thought would make a good read.

Girodias thought otherwise and rejected the book. Sinclair Beiles, who was still working for Girodias, wrote to Burroughs on May 4, 1960, saying, "Girodias has refused to publish Brion's novel. 'Won't do me any good and won't do your career any good.' The notes of objection he's pencilled in here and there about grammar etc. are utter bullshit and not worth thinking about . . . It's pretty clear what kind of career Girodias along with the art dealers have planned for Brion—post mortem genius career (just a picture out here and there, and a bit in the magazines until they've killed him or cornered him in notoriety advertising). He refused to discuss even the third part of the novel—the real crown of the work which he dismissed as being too Burroughsian (getting to be one of Girodias's swear words)."

Brion was outraged and compared Girodias to Herodias (who had asked her daughter Salome to demand St. John the Baptist's head on a plate as a reward for her dancing). Brion clearly felt martyred. Beiles, acting on Brion's behalf, sent the book to a New York literary agent as "the book that Girodias found too hot to handle" but no one was interested and the book was never published.

Remembering Brion's description of having had an optical hallucination in the bus on the way to Marseilles caused by the flicker effect of trees along the roadside, Ian wrote to Brion from Cambridge and introduced him to a book by W. Grey Walter, called *The Living Brain*, which explains the phenomenon of flicker. Walter came from Kansas City, but his English father brought him to Britain at age seven and he studied Natural Sciences at Cambridge. As the Head of the Physiological Department of the Burden Neurological Institute at Bristol he discovered "delta" rhythms and "theta" waves as well as inventing an artificial mouse that could learn things. He was experimenting with artificially induced epileptic seizures when he encountered the phenomenon of flicker and found that " 'epileptic' phenomena can be evoked in normal people by physiological stimulation of a certain type . . ." and he cited a number of examples, including several where the flicker effect of rows of trees had caused them to "pass out" or have fits. The reason was that the flicker was reproducing the alpha rhythm of the brain: between 8 and 13 cycles per second.

When created in the lab, Walter found that "in more than fifty percent of young normal adult subjects, the first exposure to feedback flicker evokes transient paroxysmal discharges of the type seen so often in epileptics." Walter mused on the effects of fluorescent lighting and other artificial forms of flicker but concluded, "Oddly enough it is not in the city, but in the jungle conditions, sunlight shining through the forest, that we run the greatest risk of flicker-fits. Perhaps, in this way, with their slowly swelling brains and their enhanced liability to breakdowns of this sort, our arboreal cousins, struck by the setting sun in the midst of a jungle caper, may have fallen from perch to plain, sadder but wiser apes."

Ian and Bill attended a lecture by Walter and conversed with him afterward, but Brion had no contact with the discoverer of the effects of flicker: "I never met him and he never had any other effect on me except that one thing he said, just in half a sentence, that people who are subjected to interruptions of light between eight and thirteen times a second reported experiences of color and pattern. I said, 'Oh wow! That's it!' So Ian was back studying mathematics at Cambridge and I wrote to him and said, 'How can we make it at home? I mean, this is the problem. How can we do it with just what we've got?'"

On February 15, 1960, Ian replied to Brion from Cambridge telling him, "I have made a simple flicker machine; a slotted cardboard cylinder which turns on a gramophone at 78 rpm with a lightbulb inside. You look at it with your eyes shut and the flicker plays over your eyelids. Visions start with a kaleidoscope of colors on a plane in front of the eyes and gradually become more complex and beautiful, breaking like surf on a shore until whole patterns of color are pounding to get in. After awhile the visions were permanently behind my eyes and I was in the middle of the whole scene with limitless patterns being generated around me. There was an almost unbearable feeling of spatial movement for a while but it was well worth getting through for I found that when it stopped I was high above earth in a universal blaze of glory. Afterward I found that my perceptions of the world around had increased very notably. All conceptions of being dragged or tired had dropped away."

Brion recalled, "And that's where it first started. We made some very beautiful machines that got lost. I made them, and Ian was very good with all that sort of cutting and handling, very expert. We did a lot of shit together, a lot of remarkable things." One of their early machines was exhibited in the window of Gaït Frogé's bookshop, and though many people were interested in it none came forward to buy.

Another Dreamachine was on display in the window of Helena Rubinstein's beauty salon in Paris, where Brion hoped it would interest the rich and fashionable. Brion had known Rubinstein in Paris before the war and they were friends but, though she was intrigued, she did not buy one, nor did any of her rich customers.

Brion: "What we had done originally was a cylinder with just the exact slots. And then I made one like a coliseum where each row was a different speed. And then I developed this one whereby the incidence of curves produced every one of those gradations between eight and thirteen flickers a second, because that's where it is, it's in the alpha band. And you see so many things in there after the hundreds of hours that I have looked, that you get to a place which is real dreaming, where apparently it affects the hypothalamus, in the very back part of the original bottom brain . . . and that rarely happens the first time round. The only person that it ever happened to the first time around was old Helena Rubinstein, with whom I had a long romance about the Dreamachine. And Madame would say, 'Oh yes, I had a boat trip. Oh, I'm taking the train in Venice. Ooh, I'm on a . . .' But she's the only person that I've known who really just saw them all like movies."

Brion loved to read deep significance into things, particularly in his own inventions. Aided by the smoking of a good deal of hashish, Cut-ups were discovered to be a supreme weapon against authoritarian control, and thus the Dreamachine was soon credited with being able to access the seat of all vision. Brion expanded on this in an interview with the writer Jon Savage. "The experience can be pushed a great deal further," he said, "into an area which is like real dreams. For example, very often people compare it to films. Well, who can say who is projecting these films? Where do these films come from? If you look at it as I am rather inclined to now—like being the source of all vision—in as much as within my experience of many hundreds of hours of looking at the Dreamachine, I have seen in it practically everything that I have ever seen—that is, all imagery. For example, all the images of established religions appear: crosses appear, to begin with; eyes of Isis float by, and many of the other symbols . . .

"And then one goes very much further; one gets flashes of memory, one gets these little films that are apparently being projected into one's head . . . one then gets into an area where all vision is as in a complete circle of 360 degrees, and one is plunged into a dream situation that's occurring all around one. And it may be true that this is all that one can see . . . that indeed the alpha rhythm contains the whole human program of vision. Well! That is a big package to deal with, and I don't think anybody particularly wants amateurs sitting in front of Dreamachines fiddling with it."

Dream research and sleep research were popular areas of study at the time and Brion and Ian read extensively into these subjects as well as anything they could find on epilepsy, visions, and hallucinations. They found there is a link between alpha brain waves and dreaming and also a link between the mechanism of dreaming and that of creativity. They also found that there is a history of the use of flicker to produce visions. In France, Catherine de Medici had Nostradamus sit at the top of a tower in Paris on sunny days where, spreading the fingers of his hand, he would flicker his fingers over his closed eyes in order to give himself visions. These he would interpret for her in political terms because they both regarded them as instructions from a higher power. Peter the Great had also seated someone at the top of a tower and had him flicker his fingers across his closed eyelids to produce prophetic visions.

The most famous example was, of course, Saul of Tarsus, who may have been subjected to flicker while riding on the buckboard wagon down a bumpy road on his way to Damascas. The horse was apparently moving at just the right speed past an avenue of trees to create flicker and produce the vision that converted him. He closed his eyes against the setting sun and saw crosses. Brion: "He said 'Wow!

that's it!' because the first thing you do see are crosses. Because of the formation of the brain and of the eye, you see visions on these two levels."

Brion's final thoughts on the Dreamachine were set out in the brochure produced by Editions Carl Laszlo in Basel in the 1980s when they made twenty of them in an expensive limited edition. His claims may seem highly extravagant, but they do in fact describe the reaction of most people to the Dreamachine (a small percentage of people get no reaction at all).

In the history of the world, Dreamachines are the first objects made to be viewed with closed eyes. In the history of art, Dreamachines bring to a conclusion the period of kinetic invention in modern painting and sculpture. Dreamachines open a new era and a new area of vision . . . interior vision.

"Dreamachines make visible the fundamental order present in the physiology of the brain."

You are the artist when you approach a Dreamachine and close your eyes. What the Dreamachine incites you to see is yours . . . your own. The brilliant interior visions you so suddenly see whirling around inside your head are produced by your own brain activity. These may not be your first glimpses of these dazzling lights and celestially colored images. Dreamachines provide them only just as long as you choose to look into them. What you are seeing is perhaps a broader vision than you may have had before of your own incalculable treasure, the "Jungian" store of symbols which we share with all normally constituted humanity. From this storehouse, artists and artisans have drawn the elements of art down the ages. In the rapid flux of images, you will immediately recognize crosses, stars and halos . . . woven patterns like pre-Columbian textiles and Islamic rugs . . . repetitive patterns on ceramic tile . . . in embroideries of all times . . . rapidly fluctuating serial images of abstract art . . . what look like endless expanses of fresh paint laid on with a palette knife.

Dreamachine visions usually begin by the meteorically rapid transit of infinite series of abstract elements. These may be followed in time by clear perception of faces, figures and the apparent enactment of highly colored serial pseudo-events. In other words, dreams in color. The Dreamachine *is* a dream-machine. These dreams can be immediately interrupted and brought to an end simply by opening your eyes.

However you look into a Dreamachine, in a short time you will have acquired greater self-knowledge, extended the limits of your vision, brightened your perception of a treasure you may not have known you own.

Ian had returned to England to continue his studies after the Easter break so Bill decided that it might be prudent, given the interest in him from the U.S. Embassy, as well as more convenient, to move to London, where he could see Ian on the weekends; Cambridge is only an hour's train ride from London. At the end of April, Bill moved into the Empress Hotel at 25 Lillie Road in Earl's Court, near the Brompton Cemetery and the Earl's Court Exhibition Building, an anonymous, soulless part of London filled with cheap hotels and rooming houses, which in those days was best known for its transient population of Australians. The Brompton Cemetery was a few blocks away on Old Brompton Road and Bill often went there when it was sunny. "You couldn't find a pleasanter place to sit in your June time," he recalled. For the next few years Bill was to divide his time between London, Paris, and Tangier.

By the spring of 1960, the beginning of the most explosive decade of cultural experimentation since the turn of the century, the Beats of the Beat Hotel had already paved the way with routines, Cut-ups, flicker, and scrying; they had had visions and hallucinations, experimented with hashish, marijuana, Diosan, codeine, morphine, and heroin, and had engaged in orgies and other sexual practices that were probably illegal and were certainly frowned upon in their own countries. Within the shelter of the Beat Hotel they had mapped out many of the paths that the "sixties generation" was to follow: the recreational use of drugs and experiments with psychedelics; investigations into magic and mysticism in all its forms; gay rights and sexual freedom for young people, as well as the legalization of "pornography" and challenges to obscenity laws. It was not quite sex and drugs and rock 'n' roll (there was no rock 'n' roll yet) but their experiments certainly became an influential blueprint for what was to follow.

9 **Soft Machine**

"The Beat Hotel period was certainly a peak creative experience in my life and I know that Brion felt the same way."

Harold Norse

Burroughs was not involved in the early Dreamachine experiments, as he was living at the Empress Hotel in London at the time, but he was very intrigued by Ian's prototype, which he saw in Cambridge. Ian went to Paris that Easter to work on the Dreamachine and Bill joined them a few days later. Bill moved into room 32 in the back of the hotel, of which he said, "I didn't like that. It was on the back of the hotel, opening on a stairwell, it was a dank dark place. I couldn't reserve a room."

Bill moved to and fro between Paris and London, staying in rooms 15, 18, 29, 30, 31, and 32 at the Beat Hotel, and rooms 7, 8, 28, 29, 35, and 37 at the Empress in London. Brion remembered, "He was as free as the wind. He could grab his hat and portable typewriter and split with nothing more than a toothbrush, abandoning his manuscripts like old autumn leaves, great shoals of them to scoop up out of the basket or sweep across the floor and put away for a rainy day, safe in my footlocker." When Brion saw the disorder of Bill's papers he bought him a set of four wire trays, in a filing stack, which he attached to the wall above Bill's desk. This way Bill was able to maintain some control over his work. When Ian moved into Bill's London apartment in 1966, he found that Bill's file cabinet contained five labeled folders and 17 folders marked "miscellaneous." Bill always had trouble with his filing.

Were it not for Brion's foresight, all of Bill's early manuscripts and correspondence would have disappeared. In the early '70s, it was the sale of their combined archive that saved them both from financial difficulties, and in the 1980s it was from that archive that the only surviving manuscript of *Queer* was delivered. Brion: "William had always just thrown, practically abandoned, his manuscripts everywhere. Lots of manuscripts have disappeared and god knows if they'll ever see the light of day. The suitcase full of material that never went into *Naked Lunch* was left behind in Tangier and the street boys were selling it for a dollar a page!"

In 1960 Brion's paintings were featured in the Salon Réalités Nouvelles group show at the Galérie de Seine, just around the corner from the hotel. This would prove to be an important year for Bill, Brion, and Ian because it was in 1960 that they would literally take their show on the road. Brion would join Bill and Ian in a multimedia evening of action painting, poetry, and slide projections held on Thanksgiving Day at the Heretics Club of Corpus Christi, Cambridge University, organized by David Bonavia. Bill read his article "The Cut-up Technique of Brion Gysin." The three of them would also put on a performance of readings combined with a light show at the ICA in London and an evening of "Verbal Theatre" at La Bohème, in Montparnasse. And it was in this year that Brion would write "Cut-ups Self Explained," the manifesto of the movement.

It began in January 1960, when George Macbeth, the British poet and novelist, read *Minutes To Go*. He worked for the Talks Department of the BBC Third Programme and was sufficiently impressed to write to Brion asking if he would like to come over and read some of it on one of his programs. At that time Brion was busy with the Dreamachine but he told Macbeth that he was interested and that he had many ideas for performance poetry but that he didn't have equipment sophisticated enough to realize them. When Brion was next in London, Macbeth introduced him to Douglas Clevedon, who had produced the elaborate soundstaging for the radio version of Dylan Thomas's *Under Milk Wood*, and they fixed a date for that summer to record something. By then the BBC was hoping to have installed some new state-of-the-art sixteen-track tape machines. The idea was to work at the "Footsteps" studio in Shepherd's Bush, where the BBC made all the sound effects for haunted houses, wind, waves, birds, and creaking doors for their plays and documentaries. The technicians there specialized in complex sound overlays—which in those days required considerable sound-engineering skills—and were able to rise to any challenge.

In the course of making the early Cut-ups, Bill and Brion had used material from Aldous Huxley's *The Doors of Perception*, and it was here that Brion claims he found the famous divine tautology, "I am that I am," as God told Moses, as quoted in the Bible. Brion looked at the words as a graphic image on the page: "I-am-that-I-am," and thought it looked a bit like the front of a Greek temple, only that it needed the last two words reversed—"am I"—to balance the corners of the architrave. Brion: "I realized as soon as I did this, it asked a question. 'I am that am I?' And I said, 'Wow, I've touched the oracle!' So then I turned the next one." He wrote out all the possible permutations of the phrase, then found other phrases that he liked and began to explore all their possible permutations. This interested him more than regular Cut-ups, and Brion's contribution to both *Minutes To Go* and *The Exterminator* consisted primarily of permutated poems, rather than the found words and phrases that Bill so delighted in.

The sixties were to see an explosion of interest in sound poetry, which existed only on tape, cut up, speeded up, echoed, utilizing all the effects possible in a recording studio. To Brion this was the only poetry that was of any real interest, and many people saw him as the originator of the movement. Brion said of his permutated tapes, "Poetry, of course, exists not necessarily on a printed page, nor even in the spoken word—nevertheless, as a so-called Father of Sound Poetry, I do believe that it's more in the spoken word . . . I understand poetry really mostly as it's called in French *poesie sonore*, and what I preferably have called 'machine poetry' . . . actually putting it through the changes that one can produce by tape recording and all of the technology, or even the just *minimal* technology that one has had in one's hands in the last few years . . . and that all the rest is really a terrible waste of time, I think."

The first poem they worked on at the BBC that summer was "Pistol Poem," a permutated revolver shot. Brion brought with him a recording of a cannon firing that he had made in Morocco, but the sound lasted too long. Brion: "They said, 'We have a pistol here that we use for haunted houses, murder scenes, and things like that. Would you like to hear it?' So I said, 'Is that the only one you've got?' They said, 'Well no, we've actually got another one.' I listened to all of their pistols and I picked one and said, 'Record it for me at one meter away, at two meters away, three, four, five. And then we'll just play them and permutate that.' Then we take the whole thing and double it back on itself like that. And it was, 'Oh . . . wow . . . there . . . ah!' So it took quite a while to do, as you can imagine."

He continued, "Here we began dealing with sound as material measurable in centimeters, even in feet and inches, and the whole point of the exercise was to do things treating sound as if it was material . . . tangible material; as indeed it had become since the invention of tape. And so we went to work and produced 'A Pistol Poem.' Then later, on the same principle but with speed changes, which were very difficult to achieve in those days . . . I mean Douglas himself had to put his finger in some place; to slow up the machine gradually, or speed it up or vice versa. Or slow it down and rerecord in the opposite direction and all sorts of things. So that took a whole day or more, and that was 'I Am That I Am.' We also did 'Junk Is No Good Baby' and 'Kick That Habit Man.'" According to Brion, the BBC technicians were quite shocked by the results that were coming back to them out of the speakers and were only too glad when the experiment came to an end. Burroughs commented, "Well, what did they expect? A chorus of angels with tips on the stock market?"

The Permutated Poems was a twenty-three-minute radio program, and it had the distinction of getting the second-worst reception that the BBC had ever had from their panel of listeners. (The lowest was a program about Britain by W. H. Auden, so Brion was in good company.) Brion commented, "The sort of people who were not startled by it were ladies who had worked in textile factories and found it very like the sort of thing they were used to with the warp and the woof, weaving things, and they wrote a lot of charming letters . . . they realized semiunconsciously that this was sound being used as material, so they compared it to their work with material. And the most interesting person that answered wrote me first, then came, and moved into the next room at the Beat Hotel, even got married in there the first time, was Daevid Allen who then went on to found the rock groups Soft Machine and Gong."

The first multimedia performance, at Ian's college in Cambridge, used very basic materials. Brion had seen an epidiascope, or overhead projector, used as a teaching aid when he was in the U.S. Army during the war and Ian made one to his specifications. It is a simple device in which any image or document placed on the active surface is projected onto a screen. They used it for projecting collages and arrangements of photographs and objects onto the ceiling. Brion: "We started it about 1960, doing things with just a small projector in one room . . . I played into my own image, and out of it, or I was surrounded by an image that was partly projected onto me, depending on what color I was wearing. I would wear black, for example, and then open a zipper and by wearing a white T-shirt underneath I would be somebody else . . . I would be another projected person, into which I could walk or out of which I could walk."

The news of these events soon spread. Brion and Ian were approached by two French artists, Bernard Heidsieck and Henri Chopin, whom Brion already knew, who were interested in their work with projections and sound collage and who suggested that they combine their efforts. Brion: "In La Bohème William and I had done some very strange things along that line, reading poems off shuffled cards along with tapes running, and stuff like that. And they said, 'Wouldn't you like to join in with us?' And I did, and Ian was there, and we sort of jumped in on this and said . . . it's got to be theater. I mean me, with my old Broadway background . . . and the only thing that we hadn't got together was the box office, and that was continually escaping us. This was at several places . . . and I should have known better."

Heidsieck and Chopin's organization was called *Domaine Poetique*, a take-off on the Domaine Musicale, which had recently introduced electronic music to Paris. They were both concerned with the area in which concrete poetry, electronic music, *poesie sonore*, machine poetry, happenings, and performance art meet and in many ways they paralleled the development of the Fluxus Group, which was founded in October 1960 by George Maciunas, with its multimedia events and attacks on bourgeois art and culture. In fact there was considerable overlap in their activities, particularly through Fluxus artist Emmett Williams, who performed at the Domaine Poetique event, and even wrote sleeve notes for Burroughs's first spoken-word album, *Call Me Burroughs*, which was released by Gaït Frogé's English Bookshop in 1965.

George Maciunas attended a performance in Paris and categorized Brion's work as "Expanded Cinema" in his Expanded Arts Diagram. Though Brion later claimed that Maciunas had made a mistake and thought they *had* made films, saying, "At the time the slides . . . were part of a show that we put together so seamlessly as manipulated by Ian Sommerville, that he may have thought it was a movie . . . The permutated poems were both recorded and given live by me, and images of myself were projected on myself, as you see on the poster for the show. It's a photograph of myself three times—two projections of the same face—one on the wall, one on my face, and a photograph across my face too. Looking ten years older. That's what I really looked like that day, and that's exactly the same face projected on my own real face . . . So this is playing with time . . . with my own age." Brion is in fact listed very specifically in Macienas's article as "subject slides on same subject" (i.e., pictures of Brion projected onto Brion). Ian's experiments done with two projectors were very much the precursors of rock 'n' roll light shows. The soft-focus fade-ins and fade-outs, passing back and forth from one to the other, made in effect a continuous light show.

These performances were not as arbitrary and random as some people have since made them out to be. One performance, held at La Bohème, Montparnasse, on July 16, 1962, had a nine-page script written by Ian Sommerville, giving detailed instructions for the complex lighting and slide-projection sequences and the timings for Bill's readings: a piece called "Subject Virus" and another called "Word Falling—Photo Falling."

As Bill spent quite a bit of his time in London and in Tangier, he was not always able to participate in the events. At one Domaine Poetique event, Brion, assisted by Ian but without Bill, put on a performance in homage to Kali, the Indian goddess of creation and destruction. A roll of white screen paper that photographers use to make a neutral background had been mounted on the wall behind the stage about two yards high. Brion pulled down the roll until the edge reached the floor, to make himself a blank sheet as tall as himself. Using three Japanese brushes and a house-painting roller into which he had incised the elements of a grid, he painted fast and furious: a field of squirming yellow glyphs was followed by large orange splashes and then the green brush drew leaflike forms. Finally he charged the roller with so much blue paint that it dribbled Pollocklike curves as he swished it over the surface, imposing a restraining grid on the vibrating glyphs. The painting finished, Brion turned, took a bow, then tore the painting from the rest of the roll at the top. The paper fell to ground and began to curl into a tube. Brion took it up, unrolled it, and began tearing it into pieces from top to bottom. Its destruction complete, he left the stage. "There is no creation without destruction / there is no destruction without creation."

Brion's use of the roller grid was an attempt to repeat graphically what he had been doing with the repetitive poems. He'd bought a housepainter's roller in Rome in 1960 and had cut a grid pattern into it. The next year he used it to paint a series called "Plans," recalling, "It came out of the permutations of the poems you see . . . I cut the grid out of that roller so I could make these things . . . so then I thought I was going to rebuild the world like that." The roller was designed to create the same effects as the Dreamachine except on paper or canvas. The grid formation was used as a template into which Brion dropped glyphs, letters, symbols, or words in a random order, making a collage. Later he added photographs, possibly influenced by Burroughs's and Sommerville's photo collages.

The biggest Domaine Poétique event was a three-day affair organized at the Centre Américain des Artists at 261 Blvd Raspail on May 18, 21, and 22, 1963, featuring works by William Burroughs, Brion Gysin, François Dufréne, Robert Filliou, Bernard Heidsieck, Jean-Clarence Lambert, Gherasim Luca, and Emmett Williams, who all performed their own works. Mise-en-scène was by Jean-Loup Philippe, with visual accompaniment by Brion Gysin and Ian Sommerville. The American Center, across from the Montparnasse cemetery, was built in 1934 as a place where American students could go to swim, do calisthenics, and study in a library. Brion liked performing there because it was such a grand space with colonnades, huge windows, an auditorium, and 4,000 square meters of gardens, including a huge cedar of Lebanon planted by Chateaubriand, who once lived in a house on the site. To Brion it provided suitable gravitas for his art.

During the war it was taken over by the Nazis, and afterward it became the American community school providing an American education for the children of diplomats and the American military. In 1946, when Jean-Jacques Lebel returned to Paris with his parents, he was sent there to study and it was through him that it became the venue for the Domaine Poetique. Jean-Jacques remembered with amusement, "I went to school there for three years, and in '61–'62, we were looking for a place to have poetry readings and happenings so I went to see the director, and I said, 'I went to school here and I'd like to do some theater,' I didn't tell him what it was, and that's how we did the first happenings. In that place which had been my study hall I did the first poetry reading of Lawrence Ferlinghetti and Harold Norse, then the Domaine Poetiques of William and Brion and Ian and Bernard Heidsieck and Henri Chopin and all the European sound poets who came from the Schwitters background, and that was a good thing. It was sort of like the English Bookstore—it was an English-speaking island in the middle of Paris."

These multimedia experiments would continue up until the summer of 1965, ending with a performance at the ICA in London, in which Brion created and then destroyed a six-foot-by-nine-foot painting while Bill sat onstage in his hat and Chesterfield overcoat, bathed in deep blue light, and stared fixedly at the audience. Stills from *Towers Open Fire* (1965), a film by Bill and Antony Balch, were projected on a screen above his head and Cut-ups of radio static, Moroccan drumming, and Bill reading disaster stories from the American newspapers were played at earsplitting volume by Ian.

All through 1960 and '61 Bill applied himself to Cut-ups, processing the enormous pile of manuscript material left out of *Naked Lunch*, and making new texts, which eventually were to become his next novel, *The Soft Machine.* His powers of application and concentration were remarkable as he methodically refined the Cut-up method into a working system so that he was no longer producing one-off poems or short prose fragments but an entire novel. Though he often used other people's words and texts as a starting point for his own texts, it proved almost impossible for anyone else to use *his* texts for their own. As Brion told his biographer Terry Wilson, "Used by another writer who was attempting Cut-ups, one single word of Burroughs's vocabulary would run a stain right through the fabric of their prose, no matter how they cut it. One single high-powered Burroughs word could ruin a whole barrel of good everyday words, run the literary rot right through them. One sniff of that prose and you'd say, 'Why, that's a Burroughs.'" Whenever they worked on a performance together, Brion made sure that his work was radically different from Bill's; in fact this may be the reason why he preferred to work with permutations and leave the Cut-ups to Bill.

Bill refined his images until they became a rich quintessence of the original texts, like images from Huysmans's *Against Nature*, so intense that they could only be read a few pages at a time: "The jissom of hanged youths gave rise to interesting innovations: a species of green newt boy with purple fungoid gills that breathe carbon dioxide and live on your exhaust like it was very chic to have A Greenie curled into you and a translucent pink water dog that ate jissom and had to be kept in crystal cylinders of spine juice known as Hydraulic jacks."

Other texts were deceptively normal, more like *Naked Lunch*, until unusual word shifts intruded and caused a rift in the sentence and meaning: "Up a great brown tidal river to The Port City stuck in water hyacinths and banana rafts. The City is an intricate split bamboo structure in some places six stories high overhanging the street propped up by concrete pillars and beams and sections of railroad track, an arcade from the warm rain that falls at half hour intervals. The Coast People drift in the warm steamy night eating colored ices under arc lights and converse in slow catatonic gestures punctuated by periods of immobile silence."

While Bill reduced these and other longer sections to their Cut-up bones in a series of progressively more condensed images—"You win something like jellyfish Meester" or "wind hand caught in the door"—other Beat Hotel residents were turning their hands to Cut-ups. Harold Norse had finally moved into the hotel in April 1960, where he was immediately subjected to the Burroughs-Gysin third degree. He became a convert and began cutting up his own work.

It was through Gregory that Norse had met Burroughs and through Norse that Burroughs had met Sommerville. However, when Norse moved into the Beat Hotel he was not a part of the inner circle of Beats, though he and Burroughs were friends. Norse discussed Burroughs and the Beat Hotel with Winston Leyland for the distinguished *Gay Sunshine* interview series. In it Norse described Burroughs as "the brains of the gang," and said "it took a long time for me to get over an uncomfortable feeling in his presence. Though very articulate, he's tight-lipped and taciturn. I always had the impression that he was evaluating and assessing everything you said." He described Bill as "very fun-loving" and a "fabulous raconteur. As we got to know each other in the early days this came out in both of us. I used to amuse him with crazy stories I heard around Paris. We joked a good deal. . . . He could go on for hours, in his room or Brion's or mine or Ian's, like in *Naked Lunch*, telling stories of his earlier experiences, reliving each part, with a thousand different faces and voices, until you thought you were hallucinating. I'm sure he had total recall. He made every scene come alive. I'd often hear his voice rumbling in the room next to mine where Ian lived. One night in Ian's room, lit only by candlelight, Bill read from the manuscript of *The Soft Machine*, which he was working on, and we were all zonked by that incredible prose and the way he read it. Brion knelt and kissed his hand and called him Master."

Norse told Leyland that his first Cut-up alarmed him so much he thought he was going crazy: "There was no precedent for what I'd written, or what was being written through me. At times I felt possessed, occupied by another being, someone else's voice speaking through me . . . When I was first doing Cut-ups in the Beat Hotel, I found out a month later that an English poet in the room next to me had been writing similar things. Whole phrases and words were identical, although we did not know each other at the time of writing. I had the same experience time and again with Burroughs, who lived upstairs."

Though he missed the initial excitement surrounding Cut-ups and so was not a contributor to *Minutes To Go* or *The Exterminator*, in subsequent years Norse was one of the few writers who continued to use the technique. He remembered, "'Sniffing Keyholes' was the first Cut-up that I did and I showed it to Brion Gysin who flipped over it and he said 'You've got to show it to Burroughs' and I said, 'No, I think I'm crazy, I don't know how I could have written anything like this,' and he said, 'No you're not crazy, this is a whole new experiment that you've broken through,' and I showed it to Burroughs and he said, 'Yes, you have broken through to something new.'" "Sniffing Keyholes" takes place in Tangier: "ZZ flipped saying, 'I gonna learn how to use words . . .'" It was written as an Olympia Press–style description of a heterosexual romp, which reads much like the "John and Mary" section of *Naked Lunch.* The lines were then progressively Cut-up until Norse had reduced the text to a few fragmentary core images: "nothing but flow change lust desire flame . . . Potent is come."

Burroughs said, "I recall my enthusiasm and laughter when Brion and I read 'Sniffing Keyholes.' 'What a gas!' Brion exclaimed, and coming from him that was high praise indeed."

To Burroughs, Sommerville, Gysin, and now Norse, the Cut-up was more than a new literary technique. Cut-ups had the power to decondition by cutting through the normal syntax, fracturing the expected patterns and revealing a new set of relationships and meanings. Burroughs believed that the operations of chance made available messages from the collective unconscious, or even from elsewhere— outer space, the beyond. As Norse said, by cutting a text, "A voice that is not your voice comes through. The words are not your words; they are everybody's words. They are words that belong to, come from, everybody . . ."

Bill believed that by fracturing the surface of reality, by subjecting the "image track" of everyday life to random factors, Cut-ups could be used as weapons against control agencies. This, combined with his growing belief that he had psychic powers, honed from hundreds of hours of scrying, becoming invisible, and experiencing out-of-body states, made Bill feel that he was in possession of tremendous skills, able to control events by sheer willpower. One day an incident occurred that proved this to be the case, at least in his own mind.

Each day Bill walked down the rue Git-le-Coeur, turned left into the tiny rue de l'Hirondelle, climbed the flight of steps at the end, and came out through an old stone archway into Place St. Michel. There he approached a round newspaper kiosk, the nearest place that sold the *New York Herald Tribune.* It was occupied by a malevolent old woman who looked as if she'd been there since the French Revolution. The floor of her tiny domain was covered with a layer of thickly matted old newspapers to keep out the drafts and the damp. She viewed Bill with ill-disguised hatred, and each day managed to aggravate him by pretending not to understand his request or getting his change wrong or finding ways to cause him some new discomfort, until finally Bill had had enough. He snarled to Brion that he was going to "take care of the old woman." The next day, when he went to buy his *Tribune,* all that was left of her kiosk and of her was a pile of ashes. The kiosk had burned to the ground.

Bill remembered, "The most casual curse is the most effective. I wasn't even conscious of doing this. She annoyed me. I was going to buy a paper at her kiosk and this dog jumped up on me from the street and I shoved it off and she said *'Pour quoi vous battez les petites betes?'* and I said it was jumping up on my coat and she said, *'Quand meme . . .'* I was conscious of considerable ill will on my part. Some days later she was filling a primus stove and it blew up . . . she was in the hospital for a long time."

Bill was slightly conscience-stricken but rather satisfied with the result, as it proved the efficacy of his methods. He was surprised at how strong his powers were. The pile of ashes remained there for months for no one bothered to clean them away. Bill and Brion often sat outside a café on Place St. Michel, looking at the spot where the kiosk once stood. One day, as they were sipping their coffee, they witnessed a young Vietnamese boy dig among the ashes with his bare hands and pull out a whole hatful of slightly blackened coins. As both Bill and Brion were short of funds at that time, Brion said to Bill, "William, I don't think your operation was a complete success." But Bill replied, "I am very glad that that beautiful young Oriental boy made this happy find at the end of the rainbow . . ."

Allen and Bill had been in constant communication ever since Allen had returned to New York. Since then Allen had traveled in South America, following Bill's footsteps in search of yagé (ayahuasca), a hallucinogenic vine used by local Indians. Allen, surrounded by the jungle's screaming monkeys and mosquitoes, had received some encouraging letters from Bill, reassuring Allen that everything was all right when he thought the drug was driving him mad. "There is no thing to fear," Bill reminded him. "Vaya adalante. Look. Listen. Hear. Your AYUASKA consciousness is more valid than 'Normal Consciousness.' Whose 'Normal consciousness?' Why return to? Why are you surprised to see me? You are following in my steps. I know thee way. And yes know the area better than you, I think." These, along with Bill's letters to Allen *from* the jungle, were published by City Lights in 1963 as *The Yagé Letters*.

At Bill's request, Allen sent him a gram of mescaline from New York. Bill sent him copies of *Minutes To Go* and *The Exterminator* and kept him informed of his progress with Cut-ups. Bill was used to discussing his work to Allen by letter—most of *Naked Lunch* had been written that way. Now Bill explained what he was doing with his new novel, *The Soft Machine.* In a letter written September 5, 1960, from

London, he told Allen: "The cut-up method is a tool which I am learning to use after a year of intensive experiments. There is no reason to keep cut-up material that is not useful to the purpose. Often from a page of cut-ups I will use one or two sentences. It depends on the material cut and the purpose in cut. In *Minutes To Go* and *The Exterminator* I was using cut-up material intact. At the time I had not learned to select. Also was more concerned with using the cut-ups as fact assessing instrument. When used for poetic bridge work procedure is different. Like I write a page of prose or prose poem straight. Then cut once or twice or more. And select from all sections what I find most valuable. A sifting panning process."

The letters continued to pass between Allen and Bill: an offer from Bill to lend money, an offer from Allen to find Bill a publisher for an article. Early in 1961 Allen told Bill of the plan that he and Peter Orlovsky had to live in India for several years. The idea was to go first to Paris, then make their way across Europe, visiting many of the countries and cities that they had missed on their first tour, then continue to the Middle East, East Africa, India, and eventually go on to the Far East. Allen told Bill he would see him in Paris in March.

Allen and Peter left New York on the *S.S. America* on March 23, 1961, bound for Le Havre. Despite the cold and flurries of snow, a small group of their friends gathered on the dock to wave them off, knowing that they would not see them again for several years. Shortly before they left, Allen received a letter from Bill saying that he would not be in Paris after the 15th of the month: "I am leaving for Southern Spain or Tangier so will see you there? Or what are your plans? . . . Right now I want to get out of Paris as quick as possible. Don't like it. Never did." He asked Allen to write him at the Beat Hotel and the letter would be forwarded. It appeared to have been a sudden decision because Bill had written a very chatty letter to Allen only three days previously, which made no mention of a trip south, though in a letter written back in January he had stated that he might soon make a move south.

Brion had gradually supplanted Allen in Bill's affections and for several years now had been his mentor, fulfilling the role that Allen normally assumed as editor, friend, and business adviser. Brion had felt threatened by Allen's imminent arrival and, as Bill had to leave France anyway because his three-month visa was up, Brion made a convincing case that Bill should go to Morocco instead of making his usual day-trip to Brussels to get a new entry permit. This would leave Brion to explain Cut-ups to Allen, something that was essential if Allen was to understand properly what Bill doing in his work. Bill agreed. As far as he was concerned, Cut-ups were a deconditioning agent, almost a new form of psychotherapy, a way to see reality clearly without nostalgia or sentimentality. In his letter explaining his work on *The Soft Machine*, Bill had told Allen, "The 'pain' referred to is pain of total awareness. I am not talking mystical 'greater awareness.' I mean complete alert awareness at all times of what is in front of you. LOOK OUT NOT IN. No talking to SO CALLED SELF. NO 'INTROSPECTION.' Eyes off that navel. LOOK OUT TO SPACE. This means kicking ALL HABITS. Word HABIT. SELF HABIT. BODY HABIT. Kicking junk [a] breeze in comparison. Total awareness = Total pain = CUT."

Cut-ups had changed Bill. He had come to believe that the only way to find out what someone was *really* saying was to cut up their words and get at the deeper meaning hidden inside. After working intensively with words, photographs, and tape recordings, he now applied this technique to people themselves, metaphorically dissecting his friends and acquaintances to "see who was inside," who they *truly* were, or, more important, who they were an agent for. Having dabbled with Scientology and been trained as an anthropologist at Harvard, Bill was able detach himself from his old friendships and dissect them with a cold, unsentimental methodology, which horrified Ginsberg when they finally did meet again.

In that Cut-ups prefigured Antonia Gramsci's concept of deconstruction of the text, this was yet another example of Burroughs's autodidactic explorations leading him in a direction that others would later investigate. In his *Prison Notebooks* Gramsci states, "The starting point of critical elaboration is the consciousness of what one really is, and is 'knowing thyself' as a product of the historical process to date, which has deposited in you an infinity of traces, without leaving an inventory, therefore it is imperative at the outset to compile such an inventory." It was such an inventory that Burroughs was looking for, both in others and in himself.

Allen and Peter arrived in Paris and were welcomed by Madame Rachou. They went immediately to Brion's room to find out what was happening. Brion had not previously met Allen and behaved in a very standoffish manner toward him. Allen thought he was being unnecessarily mysterious and furtive, as if he knew some great secret but wasn't telling. Brion told Allen bluntly that Bill had left town because he did not want to see him, and in the course of conversation Allen realized that there had been some dramatic changes in Bill in the three years since he'd last seen him and that Cut-ups were clearly far more than a literary device to Bill and Brion. Allen decided to tread warily around Gysin, who appeared to Allen to be very paranoid. Slowly he began to piece together what had been going on in Paris: the mirror-gazing, the scrying, the manifestations of psychic energy, the Cut-ups, the controlling agents, and the massive drug use on Bill's part (Brion smoked hashish but disapproved of junk). Allen thought it best to bide his time and see what happened.

Reeling slightly from these peculiar developments, Allen and Peter unpacked their bags and went out for a walk along Blvd St. Germain. As they neared the Deux Magots, they ran into Gregory, who had arrived that day from Greece. They had made arrangements to meet in Paris but had not expected to see him for another week. Gregory explained more about Brion and his paranoia, Cut-ups, the Dreamachines, and Bill's latest theories about everyone's being an agent, and the picture began to make more sense. Allen knew that he would see Bill soon, so he decided to make the most of his Paris stay and worry about Bill later.

Allen found that John Hohnsbeam, an old friend of his from his college days at Columbia, had taken a large luxury penthouse in the sixteenth-century apartment building on the corner of the rue Git-le-Coeur, overlooking the Seine. To mark their reunion Hohnsbeam gave a big cocktail party. They also found that tenor saxman Allen Eager was staying at the Beat Hotel, as well as two other old friends from New York, Bob Thompson and Stan Persky. Brion introduced Allen to Harold Norse, whom Allen remembered from an encounter on the New York subway eighteen years earlier when Allen was a freshman at college. Norse had an exhibit of his paintings in the small basement art gallery beneath the English Bookshop, which they all attended. Norse called his paintings "Cosmographs" or cosmic writings because he used the principle of chance in their creation. He threw different-colored Pelikan inks over sheets of Bristol paper at random and then washed them off in the bidet. The ink swirled and settled on the paper, giving strange psychedelic shapes and details that looked as if they had been meticulously drawn, despite the fact that they were untouched by human hand. Burroughs had liked them very much for the way they incorporated random elements and chance operations, and he wrote the following text for the announcement card:

> The ink drawings of Harold Norse are charged with a special intensity of messages from unexplored areas spelled out in color. These are maps of psychic areas, that is to say they have a definite function. Art for its own sake is no longer a tenable position. The artist is a map maker and his work is valid in so far as his maps are accurate. Poetry is a place. The drawings of Norse map a place. And anyone can go there who will make the necessary travel arrangements. Poetry is for everyone. Harold Norse reached the place of his pictures by a special route which he is now prepared to reveal so that others can travel there. So that others can reach the same area on paper or canvas or mixing colors in the street, you can paint anywhere. Pick out the blues as you walk and the reds and greens and yellows and mix them according to the method of Harold Norse and you will reach the area where painting occurs. What is painting? What is writing? Art? Literature? These words have no meaning now. This is the space age and we need

precise maps of space areas. Only the painting and writing that give us precise maps of some psychic areas serve a function at this intersection point of word and image that we call present time.

Norse had been working with the Greek sculptor Takis, whose work consisted largely of metal objects attached to thin wires and suspended in the air by the use of large electromagnets so that they appeared to be defying gravity. Takis designed the installation of Norse's show using the same system. The pictures hung in the air, tethered to the wall by wires, which appeared to be the only thing preventing them from flying away. By attaching metal sheeting to Norse himself beneath his clothing and positioning him over some carefully arranged magnets, Takis took photographs of the artist flying, which were often reproduced. Takis was a frequent visitor to the Beat Hotel and Burroughs had written the text for his *l'impossible* exhibit at the Iris Clert Gallery in Paris in 1960.

Guy Harloff, who had left the hotel and was living in an apartment around the corner in the rue Saint Andre des Arts, was apparently outraged that Norse should get a show when he had been trying to exhibit for years without success. He was rude to Norse and a fight almost erupted on the steps leading down to the *cave*. Despite Harloff's great height, Norse pinned him to the wall with his arm across his throat, and Gaït Frogé's boyfriend, Norman Rubington, had to intervene. One of the many guests at the opening was Henri Michaux, who had remained interested in the activities of the American expatriates.

Allen and Peter arranged to see Michaux soon after they arrived. They met on an agreed-upon street corner and walked about a mile with him to a café he particularly liked, where they had lunch. As before, they talked about drugs. Michaux said that he had been taking mushrooms but he told them, "I am less interested in the visions that people have with drugs. Now I am more interested in how they manifest their experience afterward, what they do with it later." Through Michaux, Allen and Peter were able to get ahold of some mescaline and Peter shot 250 mg in the vein. It came on very fast but it wasn't as frightening as he thought it would be. After six hours, he took a shot of heroin to level himself out again.

Peter enjoyed Paris. He enrolled in French classes but they didn't go very well—for example, on a test he wrote, "Je suis un livre" instead of "J'ai un livre"—but it didn't upset him; he was much more interested in learning Hindi since India was their ultimate destination. Healthy and active, Peter went to the gym and worked out, and soon found a number of girls to go to bed with. He was letting his hair grow long and wrote to LeRoi Jones, "Soon I will have enough. My long hair will cover my window."

Allen, too, was thinking about girls, but only thinking about them. One April morning, at 4 A.M., high on heroin, he wrote a draft of the poem that later appeared as "This Form of Life Needs Sex," in which he returns to the familiar theme of his fear of women:

> *I will have to accept women if I want to continue the race.*
> . . .
> *Between me and oblivion an unknown woman stands:*
> . . .
> *I'm stuck having to unlearn Peter's gaunt cheeks & my liberties inside it, and his growing hair—and how does one learn to like girls anyway—I like the feel of getting my naked prick covered by cunt and I like the feel of the man doing it.*
> *But I'm frightened to look into the eye*
>   *of real creation*
> *Frightened to know that God's a girl.*

Another day, Allen, Peter, and Gregory drove out to visit Céline in Meudon in a friend's car, but he was sick and in the hospital and they had to content themselves with examining the rusty bedsprings in the overgrown lawn. They would not get to see Céline again as he died later that year. Other days they all got high and visited the stained glass of Notre Dame and Ste. Chapelle, and felt nostalgic about their past times in Paris. Ginsberg felt quite sentimental about his return to the city. He wrote in his journal, "In bed naked in chamber of 9 rue Git-le-Coeur again—all the gray stains of Paris buildings familiar outside, cars racing around the corner down the cobble roadway along the Seine."

By now, Allen had heard from Bill, who wrote on April 7 from Tangier, "Sorry I could not have been there to greet you in Paris but my time there was up in more ways than one . . . hope you are digging Paris and write me your plans. Love Bill." He did not sound in bad shape, and there was nothing in the letter to indicate that he did not want to see them. Allen assumed that it was all Brion's fault and continued to tread carefully around him. Allen wrote to Bill, voicing his unease at Brion's talk of "psychic forces" and identification with Hassan-i-Sabbah and asking if it was true that Bill did not want to see him. Bill replied, "No I do not think Brion superstitious. All novelists of any consequence are psychic assassins in a very literal sense . . ." He went on to say, "Yes, Allen I do want to see you but I did want you to see Brion first . . . come on down any time." Allen felt relieved and devoted himself more thoroughly to enjoying the pleasures that Paris offered.

Jack Gelber's "Beat" play *The Connection*, about junkie jazz musicians, had been an off-Broadway success for the Living Theatre in New York and filmmaker Shirley Clarke had filmed it in performance. Clarke and the cast of the play were all in Paris, en route to the South of France, where her film was entered that year in the Cannes Film Festival. Allen, Gregory, and Peter knew them all from the San Remo bar and other downtown Manhattan hangouts. In general they found that, despite leaving New York for foreign shores, they had stepped into a ready-made community since much of Manhattan seemed to be there with them. Even Allen's friend, the great pianist Thelonius Monk, was in town and invited them to see him play the Olympia. Paris was full of drugs and it was a very stoned audience.

Although Bill was not there, Allen still felt the familiar need to assume responsibility for Bill's manuscripts and, despite his suspicions about Brion, he quickly joined him in the task of editing Bill's new book, *The Soft Machine*, retyping sections and arranging and assigning sections to chapters, as previously it had been one long unbroken text. Brion had been trying—unsucessfully—to knock it into shape for publication before Allen had arrived and was happy to have Allen share the task. In fact they were a good team. Brion had been there during the book's creation, so he knew the genesis of most of the pages and which sections belonged together, whereas Allen had a vastly superior literary knowledge and understanding of book production and editing. Together they produced a workable manuscript. Brion produced a design for the cover and Allen wrote an unsigned blurb for the cover flap. Having done all they could, they delivered the book complete to Maurice Girodias. By the end of April they were already revising the proofs and making corrections. Allen wrote to his friend Ted Wilentz, the owner of the 8th Street Bookshop in New York, describing the new book as "very weird and wonderful far out," but Allen did not think it was of the same standard as *Naked Lunch*, largely because of his reservations about the Cut-up technique, which to his way of thinking simply spoiled Bill's wonderful routines. Some of his hesitancy showed through in his cover blurb, in which he expressed his feeling that good Cut-up texts were only possible in the hands of good writers, using good material. His unstated opinion was that the material used in Cut-ups should be the author's own:

> Starting with old and new routines—Lee the Agent, Carl in Freeland, Dr. Benway, Johnny Yen the Image Pusher, Blue Movies, the Meat Grotto, Terminal City and Cut City, TRAK Service, Minraud and the Brass & Copper Street, Permutated Sex, etc.,—William Burroughs presents the original texts and then cuts them up, shifts and recombines them, permutating imagery until it flashes with kaleidoscopic brilliance and sets up a new 3D field in the imagination wherein the secret message behind the routines emerges stronger than ever.
>
> Burroughs uses new methods of writing derived directly from painting techniques as first suggested to him by Brion Gysin—Cut-ups and Permutations—extensions of the collage mosaic structure of *Naked Lunch*. . . . Methods which would

be vain unless the author had something to Cut up to start with: in the hands of a master, the Cut-up technique produces scenes of inhuman beauty and vast eocene nostalgia. This book is a work of art fitting to the mutant moment of the human race as it prepares to leave Earth.

Stroboscopic flicker-lights playing on the Soft Machine of the eye create hallucinations, and even epilepsy. Recurrent flickering of Cut-ups opens up the area of hallucination and makes a map for the human race to invade.

Girodias published *The Soft Machine* in June 1961, and, even though Bill was not in town, it was launched with a party at Gaït Frogé's bookshop.

In April, Jean-Jacques Lebel arrived at the hotel filled with excitement. He had managed to steal a copy of Antonin Artaud's legendary recording *Pour en finir avec le jugement de dieu* (usually translated as "To have done with the judgment of god"—Artaud always spelled "god" in the lower case to show his contempt for organized religion). In 1947, shortly before he died, Artaud had been commissioned to write a radio play by the French State Radio. It was produced by Roger Blin and featured Maria Casares and Artaud himself. Artaud's performance is so tortured, compelling, shattering that the recording was officially banned and was not broadcast until after the 1968 revolution. Jean-Jacques explained how he came to have a copy: "I had a girlfriend who was working for French Radio, and we went into the archives. And there was this thing where certain things were censored, but by getting a key we did an anarchist hijack. It wasn't on tape, it was a record, the archives of the French Radio were all stored on large records, and I hijacked that." Jean-Jacques's girlfriend had a tape copy made and Jean-Jacques invited Allen, Peter, Brion, Harold Norse, and several others to his apartment in Montmartre to hear it.

Jean-Jacques: "So we were in my house, and I didn't know how to use a tape recorder. I had borrowed an old German Grundig, like a suitcase, and all the buttons were written in German and I couldn't understand German. Anyway, we were so stoned out of our heads from hash so we didn't know what the fuck we were doing anyway. We were sitting on the floor and Allen says, 'What are we waiting for? Let's go.' I'd never heard the tape, nobody had heard the tape. It was like having Rimbaud, or Walt Whitman. Can you imagine? We were going to at last hear the great Artaud. Allen, Peter, Gregory, and Harold Norse came, thrilled at the idea of hearing Artaud's actual voice."

Jean-Jacques threaded the tape through and pressed the Play button. Artaud was famous for having invented a new language for this theater piece, but no one was quite prepared for what they heard: "Islsshle dkslishs mmskiels dakjdllai . . ." For twenty minutes they sat in a stoned trance listening to Artaud's unintelligible ranting. Jean-Jacques continued, "Allen says, 'Phew! This guy, he's invented a completely new vocabulary. A new grammar. It sounded like something from another planet, perhaps from inside the memory of all the human minds forever.' We were holding a joint in our hands and we didn't even pass it, it was a total celebration of the language above all languages, the universal tongue, you know. Silence. Even Gregory wasn't vomiting. He was really very very deeply moved. One of the great moments of a lifetime. And all of us really holding our breath. Gregory says, 'Okay, I gotta take a piss,' so he gets up, takes a piss. Allen says, 'Let's hear it again,' typical Allen, studying, serious, you know. And then we realized the tape was backwards. I didn't know how to work this damn thing. The girl who gave it to me at the radio station didn't tell me, so I didn't know. So we put it on. And then we heard Artaud's voice and there are parts in the play that are invented but not all, there are certain parts where you hear actual words and sentences. Actually both versions were extraordinary on a higher level of sound, like Tibetan chanting. When you hear the Tibetan monks chanting, you don't know what they are saying, but you get the message. It just goes through you. It was that kind of thing. So we listened to it carefully, over and over again, trying to translate certain passages."

Allen borrowed the tape and, through Allen Eager at the hotel, who had a friend with a recording studio, he had five tape copies made. There were certain people he knew had to hear the tape. One went to Julian Beck and Judith Malina, where it had a tremendous effect upon the future work of the Living Theatre. Another went to poet Michael McClure, who played it to all the San Francisco poets, including Lawrence Ferlinghetti and Philip Lamantia. McClure's book *Ghost Tantras* was directly influenced by the tape. Jean-Jacques has said "Michael has wonderful things to say about that how getting that tape completely reoriented his whole life work." Allen sent a copy to LeRoi Jones, describing it as "Hairraising screams and recitation by Artaud." It had a profound effect on Jones aas well, particularly his novel *The System of Dante's Hell*, and his early plays.

That same month, on April 24, Olympia Press finally published Gregory's first, and only, novel, titled *The American Express*, complete with a dust jacket drawn by Gregory himself. It was launched with a party at Girodias's plush nightclub Le Grand Séverin, in the rue Saint-Séverin. Girodias remembered the book launch: "When *American Express* came out I gave a great party in the nightclub. There was a lawyer from American Express who came and wanted to stop the book from being published; didn't understand what the book was about. It would have been wonderful publicity if he pressed charges but he got chicken, got annoyed when Allen and two or three of his retainers started to undress."

Someone put some sort of hallucinogen into the drinks and many of the guests freaked out. Some passed out in the bathrooms and on the floor. Maurice panicked and told Gaït, "You've got to help me clean up this mess before the police get here." Gregory said, "Of course this has to happen at my party." Maurice, adamant, "Never again." Gaït suspected Peter Orlovsky was the guilty party but he denied it. They carried and dragged bodies to the street and all went to the café next door.

Gregory remembered, "That book was written in one month, and it's the one I hate because I really did a fast job on that. It's written so awkwardly, I would have loved to have worked on that one. . . . Syntactically and grammatically it's fucked up. That's what I'm getting at. It's not so much the theme, you know, [but] too many 'he says' and 'she says.' I should know how best to cut that kind of thing out, and just know how the dialogue flows. I could do it in a play fine."

Like Burroughs and Kerouac, Gregory used his friends as the basis for some of his characters. In *American Express*, Burroughs was "Mister D." The female protagonist, Shiva, was Gregory's old girlfriend Sura, who went to India in 1958. She was a brilliant, poetic girl whose parents mistook her introspection and creativity for madness and made her take electric shock treatment. Her given name was Hope, but she changed her name after the shock treatment. She was among the first of the new generation to take off to the subcontinent in search of spirituality and enlightenment.

Gregory appeared in his own book as the unnamed character who was born in the basement beneath the American Express office in Paris and who wanders the world, penniless. There is a poignancy to the description of the character's birth, with its echoes of rape, brutal rejection, and abandonment, which must certainly parallel Gregory's feelings about his own troubled childhood:

> They wheeled her into the basement of the American Express, they held her down, they spread her legs, they plunged into her womb, they yanked the child from her, they punched it into life, they threw it out into the street, it lay there until dawn—
>
> Dawn, and something small and sad rose and walked into the world.

At one point it seemed as if Girodias had managed to sell *American Express* to Doubleday Anchor, causing Gregory to write excitedly to Allen, "That will be florins galore, so I will keep mine responsibilities to thee . . . if Anchor Books takes then I must insist on revising grammar of book which was done in months time speed and heart soul but after months of rest looking at it much much has to be changed."

Unfortunately the sale did not go through and the book has been out of print for thirty years. It is an uneven book, described most aptly by Lebel: "He didn't want to publish it. He didn't put his soul into it at all. He was on junk most of the time anyway."

Bill wrote Allen from Tangier asking him to "come along as soon as you can make it," and to wire the approximate date of arrival in case he took a trip out of town. This seemed further proof that Bill was not hiding from Allen, as Brion had suggested, so Allen, Peter, and Gregory prepared to travel on.

At the beginning of May, Shirley Clarke and the actors from *The Connection* were due to leave for Cannes for the 1961 film festival and invited Allen, Peter, and Gregory to go with them. Clarke had taken a small house just outside town for them all and offered the three poets the use of the basement for the duration. Alan Ansen was also in Paris so he, Allen, Peter, Gregory and his girlfriend Annie Campbell, Allen Eager, and several of the actors from *The Connection* all took the train down together. In a move that added further authenticity to their publicity efforts on behalf of Shirley's film, they brought with them a substantial amount of heroin.

In Cannes, both Peter and Gregory were strung out; Allen was using heroin from time to time but was not hooked. Periodically new supplies would arrive by mail. When Gregory was not arguing with Annie, he was usually in the casino. Once he had lost all of his money, he began to borrow from Allen. After two weeks of watching movies and hanging around the festival, they borrowed a car and drove thirty miles down the coast to St. Tropez, sightseeing. In St. Tropez they ran into Jacques Stern, who was delighted to see them and invited them to come and stay. He had rented a large farmhouse outside the town, but thinking they would be happier closer to the action he rented rooms for them in the best hotel in St. Tropez. For the next two weeks they spent their time mixing with French film stars, sniffing ether and junk, going swimming with the chauffeurs at the Beach Club, and spending their nights eating lobster and drinking champagne at Stern's expense at their hotel. Time drifted and Allen wrote:

A famous personal American in the Port
of Saint Tropez among the rich
eating lobster & scotch and worried about
my figure in a cute blue bikini—
with all my problems solved except
what am I doing here?

The idyllic setup was ruined by Gregory, who argued constantly with their host. Allen wrote to Kerouac, "Gregory quarrelling with Stern ('You stinky cripple'—'You stupid loudmouth poet') until that's unbearable . . . With Gregory drinking it's impossible to maintain amiable calm—finally he gives us boat fare from Marseilles to Tangier and says he'll maybe join us later." Allen, Peter, and Gregory booked passage on a boat that left June 1, which gave them a few days in Marseilles before leaving France. They wired Bill with details of their arrival time and sent him several letters.

They shipped second class to Tangier on the *S.S. Azemour* and looked for Bill at the harbor, expecting to see him standing on the quay with his binoculars, but there was no sign of him. At Moroccan immigration, the police found that Gregory's passport had expired. Gregory wept on the dock and screamed at the American consular official, who did nothing to help. Eventually Gregory was taken back on the boat and thrown in the hold to be held under police guard until the ship reached Casablanca, the capital, where there was an American embassy. As the ship was preparing to depart, Allen leapt back onboard to keep Gregory company while Peter took care of the luggage and the hotel and wired money on ahead for them in Casablanca. For thirty hours Gregory lay on his straw bed below deck. He refused to eat, but some friendly African cooks persuaded him to drink some coffee. At Casablanca, Allen went at once to the embassy, where the staff people were sympathetic and helpful and rushed to the dock to rescue Gregory with a new passport. Gregory meanwhile remained in hysterics.

They took the bus back to Tangier and finally met Bill at the Hotel Muniria. Paul Bowles was there as well, waiting for them in Bill's garden. A year later Allen wrote Kerouac, "There was Bill, I must say rather indifferent to all our dreary hegira. Anyway that began two and a half months of (looking back on it) incomprehensible petty jealousies and horrors, actually a great weird scene."

Allen, Peter, and Gregory took rooms at the Hotel Armor, just around the corner from Bill. For $20 a month, Allen and Peter had a tiled room on the roof, which led to a glassed-in conservatory and a terrace looking out over the rooftops to Tangier Harbor and to Spain. The view of the sunrise was quite spectacular and in the cool of the predawn morning Allen would sit out on the patio at a wooden table with his typewriter and a bottle of cold soda to answer letters as the eastern sky grew rapidly lighter. Cocks crowed and a few blue lights would be on around the Hotel Cecil down on the beach. Gregory had a larger room, downstairs, for $14 a month.

Bill was strung out, with sunken cheeks, shiny protruding cheekbones, and a thin body. He gestured with jerky junkie movements and appeared indifferent to their arrival. Bill was still obsessively investigating Cut-ups and had extended Cut-up theory into every aspect of his life. He coldly interrogated Allen, demanding to know who had sent him, who he was an agent for: "If we cut you up, who would we find inside? Lionel Trilling!" Bill found a lot of programming from Allen's days at Columbia University. He found ideas internalized from Allen's father and claimed to find traces of ancient Jewish culture, though Ginsberg had had little in the way of a traditional Jewish upbringing and had not been indoctrinated in the religion.

Allen, as usual, was prepared to go along with Bill's ideas but was shocked when Bill insisted that Allen should interrogate him, since everyone, including Bill, was an unwitting agent for someone else, propagating their received ideas. Bill was aided in all this by Ian Sommerville and Bill's new acolyte, a handsome aimless wealthy seventeen-year-old gay English junkie named Mikey Portman, who was besotted with Bill and slavishly imitated everything Bill did—choosing the same food, drinking mint tea whenever Bill had it, and, of course, advocating the same ideas, which he would trot out before Bill himself had even had a chance to speak. Mikey had turned up the year before, arriving unannounced at Bill's door at the Rushmore Hotel, where he was living at the time, and inveigled his way into Bill's life, much to the irritation of Ian, who was still at Cambridge. Mikey normally liked black men but after about six months he and Bill did go to bed together. Ian knew immediately and was sulky for weeks. Ian and Mikey did not get along and, out of respect for Ian's feelings, Bill did at least manage to stop Mikey from moving into the hotel, though he was not strong enough to prevent him from constantly hanging around. Bill, Ian, and Mikey had evolved a complex series of in-group routines involving Cut-ups, and Allen and Peter found it hard to distinguish Bill's actual ideas from these fictional rants, one of which was that women were in fact alien agents put on earth by a trust of giant insects from another galaxy. Allen was irritated by Ian and Mikey and wrote to Kerouac, "My feeling was that they had replaced us in Bill's affections and intimacy," and described them as "scampering and skipping behind his elbows like demons, simpering at us all."

Mikey made it very difficult for Allen to have any time alone with Bill as he was always there, interrupting, telling Allen Bill's views on this or that. Allen wrote Lucien Carr, "Bill's all hung up with 18 yr. old spoiled brat English Lord who looks like a palefaced Rimbaud but is a smart creep—Apparently Lady Portman his mother gave him into Bill's hands to look after here—platonic anyhoo—But Bill got some kinda awful relation with him and the kid bugs everyone so intimacy with Bill is limited and Bill absentminded all the time—however very busy with his Cut-up experiments and applying it to pictorial collages and taking brownie photographs and very busy and creative—also did new book in Cut-up method, very pure experiments and strangely good reading tho oft toneless, 'The Soft Machine.'"

Allen had also changed in the years since he and Bill had lived at the Beat Hotel. He had experimented with psilocybin with Timothy Leary and of course had taken yagé. In addition to extensive experimentation with drugs, Allen and Peter had worked hard at extending the idea of the "big communal love-brain" that Ginsberg and Burroughs had discussed at the Beat Hotel. They organized orgies and had a series of multiple sex partners. It came as a shock, then, for them to find that Bill had done an abrupt turnaround and rather than try to extend his love circle he no longer believed in love, affection, or even in friendship, claiming that he was beyond such things. Bill felt at the time that he was no longer controlled by passions, emotions, friendships, fantasies, or even by language itself.

Peter in particular was appalled by Bill's pronouncements that all women should be exterminated just as soon as males had found some form of parthenogenesis. Peter argued strongly in favor of sex and women, getting red-faced and angry, remonstrating with them until his voice grew hoarse, not realizing that Burroughs and the boys were purposefully goading him. They taunted Peter mercilessly for his love of women, claiming that if they cut him up they would find a Venusian inside. Allen tried to get Peter to stop but Peter felt so strongly that love and open sexuality between men and women was the answer to most of the world's problems that he believed it was an obligation to argue in defense of heterosexuality. He refused to give in, which of course only provoked Bill and the boys to come up with even more outrageous suggestions and proposals. Peter was no match for the cynicism and sophistication of Burroughs, and at the end of each bout he retired feeling hurt, frustrated, and persecuted.

When Allen tried to get him to ignore their taunts, Peter interpreted this as Allen's giving support for Bill's anti-women position and this in turn led to arguments between Allen and Peter, which went right to the heart of their complex relationship. Peter believed that Allen had made him a homosexual and often felt swamped by the sheer force of Allen's will, sometimes feeling that he was being made to do things he did not want to do. The arguments provoked by Bill enabled Peter to get a clear look at the situation and made him think that it was time for him to spend some time away from Allen.

Allen, for his part, was horrified at how inhuman Bill had become and was distraught at the thought of Peter's leaving. He was unable to coldly dismiss his years of friendship with Bill or his seven years of "marriage" to Peter, despite Bill's criticism. Bill told Allen that he was grasping and dependent on his old friendships and criticized him for his attachments to both Peter and himself. Allen had always regarded Bill as his guru and suddenly did not know what to think. Allen wrote to Lawrence Ferlinghetti about Peter's leaving, "We had big arguments about future of universe in Tangier. He wanted it to be sex-love, Burroughs wanted it to be unknown Artaud mutation out of bodies. I was undecided, confused. I still am except Burroughs seems to have killed 'Hope' in any known form. The Exterminator is serious. Peter wanted innocence and sex apocalypse. It got very serious. I was vomiting."

Throughout all this Bill continued to work on tape Cut-ups with Ian, dropping in layer upon layer of random interruptions dubbed over recordings of speech and radio static. He sat around his room for hours, listening to the "messages" on his three transistor radios, all tuned off-station and blaring white-noise radio static. He sat for hours, eyes closed before the Dreamachine that Ian had built, and had powerful joints burning in ashtrays all over the room. The photo collages that Bill first began while working on *Naked Lunch* had now become collages of photographs of collages of photographs of collages. He was trying to reduce the image to its purest essence and get at the message hidden in all the blur. With the aid of good strong majoun, Bill's home-made hashish candy, he often found interesting blobs and phantoms hidden in the picture, which he would point out to Mikey or to Allen, though most people could see only the grain of the photographic paper itself. He made collages of newspapers and *Time* magazine, sticking Khrushchev's mouth on Kennedy's forehead in the classic photomontage tradition of John Heartfield and the Surrealists.

Bill told Allen that poetry and words were finished, and Allen was saddened to find that Bill had not even bothered to read the copy of *Kaddish* that Allen had sent him when it was published. Allen began to resent the whole Cut-up theory, though he did try it himself. Using speeches made during the Bay of Pigs incident, Allen cut up a speech by Khrushchev with one by Kennedy. The result read: "The purpose of these maneuvers is offensive weapons."

The situation was further exacerbated by Gregory, who each day tried to borrow $10 from Peter. Each day Peter refused, saying that his $100 from the Veterans Administration should be spent only on food and essentials. His refusal inevitably resulted in an argument, during which Gregory put him down. When Alan Ansen arrived on July 13 to join in the fun, Peter complained to him that Gregory had told him he shouldn't write poems or paint but should do something physical like swim or play baseball instead. Allen, who was listening, couldn't believe that Gregory would say such a thing, but Peter insisted that he had recognized Gregory's antipathy ever since 1959, when he wrote his first two poems. Gregory, who was drunk, soon clarified his position by telling them all outright that he had never liked Peter's poems, though he was later to write a laudatory introduction to Peter's 1978 Pocket Poets volume *Clean Asshole Poems and Smiling Vegetable Songs*.

Minutes later Gregory and Allen were in the middle of a huge drunken argument, with Allen pointing out that he had supported Gregory in Paris, paid his train fare to Cannes, and lent him even more money after he'd spent $100 on clothes and lost the rest of his own money at the casino. Gregory now owed Allen over $200. Allen eventually gave up after the argument degenerated into a mud-slinging match between Gregory and Peter. Peter was fed up with all of them. He wrote to Kerouac, "Will buy my ticket today or tomorrow for boat to Istanbul on July 27, 150 bucks—10 days trip. I'm very glad I'm leaving. Want to be on my own—feel Allen and Gregory are creeping cancer to my soul. That's that."

In August everyone began to go their separate ways. Alan Ansen returned to Venice. Allen took a boat to Athens, his life shaken up by Burroughs and the Cut-up technique, his arrangements in confusion, separated from Peter. His only plan now was to meet Gary Snyder in India on New Year's Day. In fact, however, two months later he met up with Peter in Tel Aviv, and they continued their journey together as planned to Bombay, Calcutta, and Benares, where they were to live for the next two years.

Bill, Ian, Mikey, and Gregory went to London. From there Bill continued to Cambridge, Massachusetts, to take part in a conference on psychedelic drugs organized by Timothy Leary at Harvard. Bill was not impressed with the way that Leary handled things and left Cambridge as soon as the conference was over. After a few months in New York City, he returned to the Empress Hotel in London, then took a sublet on a flat from his English publisher, Marion Boyers, at 52 Lancaster Terrace. Mikey moved in to share the rent but proved to be such a nuisance that Bill quickly moved on, and by the beginning of March 1962, Bill was living with Ian in a basement flat at 5 Lancaster Terrace.

But by the beginning of June, Bill was back in the Beat Hotel, where he remained for the rest of the year.

10 Fade Out In Gray Room

In Heaven they have rooms
very much like yours
—perhaps a little shabbier—
this one has 3 chairs and an ancient tile floor
. . .
But everyone in this Hotel lives.
Nobody ever dies.
Kaja, "In Heaven at 9 rue Git-le-Coeur"

Brion was the only member of the group who had remained at the Beat Hotel, holed up in room 25, instead of visiting Bill in Tangier. While the others were away, a new vehicle had started to publicize the work of Bill, Brion, and Ian. Toward the end of 1961, Maurice Girodias launched *Olympia*, a literary magazine in which his authors and friends were heavily featured. The first issue included ten episodes from *The Soft Machine*, the chapter from J. P. Donleavy's *The Ginger Man* that was censored from the British and American editions, an excerpt from Terry Southern and Mason Hoffenberg's *Candy*, and a section from Iris Owens's *The Woman Thing*. The second issue, published in February 1962, had a full-color cover photograph of Brion Gysin and Ian Sommerville looking at a Dreamachine, and included not only essays on flicker by Sommerville and the Dreamachine by Gysin but cut-out plans to enable readers to build one of their own. *Olympia* was, in a way, the house journal of the Beat Hotel: Kay Johnson, known as Kaja, a writer, painter, and poet from New Orleans who now lived in Gregory's old attic room 41, had a long poem entitled

"I Worship Paperclips" in the third issue, and the same issue featured a short story by Jonathan Kozol called "The Contest."

Bill returned from the States and continued to spend much of his time at the hotel, drifting in and out in his suit and tie, so anonymous-looking that most people did not notice his presence at all—just as he liked it. At one point, when Bill and Bill Belli were sitting in the Club Chameleon just around the corner from the hotel in the rue St. Andre des Arts, Burroughs told Belli, "My goal in life is total anonymity." Right then Gregory Corso burst through the door, having just arrived back from a trip to Assisi, and yelled at the top of his voice, "Bill Burroughs! I love you! I love you!" Bill pursed his lips and sank deeper into his chair and muttered, "All right Gregory. Calm down." It was hard not to draw attention when Corso was around. There is an evocative description of Burroughs from this period, written in the latter half of 1962 by Ann Morrissett:

> Nine Lies-the-Heart: the door opens on a narrow cell with a bright window. A high figure is silhouetted against the light. Gradually I make out its features. Stretched over the skeleton and meat is a fine yellow parchment on which have been written many things now carefully erased. Dark rimmed glasses are painted around the eyes.
>
> Will you have some tea, he says . . . A fat brown pot sits cold on the gas burner. Wedged in the radiator on the other side of the window is a thin smouldering stick. . . .

While the others were away, Brion had continued to try and market his Dreamachine. The Philips Corporation sent an executive from Holland to discuss marketing the machine but he slipped on a dog turd in the hallway, turned on his heel, and left. Brion looked to be on the verge of a breakthrough when the Musée des Arts Decoratifs in Paris exhibited the Dreamachine in its 1962 show *The Object*, but it received a very mixed reaction. Most people get no visions on their first sitting and some people do not respond at all to the alpha band, which causes the visions. Gysin joked, "The only problem with getting the Dreamachine displayed is that all the museums curators don't have alpha waves." Privately, however, he naturally had a conspiracy theory to explain its failure to take off: "The Dreamachine should have been the great drugless turn-on of the sixties which would have solved all my financial problems and it didn't work. It was, and still is, too new. It's the opening of a whole new territory which in a way is a threat to very many people who are using the same means for control or are using the same means to make great sums of money. And when the prototype of the machine which the museum later bought was being installed, and all the museum heads were standing around, a young technician was just putting the switch in and when he turned it on and shut his eyes, at my bidding, the first thing he said was, 'Why all the museum is in here!' Well, you should have seen the looks on all of the faces." No museum wanted a machine that rendered the rest of their collection redundant.

In December 1962, just before the Beat Hotel closed, the third of Bill's Olympia Press books was published: *The Ticket That Exploded*, complete with two sections—"A Strange Bed" and "The Black Fruit"— written in collaboration with Mikey Portman, a page of calligraphy to end the book by Brion Gysin, and a dust wrapper design by Ian Sommerville. The dust wrapper is one of the few published examples of the massive photocollages that Sommerville had worked on with Burroughs. Photo collages were photographed, and then used in collages themselves, until the original image was reduced to microscopic size and lost in the grain of the photographic paper. These images were also printed in reverse to provide a mirror image.

Though Olympia Press books were paperbacks, easily recognizable by their characteristic green wrappers, Girodias tended to add a dust jacket to those titles he regarded as literary: Donleavy's *Ginger Man*, Queneau's *Zazie dans le métro*, or Philip O'Connor's *Steiner's Tour*. All three of Burroughs's Olympia books were issued with dust jackets. The jackets reflect perfectly Burroughs's time at the Beat Hotel. *The Soft Machine*, for instance, is an example of a first edition's truly reflecting the moment of a book's creation, with its Gysin-designed dust jacket and its Ginsberg jacket blurb. Bill's

262 The Beat Hotel

new book, *The Ticket That Exploded*, with its endlessly multiplying Sommerville photographic collage design, was launched with a party at the English Bookshop. Bill signed a copy of the book: "For Gregory Corso with best wishes William Burroughs." "Is that all I get?" Gregory muttered.

It was just like the old days: Brion, Bill, and Gregory all ensconced at the Beat Hotel, a new Olympia Press book to sign, another book launch in the hopelessly overcrowded English Bookshop, with Gaït Frogé squeezing past everyone, pouring drinks, laughing, handing Bill more copies to sign.

The two Cut-up books, *The Soft Machine* and *The Ticket That Exploded*, were regarded abroad as too extreme to be commercial. Barney Rosset at Grove Press had fought an obscenity case over *Naked Lunch* and was disappointed to find that Bill's follow-up was so hard to read. Bill's British publisher, John Calder, felt the same way and they both requested that Bill make the books more reader-friendly. Bill agreed and made extensive revisions to both of them before their American and British publications. In a March 1963 interview, Bill explained, "With *The Soft Machine* I had many complaints it was difficult to read and going through it again I felt this was true so I rewrote it completely introducing about 65 pages of straight narrative." Most people feel that the Cut-up books are still inaccessible, and they are, if the reader is looking for a straightforward narrative; they are best approached as prose poems.

Bill moved back into the hotel in late May 1962. He was living in room 30 on the fifth floor. There was a two-burner gas stove on a table in the corner, where Bill cooked himself bacon and eggs each morning, followed by yogurt. Bill had grown used to a proper English breakfast during his sojourns at the Empress Hotel but the nearest café in Paris that served bacon and eggs was all the way over on the Right Bank. The room also contained a bed, two chairs, and a large brown wardrobe. The room's single, bare lightbulb was suspended over the table, upon which sat Bill's battered old Spanish portable typewriter. Hanging over the table on the wall were the four wire filing trays Brion had given him. The shelf was piled with tapes spilling out of their boxes, but Bill's tape recorder was out of order, its buttons punched to death during a Cut-up tape session. The window looked out across the rue Git-le-Coeur to a confusion of sloping roofs and crooked chimney pots.

It was during the following summer that the final flowering of avant-garde experimentation at the Beat Hotel came. Brion Gysin had met the young English filmmaker Antony Balch at a friend's apartment across the street at 10 rue Git-le-Coeur. Balch described their meeting: "It was through Jacques Leiser's friend Jean-Claude de Feugas that I met Brion Gysin and William Burroughs. A chance mention of Jean Cocteau's journeys through mirrors brought instant scorn from Brion who said he traveled through every day, and would I like to phone ODE 41.66 to find out how."

Bill and Brion had known all along that the ultimate extension of the Cut-up technique had to be in film, but this was an area that neither of them knew much about. Brion remembered "saying to William that . . . we should get hold of somebody that could help us—that was in the business already. And right in that same short street which is only one block long, somebody that I knew just as a neighbor invited me to a party, and that's where we met Antony Balch."

Balch made his first amateur films at the age of ten, screening them in his living room and charging the family admission. He would always rent a bit of newsreel to show beforehand and put on a proper screening. Before he left for boarding school he always posted a screening timetable on the living room door, which he hoped that Delta, his mother, adhered to, screening the films he had made or rented even when he was away. Delta worked in the film industry and through her he acquired a knowledge of all aspects of the business. She had begun her career as a singer but claimed that she lost her voice when Antony was born. She became an actress, did stand-in parts, and worked in other organizational areas of the film business, including accounting and financing.

Antony was interested in all aspects of filmmaking, from exhibiting and distribution to directing. He worked as a production assistant on television commercials, which gave him experience in lighting, print grading, cutting, editing, and eventually to directing; his first "film" was a television commercial for Kit-E-Kat cat food. Antony: "That kind of filmmaking was a very good training ground because you really did do everything." Antony turned his hand to all aspects of filmmaking; for instance, he subtitled Alain Resnais's 1961 classic *L'Anée Dernière a Marienbad* (*Last Year at Marienbad*) as well as going on to run two cinemas in London—the Jacey on Piccadilly and the Times on Baker Street—and writing film reviews for *Continental Film Review*. He distributed European "art" films that showed bare breasts or perhaps a flash of buttocks, retitling them for the British soft-core porn market. His own first attempt at filmmaking proper was a campy short shot in Paris in 1959, which included an old man, a would-be ballet dancer prancing about under the bridges of Paris, and Antony's friend Jean-Claude de Feugas lying naked on a funeral couch surrounded by candles. He was disappointed with the footage and abandoned the project.

Antony was a rather fey young man, tall, slim, impeccably dressed with full wet lips and an upper-class English public school accent. He and Brion became very close friends. Brion introduced him to Scientology, and Antony became a "clear," but most of all it was the Cut-up technique that intrigued him. Over the next few years he was to make three experimental films with Burroughs and Gysin: *Towers Open Fire*, *The Cut-ups*, and *Bill and Tony*.

The first footage he shot with them was in and around the Beat Hotel for a proposed twenty-three-minute documentary on the lives of William Burroughs and Brion Gysin, to be called *Guerrilla Conditions*. (The number 23 had become a leitmotif in Burroughs's work.) Using a hand-wound wartime De Vry 35mm camera, he filmed Bill in the street market on rue de Buci, buying a shopping basket. He did a number of takes of Bill walking up and down the rue Git-le-Coeur, hunched over in his Chesterfield coat, and of Bill pushing through a crowd carrying a suitcase. He filmed Bill lighting a cigarette, and walking down Blvd St. Germain past the church, talking to Jean-Jacques Lebel. They went to the Paris Zoo and filmed Bill looking impassively at a vulture, both bony-faced. There were a number of other sequences, including Bill standing in front of dramatic posters for St. Yorre table water and climbing the water steps from the Seine to the quai.

Brion was filmed hurrying from the rue l'Hirondelle to the rue Git-le-Coeur and entering the hotel wearing a unique zip-up sweater that had been knitted to include four of his calligrams on the back. Most of the footage of Brion was shot indoors: Brion in room 25 doing his famous magic smoking trick, where he appears to set fire to his finger then blows smoke from his mouth; shots of Brion painting in his room, a Dreamachine behind him on a table. Further Dreamachine footage was shot at the Musée des Arts Decoratifs at *The Object* show.

Guerrilla Conditions was ultimately not completed, though Antony continued to film at the Hotel Chelsea in New York, the Villa Muniria in Tangier, and the Empress Hotel in London. The footage was not wasted because Antony used it in two subsequent films: *Towers Open Fire* and *Cut-ups*. After the Beat Hotel filming, Antony had a better idea of what he wanted to do and began shooting further footage to make *Towers Open Fire*, which was mostly done as a collaboration with Bill. In January 1963, they shot a scene in the boardroom of the British Film Institute using his De Vry 35mm. Among the "board members" was author Alex Trocchi, whom Burroughs had met at the August 1962 Edinburgh Writers' Conference. From there Bill and Antony went on to Gibraltar for the shots of radio transmission towers, and to Tangier where the garden scenes with Sommerville and Portman were shot. Antony included footage of himself masturbating in the film, filmed from above the waist in his mother's house, using his left hand to hold the camera.

Towers Open Fire was Bill's first acting job, and in it he plays Colonel Bradley, a commando figure dressed in camouflage fatigues, tin hat, and gas mask and armed with a large Ping-Pong-ball gun bought at Hamleys Toy Shop on Regent Street, London. Bill uses it to shoot down photographs of his family. The script, written by Burroughs, was based loosely on the text of the same name that finally appeared in his novel *Nova Express* in 1964. Though not a Cut-up, the film used a number of experimental techniques, including hand-painting a section of the film. Antony laboriously painted each frame of a strip of clear leader so that a series of hand-colored dots descend from the sky onto Mikey Portman in this otherwise black-and-white film. Ian assembled a sound track with Burroughs at the Empress Hotel, including Jajouka trance music recorded by Brion in Morocco, radio static, and Burroughs reading his own text. There was no synchronized sound as such, though the radio static corresponds, more or less, with white-noise static onscreen.

It is a remarkable piece of filmmaking, not just for its cast but for its confident use of experimental techniques and its craftsmanship. Balch was always very keen on film editing. Prefiguring his own film-making, Balch had written in 1961 about Henri Colpi's first film, *Une Aussi Longue Absence:* "When film technicians become directors, it is often the editors who shine. Perhaps because they, more than the others, know what concrete elements can produce an abstract emotion. They know, or at least they should, what speeds and lengths can mean in terms of drama, and what 'pieces of space' can most effectively stir the senses."

The most important film collaboration was *The Cut-ups*, which was made after the Beat Hotel period but which includes Beat Hotel footage. It is the Cut-up idea taken to its final, logical conclusion and is a very powerful piece of work. Balch had about twenty-five minutes of film from the unfinished *Guerrilla Conditions*, which he used as the basis for the film. In addition to a normal print, he had about half of it printed in negative. Lengths of film, usually from the same shot, were superimposed upon one another out of sequence. Sometimes three separate lengths of film would be superimposed, and sometimes negative film would be used. The triple and negative superimpositions were done last and included footage taken from other films, such as *Bill Buys a Parrot*, a 16mm color short filmed on August 25, 1964, at John Hopkins's house in Tangier. Burroughs and Balch simply showed up one day and asked if they could film Bill talking to Coco, Hopkins's parrot. The footage appears in black-and-white negative in *The Cut-ups*.

When he had enough film, Antony spooled it off onto four reels, which he then gave to a film-lab technician and asked her to take twelve-inch lengths from each reel in rotation and splice them together. Antony explained: "Nobody was exercising any artistic judgment at all. The length of the shots (except for the last) was always a foot." This purely random Cut-up was done with a print of the film, from which an interneg was made. The terrible grading problems presented by the master print meant that the film could be made no other way. The sound track consisted of Burroughs and Gysin reading quotes from Scientology classes that Bill was attending at that time in London.

The Cut-up technique in another form, this time as an extension of the superimposed images used by Gysin and Sommerville at the Domain Poetique events, makes an appearance in the Burroughs / Balch collaboration *Bill and Tony*, in which Burroughs and Balch, as talking heads, read from two texts: one a Scientology Auditing manual, the other the script of Tod Browning's film *Freaks*, which Balch distributed in Britain. In it Burroughs and Balch swap voices, their words perfectly synchronized to their lip movements by Sommerville. The film was shot in 70mm in full color and was the last, and most perfectly realized, of this line of Cut-up experimentation.

We are fortunate that Balch arrived on the scene in time to film the Beat Hotel because no other footage of it is known to exist. In *Guerrilla Conditions* we see Burroughs and Gysin going about their lives in what was, unbeknownst to them, the final days of the hotel. At the end of 1962 Madame announced to her guests that she was selling the hotel and that they would all have to move out. She had managed it for thirty years and perhaps her lease had ended if, as Brion maintained, she only held the *gérance*. The new owners intended to renovate it, install an elevator, bathrooms, and other amenities, and call it the Relais-Hôtel du Vieux Paris. The last to go were the old-timers: Burroughs was still there in December, and Kaja Johnson stayed until nearly the end. Harold Norse stayed on until January 1963, almost to the day it closed, as did Gysin, who helped Madame sort out her things. He was horrified to find that she had not kept any of the manuscripts or paintings she had been given—often in lieu of rent—thinking they'd never be of any value. Brion claimed, "I was the last person to leave the hotel, the new owner came in and started tearing it down around me. I left all of my stuff with this painter friend called Jett . . . and I went to Morocco. I had a show in Morocco. William was already there."

And so this fertile period in Beat history drew to a close. Though it might look as if life in the Beat Hotel had encouraged extreme forms of experimentation and investigation, this was in fact a characteristic of all the Beats. The original Beat Generation writers had a penchant for weird and untried writing styles, which they defended vehemently as the only possible way of writing. Kerouac had his spontaneous prose; he believed writing was the word of God and therefore to change it would be sacrilegious, even when his texts sometimes became streams of amphetamine-fueled babble. Burroughs was equally adamant that Cut-ups were the only way to free literature from the authoritarian control system built into the language itself. Ginsberg, for his part, drove a hole as big as a bus through conventional poetry with his long breath-length lines and attempts to capture the human voice in extreme emotion. But Ginsberg declared himself to be "straight" compared to Gregory Corso, who could write long poems about everything from hair to atom bombs. The Beats opened up the world so that everything became subject matter for poetry and art. At the hotel, Kaja even wrote about the switchboard that Madame used to monitor each room's electricity usage: "The lights go on and off. / You use too much, a light flashes."

The Beat Hotel affected each of them in different ways. For Burroughs, it saw the beginning of his life as a professional writer. His previous books, the straightforward narratives *Junkie* and *Queer*, had been written very much at Ginsberg's urging, but when Bill moved to Paris in 1958, the umbilical cord to Ginsberg was cut. Allen still functioned as editor, promoter, and chief advocate, but the emotional ties were loosened and then dropped. It was Brion Gysin who enabled Burroughs to see himself primarily as a writer. It was Gysin's unqualified support and his enthusiasm and admiration for Bill's work that tipped the scales. Bill began to work, and work hard, and did not stop until his death. He needed that support and always worked best with an assistant or collaborator. After Gysin came Ian Sommerville, then James Grauerholz, with many other friends contributing their bits along the way. The Beat Hotel was where Burroughs severed his psychic dependency on others and became a writer.

By the time he left the Beat Hotel in December 1962, Burroughs had written five books, one of which, *Queer*, would not be published until 1985. Grove Press published *Naked Lunch* in the United States in 1962, but Bill was already well on his way to becoming a cult figure in his homeland. Grove followed up with *Nova Express* in 1964, and *The Soft Machine* and *The Ticket That Exploded* followed at two-year intervals. Burroughs himself remained in self-imposed exile, living mostly in London, until he returned to New York in 1974. He had lived outside of the United States for twenty-five years. At the time of his death, he had produced seventeen novels, three volumes of letters, several filmscripts, two books of literary essays, and numerous volumes of shorter works. In addition, he had developed a separate career as a painter and exhibited widely in galleries all around the world. He recorded more than a dozen spoken-word albums and was celebrated for his film, television, and stage appearances.

Gregory Corso flowered as a writer in Paris; there he was able to be "The Poet," with his silver-topped cane, his silk cape, and his way with the ladies. He became a self-invented Byronic figure—Captain Poetry—without the money, of course. Paris respected writers and poets and the Beat Hotel gave him the base from which to operate, an English-speaking haven. In these years his poetry loosened up and blossomed. His impish humor came through in poems like "Marriage" and "Hair," and he developed a form for his serious, long meditations on authority: "Power," "Police," and "Army." It was at the Beat Hotel where Corso evolved his mature style. His volume of poems *The Happy Birthday of Death*, which consists mostly of poems written during his Beat Hotel period, remains his most popular book and has gone through more than a dozen printings. Europe agreed with him and he continued to spend long periods there, with spells in England, Italy, and Greece through the following decades. Ginsberg has described him as "a poet's Poet" and, though he never attracted the kind of fame that

Ginsberg achieved, he produced a solid body of work, including a 268-page book of selected poems called *Mindfield,* which features forewords by both Burroughs and Ginsberg.

Allen Ginsberg was perhaps the least influenced by his stay in Paris. He knew that he had to escape from the growing media attention on the Beats in the United States, and Paris was probably the best place to escape to. He began to discover the European avant-garde but unfortunately he returned to New York just as he was beginning to put faces to the legendary names. Whether these contacts would have led him to a greater sophistication or a less American-centered worldview is impossible to say. Certainly he was at his creative peak in the Beat Hotel period and wrote some wonderful poetry. He also developed a lifelong love of Paris and became a frequent performer at art and literature festivals in the city. Later in life he often spoke of a desire to return for a year or so to learn more about its culture and get a different perspective on world events. Sadly this was not to be.

After spending two years in India with Peter Orlovsky, Allen returned to the States, where he helped forge the inchoate hippie movement and became active in pro-drug, antiwar, and many other political campaigns. In 1971 he became a Tibetan Buddhist, a development that took his poetry—and his politics—into areas not always appreciated by his readers and critics. As his fame increased, Allen traveled to virtually every country on earth as a kind of countercultural ambassador, spreading his singular message of love, poetry, anarchy, and meditation. At his death, he was probably the most famous poet in America.

When the hotel closed, Brion Gysin returned to Tangier and wrote *The Process,* a superb novel that is the basis of his literary reputation. He remained in Morocco until 1973, when he joined Burroughs in London. There Burroughs, Gysin, and Antony Balch had apartments in Dalmeny Court on Duke Street Saint James's, and spent many months working on a filmscript for *Naked Lunch.* When this fell through, Brion returned to Paris, where he lived for the rest of his life, concentrating mostly on painting. He devoted much of his time to trying to penetrate the French art establishment but he was ultimately unsuccessful, though he did have a number of exhibits of his work. As Brion himself concluded, he should have concentrated on one career and stuck to it. Publishers saw him as an artist and art dealers saw him as a writer or a restaurateur or a performance artist or a screenwriter or a poet or—toward the end of his life—a rock 'n' roll performer. He was ahead of his time, a multimedia artist before anyone really knew what this was, and all that it encompassed.

Brion immortalized the Beat Hotel in the novel he completed just before his death. *The Last Museum* was a book that Brion had toyed with, on and off, for twenty years. In it the Beat Hotel becomes the Bardo of the *Tibetan Book of the Dead*, run by Madame Rachou for invisible Tibetan landlords. The hotel is shipped room by room to California, where a fictional version of the Getty Museum is reconstructing it on the San Andreas fault, ready to slide into oblivion. By the time *The Last Museum* was published, the Beat Hotel itself had been closed for twenty-three years, its contents stripped out, the rooms remodeled, and the ground floor façade rebuilt.

The hotel at 9 rue Git-le-Coeur closed for good in the spring of 1963. William Burroughs remembered when Madame and Mirtaud the hotel cat finally moved out: "There was a gray cat in the Beat Hotel. It was owned by Madame. When she retired, she moved sort of across the street. She looked so sad there, like people do when they retire. She had geraniums and an old gray chin and an old old gray cat, and she just faded out . . ."

In Memoriam

Ian Sommerville died in a car crash near Bath, Somerset, England, on February 5, 1976.

Antony Balch died in London of stomach cancer on April 6, 1980.

Michael "Mikey" Portman died of a heart attack on November 15, 1983.

Brion Gysin died in Paris of a heart attack on July 12, 1986.

Allen Ginsberg died of liver cancer in New York City on April 5, 1997.

William Burroughs died of a heart attack in Lawrence, Kansas, on August 2, 1997.

Acknowledgments

Many people shared their memories of the Beat Hotel with me for this book. In some instances I tape-recorded an interview with them but more often these were conversations at a bar, over lunch, dinner, or at parties. I went to Lawrence, Kansas, to interview William Burroughs about his time at the hotel and would particularly like to thank his assistant James Grauerholz for his friendship and help both in making the files of William Burroughs Communications available to me and for his valuable insights into all matters Burroughsian. Allen Ginsberg answered my questions about the hotel both in person in New York and in a number of subsequent telephone calls. In the course of our thirty-year friendship we had often discussed the hotel. Tom Neurath, the head of Thames and Hudson publishers, gave me an interview and valuable assistance, as did Jean-Jacques Lebel in Paris. Many thanks to them both. Jon Savage kindly gave me his original interview tapes with Brion Gysin and allowed me to quote from them. I would also like to thank Andrew Sclanders of Beatbooks.com for tracking down fugitive Beat Hotel publications, as well as José Ferez, John Geiger, Daevid Allen, Victor Bockris, Peter Wollen, Paul Smith, Lawrence Ferlinghetti, David Dawson, Damon Wise, Joseph Geraci, John Howe, Ilona Halberstam, Ira Silverberg, and the staff of the London Library for their help. My thanks to Marilyn Wurzburger and her staff at the Special Collections department of the Hayden Library, Arizona State University, who could not have been more helpful. I am very grateful to Andrew Wylie, and to Jeffrey Posternak and Rose

Billington, at the Wylie Agency. I would particularly like to thank Amy Hundley for a sterling editing job, though of course the remaining mistakes are all mine, and Michael Hornburg, the managing editor at Grove Press. As usual, Rosemary Bailey has provided many valuable suggestions.

Selected Bibliography

Burroughs, William S.

The Naked Lunch (Paris: Olympia Press, 1959)
[with Brion Gysin]: *The Exterminator* (San Francisco: Auerhahn, 1960)
[with Gregory Corso; Brion Gysin; Sinclair Beiles]: *Minutes To Go* (Paris: Two Cities, 1960)
The Soft Machine (Paris: Olympia Press, 1961)
[with Allen Ginsberg]: *The Yagé Letters* (San Francisco: City Lights, 1963)
Roosevelt After Inauguration (New York: Fuck You Press, 1964)
AQ 14: Cut Up Eine Anthologie (Frankfurt, 1973)
The Job (New York: Grove Press, 1974 [revised])
Junky (New York: Penguin, 1977)
Letters to Allen Ginsberg (Genéve: Claude Givaudan, 1978)
[with Brion Gysin]: *The Third Mind* (New York: Seaver, 1978)
Doctor Benway (Santa Barbara: Bradford Morrow, 1979)
Early Routines (Santa Barbara: Cadmus, 1982)
The Burroughs File (San Francisco: City Lights, 1984)
The Adding Machine: Selected Essays (London: John Calder, 1985)
Queer (New York: Viking, 1985)
Interzone (New York: Viking, 1989)
The Letters of William S. Burroughs 1945–1959 [Oliver Harris, ed.](New York: Viking, 1993)

Ambrose, Joe, Terry Wilson, and Frank Rynne: *Man From Nowhere: Storming the Citadels of Enlightenment with William Burroughs and Brion Gysin* (Dublin / London: The Gap / Subliminal, 1992).
Ansen, Alan. *William Burroughs* (Sudbury, MA: Water Row, 1986).
Bockris, Victor. *With William Burroughs: A Report from the Bunker* (New York: Seaver, 1981).
Caveney, Graham. *The "Priest" They Called Him; The Life and Legacy of William S. Burroughs* (London: Bloomsbury, 1997).

278 The Beat Hotel

Goodman, Michael. *William S. Burroughs: An Annotated Bibliography* (New York: Garland, 1975).
Loydell, Rupert (ed). *My Kind of Angel. I.M. William Burroughs* (Exeter: Stride, 1998).
Lydenberg, Robin. *Word Cultures: Radical Theory and Practice in William S. Burroughs' Fiction* (Urbana: University of Illinois, 1987).
Maynard, Joe, and Barry Miles. *William S. Burroughs: A Bibliography 1953–73* (Charlottesville: University of Virginia, 1978).
Miles, Barry. *A Catalogue of the William S. Burroughs Archive* (Ollon, Suisse, and London: Am Here and Covent Garden, 1973).
Miles, Barry. *William Burroughs: El Hombre Invisible* (London: Virgin, 1992).
Mottram, Eric. *William Burroughs: The Algebra of Need* (London: Marion Boyars, 1977).
Morgan, Ted. *Literary Outlaw: The Life and Times of William S. Burroughs* (New York: Henry Holt, 1988).
Murphy, Timothy S. *Wising Up the Marks: The Amodern William Burroughs* (Berkeley: University of California, 1997).
RE/Search 4 / 5. San Fransico, 1982 (William Burroughs issue)
The Review of Contemporary Fiction, Spring 1984 (William S. Burroughs number)
Skerl, Jennie. *William S. Burroughs* (Boston: Twayne, 1985).
Skerl, Jennie, and Robin Lydenberg (eds.). *William S. Burroughs at the Front: Critical Reception 1959–1989.* (Carbondale: Southern Illinois University, 1991).
Sobieszek, Robert A. *Ports of Entry: William Burroughs and the Arts* (Los Angeles: County Museum of Art, 1996).
Weissner, Carl, and Michael Köhler: *Burroughs, Eine Bild-Biographie* (Berlin: Nishen, 1994).

Corso, Gregory

The Vestal Lady on Brattle (Cambridge, MA: Richard Brukenfeld, 1955)
Bomb (San Francisco: City Lights, 1958)
Gasoline (San Francisco: City Lights, 1958)
The Happy Birthday of Death (New York: New Directions, 1960)
The American Express (Paris: Olympia, 1961)
The Minicab War (London: Matrix, 1961)
Unmuzzled Ox, 22. Winter 1981 (Gregory Corso issue)
The Riverside Interviews 3: Gregory Corso (London: Binnacle, 1982)
Mind Field (Madras / New York: Hanuman, 1989)
Mindfield (New York: Thunder's Mouth, 1989)

Stephenson, Gregory. *Exiled Angel: A Study of the Work of Gregory Corso* (London: Hearing Ear, 1989).

Wilson, Robert. *A Bibliography of Works by Gregory Corso: 1954–1965* (New York: Phoenix Book Shop, 1966)

Ginsberg, Allen

Kaddish and Other Poems (San Francisco: City Lights, 1961)
Reality Sandwiches (San Francisco: City Lights, 1963)
Allen Verbatim: Lectures on Poetry, Politics, Consciousness (New York: McGraw-Hill, 1974)
Gay Sunshine Interview with Allen Young (Bolinas, CA: Grey Fox, 1974)
Journals: Early Fifties, Early Sixties (New York: Grove, 1977)
[with Peter Orlovsky]: *Straight Heart's Delight: Love Poems & Selected Letters* (San Francisco: Gay Sunshine, 1980)
Collected Poems 1947–1980 (New York: Harper & Row, 1985)

Dowden, George. *A Bibliography of Works by Allen Ginsberg: October, 1943 to July 1, 1967* (San Francisco: City Lights, 1971).
Hyde, Lewis (ed.). *On the Poetry of Allen Ginsberg* (Ann Arbor: University of Michigan Press, 1984).
Kramer, Jane. *Allen Ginsberg in America* (New York: Random House, 1969).
Kraus, Michelle P. *Allen Ginsberg: An Annotated Bibliography 1969–1977* (Metuchen, NJ: Scarecrow, 1980).
McBride, Dick. *Cometh with Clouds (Memory: Allen Ginsberg)* (Cherry Valley, NY: Cherry Valley Editions, 1982).
Miles, Barry. *Ginsberg: A Biography* (New York: Simon & Schuster, 1989).
Morgan, Bill. *The Works of Allen Ginsberg 1941–1994* (Westport, CT: Greenwood, 1995).
Morgan, Bill. *The Response to Allen Ginsberg, 1926–1994* (Westport, CT: Greenwood, 1996).
Morgan, Bill, and Bob Rosenthal (eds.). *Best Minds: A Tribute to Allen Ginsberg* (New York: Lospecchio, 1986).
Morgan, Bill, and Bob Rosenthal (eds.). *Kanreki: A Tribute to Allen Ginsberg Part 2* (New York: Lospecchio, 1986).
Mottram, Eric. *Allen Ginsberg in the Sixties* (Brighton: Unicorn, nd [1972]).
Mottram, Eric. *The Wild Good and the Heart Ultimately: Ginsberg's Art of Persuasion* (London: Spanner, 1978 [as *Spanner* v2 no 5]).
Portugés, Paul. *The Visionary Poetics of Allen Ginsberg* (Santa Barbara: Ross-Erikson, 1978).
Schumacher, Michael. *Dharma Lion: A Biography of Allen Ginsberg* (New York: St. Martins, 1992).
Sinclair, Iain. *The Kodak Mantra Diaries* (London: Albion Village, 1971).

Gysin, Brion

To Master, A Long Good Night (New York: Creative Age, 1946)
The Process (New York: Putnam, 1969)
Brion Gysin Let the Mice In (West Glover, VT: Something Else, 1973)
[with Wilson, Terry]: *Here To Go: Planet R-101* (San Francisco: RE/
      Search, 1982)
Stories (Oakland: Inkblot, 1984)
Beat Museum: Bardo Hotel Chapter Two (Berkeley: Inkblot, c 1985)
The Last Museum (New York: Grove Press, 1986) [with a William
      Burroughs preface not in UK edition]
Morocco Two (Oakland: Inkblot, 1986)
Dreamachine (Basel: Laszlo, Editions Panderma, c 1988)
Dreamachine Plans Created by Brion Gysin (Brighton: Temple, 1992)

Soft Need 8. September 1973
Soft Need 9. Spring 1976
Soft Need 17. October 1977 (Brion Gysin issue)
Brion Gysin (London: October Gallery, 1981)
Calligraphy of Fire (Paris: Galerie Samy Kinge, 1986)
Brion Gysin (New York: Guillaume Gallozzi Gallery, 1994)

Norse, Harold

Beat Hotel (San Diego: Atticus, 1983)
Memoirs of a Bastard Angel (New York: William Morrow, 1989)

Memoirs, Studies, Anthologies

Campbell, James. *Paris Interzone* (London: Secker and Warburg, 1994).
Cecil, Paul (ed.): *Flickers of the Dreamachine* (Hove, Sussex: Codex,
      1996).
Chapman, Howard. *The Beat Hotel* (Montpellier: Gris Banal, 1984).
Charters, Ann. *The Beats: Literary Bohemians in Postwar America* DLB
      16 (Ann Arbor, MI: Gale Research, 1983).
de St. Jorre, John: *The Good Ship Venus: The Erotic Voyage of the Olympia
      Press* (London: Hutchinson, 1994).
Easton, Malcolm. *Artists and Writers in Paris. The Bohemian Idea, 1803–
      1867* (London: Edward Arnold, 1964).
Ebin, David (ed.). *The Drug Experience* (New York: Orion, 1961).
Edinger, Claudio. *Chelsea Hotel* (New York: Abbeville, 1984).

Feldman, Gene, and Max Gartenberg (eds.). *The Beat Generation and the Angry Young Men* (New York: Citadel, 1958)

Girodias, Maurice (ed.). *The Olympia Reader* (New York: Grove Press, 1965).

Gold, Herbert. *Bohemia: Where Art, Angst, Love and Strong Coffee Meet* (New York: Simon & Schuster, 1993).

Hewison, Robert. *Too Much, Art and Society in the Sixties, 1960–1975* (London: Methuen, 1986).

Himes, Chester. *The Quality of Hurt: The Autobiography of Chester Himes Volume I* (New York: Thunder's Mouth, 1989).

Himes, Chester. *My Life of Absurdity: The Autobiography of Chester Himes Volume II* (New York: Paragon, 1990).

Hopkins, John. *The Tangier Diaries 1962–1979.* (London: Arcadia, 1997).

Kearney, Patrick J. *The Paris Olympia Press* (London: Black Spring, 1987).

Lennon, Peter. *Foreign Correspondent: Paris in the Sixties* (London: Picador, 1994)

Leyland, Winston (ed.). *Gay Sunshine Interviews, v1* (San Francisco: Gay Sunshine, 1978).

Mason, Felicity [as Cumming, Anne]. *The Love Quest, A Sexual Odyssey* (London: Peter Owen, 1991).

Miller, Richard. *Bohemia: The Protoculture Then and Now* (Chicago: Nelson-Hall, 1977).

Murger, Henri. (*Scènes de la Vie de Bohème*) (*The Bohemians of the Latin Quarter*) (Paris: Société Des Beaux-Arts, 1915).

Parkinson, Thomas (ed.). *Casebook on the Beat* (New York: Crowell, 1961).

Parry, Alfred. *Garrets and Pretenders: A History of Bohemianism in America* (New York: Dover, revised ed., 1960).

Peabody, Richard (ed.). *A Different Beat: Writings by Women of the Beat Generation* (London: Serpent's Tail, 1997).

Richardson, Joanna. *The Bohemians* (South Brunswick: A. S. Barnes, 1971).

Rodman, Selden. *Tongues of Fallen Angels: Conversations with Ginsberg* [et al.] (New York: New Directions, 1974).

Rosenthal, Irving. *Sheeper* (New York: Grove Press, 1967).

Rosset, Barney (ed.). *The Evergreen Review Reader, 1957–1961* (New York: Grove Press, 1979).

Sargeant, Jack. *The Naked Lens: An Illustrated History of Beat Cinema* (London: Creation, 1997).

Sawyer-Lauçanno, Christopher. *The Continual Pilgrimage: American Writers in Paris 1944–1960* (London: Bloomsbury, 1992).

Seaver, Richard, Terry Southern, and Alexander Trocchi (eds.). *Writers in Revolt, An Anthology* (New York: Frederick Fell, 1963).

Seigel, Jerrold. *Bohemian Paris* (New York: Viking, 1986).

Solomon, David (ed.). *The Marihuana Papers* (Indianapolis: Bobbs-Merrill, 1966).
Walter, W. Grey. *The Living Brain* (London: Duckworth, 1953).
Webster, Paul, and Nicholas Powell. *Saint-Germain-Des-Pres: French Postwar Culture from Sartre to Bardot* (London: Constable, 1984).
Willey, Peter. *The Castles of the Assassins* (London: George Harrap, 1963).
Wolf, Daniel and Ed Fancher (eds.). *The Village Voice Reader* (Garden City, NY: Doubleday, 1962).

Big Table 1–4
Chicago Review v12, nos 1 and 3
Left Bank This Month v2, no 1
Olympia 1–4
Two Cities 1–9

Other articles and references are listed in the notes. If a quote is not attributed, then it is taken from an interview with the author. The following abbreviations are used in the notes:

WSB: William Seward Burroughs
GC: Gregory Corso
LF: Lawrence Ferlinghetti
AG: Allen Ginsberg
BG: Brion Gysin
JK: Jack Kerouac
PO: Peter Orlovsky

Notes

Introduction

devoted to them: The Whitney is, of course, dedicated to the presentation of American art only; however, Brion Gysin held an American passport and, consequently, was just as much an American as, say, Willem de Kooning.

1: 9, rue Git-le-Coeur

sixteenth century: The present owners claim it was built in 1480 and it is entirely possible that its foundations date from that time. **"The 'police of foreigners' . . . coveted document":** WSB: Foreword to Norse, Harold: *Beat Hotel*. San Diego: Atticus, 1983.

2: Kaddish

"Peter needs . . . paperthinwall": In Ball, Gordon (ed.): *Allen Ginsberg: Journals Mid-Fifties 1954–1958*. New York: HarperCollins, 1995. **Ferlinghetti:** AG to LF: September 3, 1957. **Picasso's minders:** AG to Robert LaVigne: Tangier, June 8, 1957. **"Why . . . you bastards?":** AG to LF: Tangier, June 10, 1957. **"I went there . . . just stared":** Corso, Gregory: "Biographical Notes" in Allen, Donald (ed.): *The New American Poetry 1945–1960*. New York: Grove Press, 1960. **"I lived . . . Clinton Prison":** Ibid. **"I had the best . . . all the words":** Cherkovski, Neeli: *Whitman's Wild Children*. Venice, CA: Lapis, 1988. **"Went home . . . stamp collection":** Corso, Gregory: 'Biographical Notes" in *The New American Poetry 1945–1960*. **"My first lay when I got out of prison":** Gregory Corso speaking at the 1982 Kerouac conference at Naropa. **"Through him . . . dear friend to me":** Corso, Gregory: "Biographical Notes" in *The New American Poetry 1945–1960*. **"I dint get . . . on straw sleep?":** GC to JK: nd [November, 1958]. **"Peter and Allen . . . Paris Beat Hotel":** Ansen, Alan: "Memories of Allen" in *Best Minds: A Tribute to Allen Ginsberg*. New York: Lospecchio, 1986. **"Just got here . . . RR stations and hotels":** AG to Louis

Ginsberg, September 18, 1957. **"Waking all night . . . the RR stations gets noisy":** AG: *Journals Mid-Fifties 1954–1958.* **"We went . . . I imagined":** AG to JK: September 28, 1957. **"It was such a mess . . . Allen was very angry at me":** Maurice Girodias interviewed by Victor Bockris. Taken from a manuscript in the Bockris archive. It is not known if this was published. **"NO ONE . . . rucksack in Paris":** JK to John Clellon Holmes, June 23, 1957. **chapter, which he had not liked:** Published in *Interzone* but at this time a part of the *Naked Lunch* ms. **"We saw *Times* . . . Fame crashing over our ears?":** AG to JK: September 28, 1957. **"Apocalypse at Les Halles":** In Ball, Gordon (ed.): *Allen Ginsberg: Journals Mid-Fifties 1954–1958.* **"I haven't heard . . . a story soon":** AG to LG: September 30, 1957. **"I know everybody puts Gregory down . . . like an Esso sign?":** AG to LF: September 28, 1957. **"We unite & give . . . even publish 'Power'":** AG to JK: September 28, 1957. **Gregory wrote a poem:** "Gargoyles," in Corso, Gregory: *The Happy Birthday of Death.* New York: New Directions, 1960. **"Julius is in the hospital . . . a year already":** In Ball, Gordon (ed.): *Allen Ginsberg: Journals Mid-Fifties 1954–1958.* **"always has girls . . . cooks good food":** PO to Ron Loewinsohn: October "could be 19 or 20" 1957. **"Correspondence mounts . . . support so great a weight of bull":** AG to LG: September 4, 1957 [misdated as September 14 in Columbia version of letters catalog]. **"Sputnik I & II . . . American, any more, as we used to think":** AG to LG: November 6, 1957 [added to a letter of October 19, 1957]. **"It seems unimportant . . . poetry, to enrich world":** In Ball, Gordon (ed.): *Allen Ginsberg: Journals Mid-Fifties 1954–1958.* **"I tend not to want to identify myself . . . it certainly isn't me":** AG to LG: nd [approx. October 25, 1957]. **"All personal and alive . . . they've published for 50 years":** AG to JK: November 13, 1958. **"A major world poet . . . new Oriental age to come":** AG to LG: January 14, 1958. **"So pure horse . . . stronger in long run":** AG to JK: November 13, 1958. **Breton's poem:** Anthologized in Jean, Marcel (ed.): *The Autobiography of Surrealism.* New York: Viking, 1980. First publication date unknown. **"[I] realize . . . with her paranoia . . .":** "I Was Walking Down the Street" in Ball, Gordon (ed.): *Allen Ginsberg: Journals Mid-Fifties 1954–1958.* **section Allen sent to Kerouac:** In Ball, Gordon (ed.): *Allen Ginsberg: Journals Mid-Fifties 1954–1958.*

3: Expatriates

"Nothing English . . . pure American": Quoted by Gregory Corso in his introduction to Orlovsky, Peter: *Clean Asshole Poems & Smiling Vegetable Songs.* San Francisco: City Lights, 1978. **"Both unmistakably . . . New poet actually to be sure!":** AG to JK: January 4, 1958. *Smiling Vegetable Songs.* **"Wile Allen & Gregory . . . hard ons because of the dope":** PO to JK: December 3–December 5, 1957. **"We're crowded . . . Peter makes ladies of the streets":** AG to Lucien Carr: December 11, 1957. **"OK for you to read them . . . expensive and rare in the US":** AG to Edith Ginsberg: December

15, 1957. **"Eerie haunting damp . . . Rimbaud on the wall"**: PO to Robert LaVigne: December 7, 1957. **"I thought, and still do . . . aggression and hatred"**: AG interviewed by Rick Fields for *Open Secret*, Naropa, Boulder, CO, 1974. **"In the long run . . . don't even vote"**: "Facsimile of Letter from Jack Kerouac on Céline" in *Paris Review* 31. **"Shlepping . . . Youth Club now"**: Norse, Harold: "Green Ballets" in *Residu* 1, Athens, 1965. **". . . in his poverty . . . even going further"**: AG to JK, November 13, 1957. **"I'm glad you dug . . . to include 'Coit Tower'"**: AG to LF: January 18, 1958. **"When I look at your poem . . . poetry is Ode To The West Wind"**: GC to JK: Paris nd [December 7, 1957]. **"Spend or waste a lot time . . . write in on toilet paper"**: AG to LG: November 30, 1957. **Jones autobiography**: LeRoi Jones / Amiri Baraka: *The Autobiography.* New York: Freundlich, 1984. **"Overtaxing of the productive person . . . brought forth his work"**: Benjamin, Walter: *Charles Baudelaire: A Lyric Poet in the Era of High Capitalism.* Trans. Harry Zohn. London: New Left Books, 1973. **"simulate blood . . . his own and his mother's"**: Parkinson, Thomas: "Allen Ginsberg at 30 and 60," in *Best Minds: A Tribute to Allen Ginsberg.* New York: Lospecchio, 1986. **similar article for his magazine:** It appeared as "Dichter Und Gesellschaft In Amerika" in *Akzente* 2 (April 1958). **Ehrenreich book:** Ehrenreich, Barbara: *The Hearts of Men: American Dreams and the Flight from Commitment.* New York: Anchor, 1983. **"I also thought . . . Satanic Bill"**: AG to PO: January 20, 1958. **"Just as between us . . . continuing the same process"**: AG to PO: January 28, 1958. **"Burroughs and Ansen . . . ripened in Europe"**: AG to Eugene Brooks: January 23, 1958. **"Sooner or later . . . served him well the last ten years"**: Ibid. **"It's very intimate and funny . . . human love-possibilities"**: AG to PO: January 28, 1958. **"It is hardly . . . demand conventional behavior"**: WSB to Alan Ansen: July 15, 1957.

4: Bomb

"Saw Joy, . . . hah that's over": AG to PO: January 28, 1958. **"Screwed Joy again . . . asia-girl mystic"**: AG to PO: February 3, 1958. **"Elgin Marbles . . . Greatest thing in Europe"**: AG to PO: February 15, 1958. **Peter Lennon quote:** Lennon, Peter: *Foreign Correspondent.* London: Picador, 1994. Lennon spells the name "Balph" whereas both Ginsberg and Burroughs use "Balf." **"Graham and his beastly . . . various electrical appliances"**: WSB to AG: nd [February, 1958]. **"That kid Dick whatever . . . shove a man out of his own bed"**: WSB to AG: February 3, 1958. **"Another 4th successive . . . sunrise over Notre Dame"**: AG to PO: April 1, 1958. **"I sit in my room . . . till death . . ."**: AG: "World! World! World!" original ms. in U of Texas, Austin, February 29, 1958. pub as "Europe! Europe!" with line six deleted and other slight changes. **"Maybe we Ball her . . . like pond water"**: AG to PO: February 24, 1958. **"I have never picked up . . . look for souls again anyway"**: Ibid. **"Analysis . . . furnace

in my presence": WSB to AG: July 24, 1958. **He cited a passage in** *Naked Lunch:* Ansen interviewed by Ted Morgan for his biography of Burroughs. The phrase "white defenders" does not appear in *Naked Lunch* though it might well have been in one of the drafts that Ansen had helped to type. **"I read** *You Can't Win* **in 1926 . . . by my peers":** WSB: Foreword to Black, Jack: *You Can't Win.* New York: Amok Press, 1988. **"The knife sharpener . . . wrong?' I wondered":** WSB introduction to *Queer.* New York: Viking, 1985. **Writing** *Junkie:* First published by Ace as *Junkie* by William Lee, reissued in an uncensored edition by Penguin as *Junky.* **oft-quoted passage:** WSB introduction to *Queer.* **manuscripts from them:** AG to Denise Levertov: January 28, 1958. **"Plus two evenings . . . was a chauvinistic whore":** AG to Robert Creeley: February [25?], 1958. **editor of his journals:** In Ball, Gordon (ed.): *Allen Ginsberg: Journals Mid-Fifties 1954–1958.* **"It was all happening . . . coffee in the morning anyway":** AG in conversation with Maurice Girodias and WSB on Charles Ruas's Conversations with Amerian Writers program, WBAI, New York. Transcribed in Ruas, Charles: *Con.ver.sa.tions with Amer.i.can writ.ers.* New York: Knopf, 1984. **"If I can ever find . . . hand in my resignation":** Gold, Herbert: *Love & Like.* New York: Dial Press, 1960. **Gold Memoir:** Gold, Herbert: *Bohemia: Where Art, Angst, Love and Strong Coffee Meet.* New York: Simon & Schuster, 1993. **read in the space of two weeks:** Larry Fagin. Speech given at Kerouac Conference, Naropa Institute, Boulder, CO, 1982. **"The dollar is down . . . franc more uppity":** WSB to JK: March 29, 1958. **"I've been serving him . . . haggard complaining wife":** AG to PO: April 1, 1958. **"A door opened . . . issued from the source":** Guest, Barbara: "Allen, Gregory, Paris" in *Kanreki: A Tribute To Allen Ginsberg. Part 2.* New York: Lospecchio, 1986. **"It was Allen . . . he was exemplary":** Ibid. **"When a pigeon moaned . . . into the March sunshine":** Moraes, Dom: *My Son's Father.* London: Secker & Warburg, 1968. **"I smoked some of it . . . every morning'":** Moraes, Henrietta: *Henrietta.* London: Hamish Hamilton, 1994. **"The whole arrondissement . . . Play it cool myself":** WSB to JK: nd [March 29, 1958]. **"Unfortunately another poet . . . I was a big success":** "Two Poets in Paris," *New York Herald Tribune.* Paris, June 26, 1958. **The running order of the manuscript:** The ms. of *Interzone* in the Butler Library of Columbia University, which is included as an enclosure to a letter from WSB to Lawrence Ferlinghetti, dated April 18, 1958, has a suggested running order of sections in Allen Ginsberg's hand with Ginsberg's East 2nd Street, New York, address. As Ginsberg did not move into this apartment until after he returned to New York from Paris, it must be concluded that new chapters and additions were made to this manuscript during the period that Ferlinghetti was considering it. At any rate, the contents list could not possibly have been sent as part of the April 18, 1958, letter. Ginsberg's cover sheet also includes a different running order, what he called a "Definitive Table of Contents for Interzone," which differs from the one given above and which I assume to be the earlier of the two, though not necessarily the order that the ms. was in when Burroughs sent it. **"I wrote 'Marriage' . . . let it jump":** GC interviewed by Michael Andre 1972: *Unmuzzled Ox* 5 / 6 New York 1973. **"I saw the kids ... I loved the Bomb"**: Ibid. **"I use it in 'Bomb' ... flower power"**: Ibid. **"I don't understand ... vulnerable to it."**: AG to LF: September 4, 1958. **"I didn't leave ... took the book"**: "I'm Poor Simple Human Bones" GC interviewed by Robert King, March 18, 1974, in *The Beat Diary*, California, PA, 1977.

5: Fellow Writers

Louis-Ferdinand Céline: Céline interviewed June 1, 1960. *Paris Review* 31. December 1963. **"who pounded the table ... colons *with pistols*"**: AG to Louis Ginsberg: March 15, 1958. **"... starved most of the time ... strike, & hungry"**: AG to Lucien Carr: May 30, 1958. **"They smoked marijuana ... to school here"**: Moraes, Dom: *My Son's Father*. London: Secker & Warburg, 1968. **"During that period ... might have committed?"**: Parkinson, Thomas: "Allen Ginsberg at 30 and 60" in *Best Minds: A Tribute to Allen Ginsberg*. New York: Lospecchio, 1986. **"BJ and Baird ... Baird is in hospital ..."**: AG to PO: June 15, 1958. **"Far and away ... I have met in Paris"**: WSB to Paul Bowles: July 20, 1958. **"A new strange cripple ... have free spirit"**: AG to PO: June 15, 1958. **"very good ... but amazing"**: AG to JK: June 26, 1958. **"His tall sexy lovely wife hates us"**: Ibid. **"hear driving raging ... mysterious basement"**: AG to PO: June 21, 1958. **"Strange to meet ... chair, arms crossed"**: Ibid. **Chopin and Voltaire once lived:** Presumably number 6, which has a room dedicated to the memory of Chopin. **"Bill probably stay ... illumination & analysis"**: AG to Lucien Carr: May 30, 1958. **"I am getting ... come to like her very much"**: WSB to AG: July 24, 1958. **"Great night yesterday ... & saw dawn"**: AG to PO: May 30, 1958. **"making serious goofy ... long vague bad novel"**: Ibid. **"But not queer ... Been thinking of that"**: AG to PO: June 8, 1958. **where he was hospitalized:** *Relevé de la conférence d'Allen Ginsberg.* [Montreal?] 1988. *Dada Painters and Poets:* New York: Wittenborn & Schultz, 1951. **"Allen and me were interviewed ... threatening gloom"**: GC to Gary Snyder: c. June 30, 1958. **Buchwald article:** "Two Poets in Paris," *New York Herald Tribune.* Paris, June 26, 1958. **"I get money from girls. ... I just use it to buy food"**: Ibid. **would arrange a meeting:** Interview with the author. **"That had a big influence ... Bill I'm sure, literally"**: Interview with the author. **"I think ... lively and very funny"**: Mikriammos, Philippe: "The Last European Interview" in *The Review of Contemporary Fiction*, Spring 1984. **collaborationist activity:** Stromberg, Robert: "A Talk With Louis-Ferdinand Céline" in *Evergreen Review* 19. July 1961. **"He was an old ... we were poets"**: "Here to Save Us, But Not Sure from What" in *Village Voice*, October 15, 1958. **"Cookstove & the great ... to Françoise, to George"**: AG: *Journals Mid-Fifties, 1954–1958.* George is George Whitman, the owner of the Mistral Bookshop. *The Beat Generation and the Angry Young Men:* New York: Citadel Press, 1958, reviewed in *Time*, June 9, 1958. **description of the occasion:** Written by AG for *L'Herne Texts: Michaux*, December 1965. **"Michaux said ... Gregory's still seeing him":** AG to LF: August 20, 1958. **"Bill downstairs, ... distinguished sanctity":** AG Journals, 1958. **for the *Village Voice:*** "Here to Save Us, But Not Sure from What."

6: Ports of Entry

"Gregory came in ... melt all the icebergs": Turnbull, Gael: "Paris and Bill Burroughs" in *Mica* 5, Santa Barbara, Winter 1962. **"When I got back ... should have gone for that":** GC to AG: August 29, 1958. **"I am going to ... visitors on my return":** WSB to AG: August 25, 1958. **"Many a queer ... shrieking from the Parade":** Ibid. **"going to put ... 'friends from Oxford'":** WSB to AG: nd [July, 1958]. **"of the most sordid, ... respectability and whiteness":** GC to AG: September 28, 1958. **"Dave McAdams gets me ... just don't go out":** GC to AG: August 29, 1958. **"I need it published ... really labored over it":** Ibid. **"I have visions now practically constant":** WSB to AG: September 28, 1958. **"there were no alcoholics ... tone of the establishment":** WSB to Paul Bowles: October 19, 1958. **"Unless I can reach ... look for another way":** WSB to AG: October 10, 1958. *Bannisteria caapi:* A hallucinogenic (the actual Linnaean name is Bannisteriopsis caapi) also known as yagé or ayahuasca. See Burroughs, William and Allen Ginsberg: *The Yagé Letters*, San Francisco: City Lights, 1963. **"Wheeled into ... under the brim of his hat":** WSB & BG: *The Third Mind*. New York: Viking, 1978. **"Hamri and I ... he was too Spanish":** Ibid. **"paranoid bitch ... Brion Gysin":** WSB to AG: November 2, 1955. **"We had just been ... practices of this dreary tribe":** WSB to AG: June 24, 1954. **"The years at ... experimental things going on":** Wilson, Terry: "Brion Gysin: A Biography / Appreciation" in RE / Search 4 / 5. San Francisco, 1982. **John Clifford Brian:** His birth certificate spells "Brian" in the conventional manner. His spelling, "Brion," was clearly a later innovation. His certificate of naturalization, making him an American citizen, states that his name was "changed by decree of Court from John Clifford Brian Leonard Gysin to Brion Gysin" as part of the naturalization process on December 16, 1946. **"There's been a mistake ... return address on me somewhere":** BG: *Family Album*. Published in France as *Legendes de Brion Gysin*, Gris Banal Editeur: Montpellier, 1983. Taken from original, unpublished English ms. **"A literary café ... sordid scene, I came out":** Ibid. **"In those great 52nd Street ... he was going to be doing":** Ibid. **Alice:** Alice B. Toklas, Gertrude Stein's lover. **"Brion Gysin gave ... danced marvellously":** Carl van Vechten to John Breon, September 20, 1949 in Kellner, Bruce (ed.): *Letters of Carl van Vechten.* New Haven: Yale University Press, 1987. **"This German lady ... First time I'd heard of him":** Ibid. **"It was not until ... from 1950 to 1973:** BG catalog notes to *Calligraffiti of Fire.* **"Brion Gysin has opened ... bowling team from Newark":** WSB to AG: December

8, 1957. **"May Ibrahim . . . smoke leaves this chimney"**: BG interviewed by Rob LaFrenais and Graham Dawes, in *Performance* magazine 11, London 1981. **"I said, 'Don't be silly, . . . place very uncomfortable"**: BG interviewed by Jon Savage. **"You ask after Brion Gysin . . . except the workingmen"**: November 27, 1958 in Toklas, Alice B.: *Staying on Alone, the Letters of Alice B. Toklas.* **"William often sat . . . masturbation, or should be"**: BG interviewed by Terry Wilson in *Here To Go: Project R-101.* San Francisco. **"I actually had . . . came into being for me"**: BG interviewed by Jason Weiss August 21, 1980, in *Reality Studios* v4 nos 1–4 [in one vol] London 1982. **"It has most of the . . . pen to the surface"**: Ibid. **Tobey at the time:** Brion probably saw his first Tobey work at the Mark Tobey show held at the Musée des Arts Décoratifs in Paris, 1961. **"GREAT painting . . . opens up in front of you"**: WSB to AG: October 10, 1958. **tape-recorded transcript:** Galerie Weiller catalog text for 1973 Brion Gysin show. Reprinted in 1976 in *Soft Need* 9 and in the catalog to a Gysin show at the October Gallery in 1981.

7: Through the Magic Mirror

epigraph: The "Pooter" column, *Sunday Times*, London c March 1969. **1984 book of photographs:** Chapman, Harold: *The Beat Hotel*, Paris: Gris Banal, 1984. **"Just about everybody and anybody . . . discovered or rediscovered:** BG interviewed by Terry Wilson in *Here To Go: Project R-101.* **"Bill looked . . . wasn't based on suggestion"**: BG to Ted Morgan. Tape transcript in Arizona State University Special Collections Library. **"I know I am . . . is way back yonder"**: WSB to AG: January 2, 1959. **"We did a great deal . . . always said we would"**: BG interviewed by Terry Wilson in *Here To Go: Project R-101.* San Francisco. **"I sat once for 36 hours . . . was nothing beyond that"**: Ibid. **"a lamprey disk . . . scar patterns of junk"**: "The Algebra of Need" in *Naked Lunch*. **"I saw it happen . . . a cold yellow halo . . ."**: *Naked Lunch*; this appears in the first section, and three pages from end. **"My God, Bill! . . . growing out of the fingers . . ."**: WSB to AG: January 2, 1959. **"Sheldon took off . . . of Sheldon than Gregory"**: WSB to AG: February 10, 1958. **"the three mystics . . . Shell, Gysin, and Stern"**: WSB to AG: May 18, 1959. **"novel . . . published eventually by Grove Press"**: Thomas, Mack Sheldon: *Gumbo*, New York: Grove, 1965. **"Toby" stories:** The first, "Magnolia," appeared in *Evergreen Review* 18, in May 1961; it was followed by "Folksong" in *Evergreen* 22, in January 1962; "Revival" in *Evergreen* 26, in September 1962; and "I'm Not Complaining" in *Evergreen* 30, in May 1963. **"Imagine that idiot . . . stupid can a man get?"**: WSB to AG: February 12, 1959. **"They were both . . . the Heavenly Twins"**: Cumming, Anne [Felicity Mason]: *The Love Quest, A Sexual Odyssey.* London: Peter Owen, 1991. **"I did not spend . . . world"**: Ibid. **"Brion, as usual . . . always the king"**: Felicity Mason: *The World of Brion Gysin. He Came, He Saw, He Conquered, and*

He Cut It Up. Typescript dated November 1986 in William Burroughs Communications archives, Lawrence, Kansas. **Norman Mailer's assessment:** Footnote 2 to "Quick and Expensive Comments on the Talent in the Room" in *Big Table* 3, Chicago 1959. **"[they] wade through . . . has a code significance.)":** WSB to AG: April 2, 1959. The whereabouts of the suitcase and its contents is unknown. It contained the early draft versions of the John and Mary hanging scenes in *Naked Lunch* that caused so much controversy in the United States when the book was published there. **"There is no . . . he saved Jack's life":** WSB to AG: June 8, 1959. **"I think it is better . . . greatest writer of our time":** Ibid. **"Showers of fading snapshots . . . hammered out new stuff . . .":** In Burroughs, William and Brion Gysin: *The Third Mind.* New York: Viking, 1978. **"We made the selections . . . *Nova Express* as well":** WSB in conversation with Maurice Girodias, Allen Ginsberg on Charles Ruas's Conversations with Amerian Writers program, WBAI, New York. Transcribed in Ruas, Charles: *Con.ver.sa.tions with Amer.i.can writ.ers.* New York: Knopf, 1984. **"Although the routines . . . a didactic frame":** Skerl, Jennie: *William Burroughs.* Boston: Twayne, 1985. **"One month after . . . record from prompt publication":** "Foreword" to Maynard, Joe and Barry Miles: *William S. Burroughs, A Bibliography, 1953–73.* Charlottesville: University Press of Virginia Bibliographical Society, 1978. **"I am sure that . . . of the whole structure":** WSB to AG: nd [late July, 1958]. **"The point is . . . manuscript published in 1959":** WSB in conversation with Maurice Girodias, Allen Ginsberg in Ruas, Charles: *Con.ver.sa.tions with Amer.i.can writ.ers.* **Publication of *Naked Lunch:*** The Olympia Press edition was called *The Naked Lunch;* subsequent editions in Britain and America were called simply *Naked Lunch.* **"not a human . . . silly word . . .":** WSB to AG: nd [late July, 1959]. **"Not for nothing . . . Invisible Man'":** Ibid. *Smiling Damned Villain:* Croft-Cooke, Rupert: *Smiling Damned Villain: The True Story of Paul Lund.* London: Secker & Warburg, 1959. **"I am writing . . . that junk wagon, boys":** WSB to AG: September 11, 1959. **"The article is . . . cold and junkless charity":** WSB to AG: October 7, 1959. **"simply run the tape . . . trauma is wiped off":** WSB to AG: October 27, 1959. **"[He] proceeded . . . had driven himself insane":** Norse, Harold: *Memoirs of a Bastard Angel.* New York: William Morrow, 1989. **"The thing about apomorphine . . . it is quite unpleasant":** Mikriammos, Philippe: "The Last European Interview" in *The Review of Contemporary Fiction*, Spring 1984. **"It's been fuckin' . . . worth it; he's getting well":** Norse, Harold: *Memoirs of a Bastard Angel.* **"Ian Sommerville was . . . tape recorders as I was":** Brion Gysin, 1982. Typewritten document in the archives of William Burroughs Communications. **"I once said to Ian . . . Rupert Brooke way":** Felicity Mason interviewed by Ted Morgan. ASU Morgan Collection. **"The first book . . . musical thing within me":** GC interviewed by Michael Andre 1972: *Unmuzzled Ox* 5 / 6 New York 1973. *Nouvelle Revue Française:* The manuscript was translated as *"Temoignage à propos d'une maladie"* by Eric Kahane, Maurice Girodias's brother. **he wrote Allen a story:** WSB to AG: October 30, 1959.

8: Cut-ups

"LIFE was around . . . Names: Snell and Loomis": WSB to AG: October 7, 1959. "The Life interviewers . . . final form of the story": WSB to AG: November 17, 1959. ". . . fade out to . . . appeared in *Minutes To Go*": WSB: "Introductions" in Burroughs, William and Brion Gysin: *The Third Mind*. New York: Viking, 1978. Gysin seems to have accepted this version, but he later gave a different account of the discovery. He told Terry Wilson: "He was away in London seeing Dr. Dent. William came back, and contact had been made with *Life* magazine. When he came from lunch I showed him these things, saying that it had happened during the last 2 or 3 weeks, during his absence at any rate." BG: "Cut-Ups, A Project for Disastrous Success" in *Evergreen Review* 32, New York, April–May 1964. "It was a readymade . . . apt and so extraordinary": BG interviewed by Terry Wilson in *Here To Go: Project R-101*. "When he came from lunch . . . That's what it's for": BG to Terry Wilson, 1976. "Cut up Rimbaud . . . if not personal appearance": WSB: "The Cut-Up Method of Brion Gysin" in *The Third Mind*. "We began to find out . . . make them a new world": BG talking to Robert Palmer, quoted in Palmer: "Brion Gysin 1916–1986." [Photocopy ms. in William Burroughs Communications archives, Lawrence, Kansas. Origin unknown.] Almost certainly from an interview conducted by Palmer for *Rolling Stone* magazine. **Dada Manifesto on Feeble Love and Bitter Love:** Polizzotti, Mark: *Revolution of the Mind: The Life of André Breton*. New York: Farrar Straus and Giroux. "It was an accident . . . the arts, let's say": BG to Jon Savage. **Cut-up Pound's *Cantos*:** in: Breger, Udo, Silke Paull and Erwin Stegentritt (eds.): *AQ14 CUT UP, eine Anthologie*. Dudweiler: Germany, AQ, 1973. "Obviously those . . . those roles after all": BG interviewed by Jason Weiss May 9, 1981, in *Reality Studios* v4 nos 1–4 [in one vol] London 1982. "Cut-Up with Jacques Stern's Telegrams & Letters": unpublished. "It seemed like . . . marvellous subjects that he had": BG to Jon Savage. "Poetry is for everyone": WSB is quoting Tristan Tzara. **an amusing routine around the idea:** WSB: "First recordings" in Burroughs, William and Brion Gysin: *The Third Mind*. "As he wrote . . . had first evoked them": BG interviewed by Terry Wilson in *Here To Go: Project R-101*. "The idea is to . . . always been my principle": BG interviewed by Jason Weiss, "Renaissance Man of Art." *New York Times*, January 12, 1983. "Then William had used . . . Nothing ever fazed him": Ibid. "Burroughs named it . . . watch and looking at it": Sinclair Beiles to Ted Morgan: March 19, 1984. "'Death of 1959' was . . . far out spatial sound": GC interviewed by Michael Andre 1972: *Unmuzzled Ox* 5 / 6 New York 1973. "I've been quoted . . . pain in the ass . . .": BG interviewed by Terry Wilson in *Here To Go: Project R-101*. **Bouthoul's Study of the Assassins:** Bouthoul, Betty: *Grand Maître des Assassins*, Libraire Armand Colin: Paris 1936. Burroughs presumably read it in translation. "Hassan: Sabbah . . . Assassin of Ugly Spirits": Burroughs, William S.: footnote to "Comments on the Night Before Thinking" in *Evergreen Review* 20, September 1961. "The purpose of my writings . . . J. Lee

Novia Police": Burroughs, William S.: "Introduction to Naked Lunch The Soft Machine Novia Express." *Evergreen Review* 22, January 1962. **"Small enough . . . be afraid to hit him"**: Transcription from a taped interview with BG by Ted Morgan. Hayden Library, ASU. **dream night of June 26, 1972**: Item 1 from Folio 60. Miles, Barry (compiler): *A Catalogue of the William S. Burroughs Archive.* London: Covent Garden Press, 1973. p. 149. **London** *Sunday Times* **review**: quoted in *Two Cities* 5, Autumn 1960. **"Ian says Bill . . . have power over people"**: BG to the author, London 1974. **"But an emergency . . . emergency has arisen since then"**: Coleridge after De Quincey: *Confessions of an English Opium Eater.* **Gysin's Cut-up parody**: Gysin, Brion: *The Last Museum.* New York: Grove, 1986, p. 88. **"Sinclair Beiles is in . . . I'm sorry to say"**: WSB to Jon Webb: January 5, 1961. **"There is something . . . first time you hear it"**: BG interviewed by Terry Wilson in *Here To Go: Project R-101.* **"Ian was an extraordinary . . . afraid, out of his room"**: Ibid. **"So when Ian came back . . . we could get enough"**: BG interviewed by Jason Weiss August 21, 1980, in *Reality Studios.* **a book by W. Gray Walter**: *The Living Brain.* London: Duckworth, 1953. **"And that's where . . . lot of remarkable things"**: BG interviewed by Jason Weiss August 21, 1980 in *Reality Studios.* **"What we had done . . . all like movies"**: Ibid. **"He said, 'Wow' . . . on these two levels"**: BG to Jon Savage. **Dreamachine expensive limited edition**: *Dreamachine von Brion Gysin*, Editions Carl Laszlo, Basel, nd.

9: Soft Machine

epigraph: Harold Norse to WSB: August 9, 1986. **"He's as free . . . safe in my footlocker"**: BG interviewed by Terry Wilson in *Here To Go: Project R-101.* **"William had always . . . a dollar a page!"**: BG interviewed by Jon Savage. **Brion claims**: The author is unable to find it in Huxley's text. **quoted in the Bible**: Exodus III, 14. **"Poetry, of course, exists . . . I think"**: BG interviewed by Terry Wilson in *Here To Go: Project R-101.* **"They said, 'We have . . . as you can imagine"**: BG interviewed by Jason Weiss August 21, 1980, in *Reality Studios* v4 nos 1–4 [in one vol] London 1982. **"Here we began . . . 'Kick That Habit Man'"**: BG interviewed by Rob LaFrenais and Graham Dawes in *Performance* magazine 11, London, 1981. **"The sort of people . . . Soft Machine and Gong"**: Ibid. **"We started it about . . . which I could walk"**: Wilson, Terry: "Brion Gysin: A Biography/Appreciation" in RE / Search 4 / 5. San Francisco, 1982. **"In La Bohème . . . should have known better"**: BG interviewed by Jason Weiss August 21, 1980 in *Reality Studios.* **"At the time . . . with my own age"**: Ibid. **"There is no creation . . . no destruction without creation"**: See Lawrence Lacina: "Rolling With Brion" in Brion Gysin 23, *I.C.B.M.* 23/ed Cactus. 1992. **"It came out of . . . rebuild the world like that"**: BG interviewed by Genesis P.Orridge and Paris Sleazy, c 1981 [unpublished transcript]. **performance at the ICA in London**:

Organized by the author. **"Used by another . . . 'Why, that's a Burroughs.'":** BG interviewed by Terry Wilson in *Here To Go: Project R-101.* **"The jissom of hanged youths . . . known as Hydraulic jacks":** Burroughs, William S.: *The Soft Machine,* Paris: Olympia Press, 1961. **"Up a great brown . . . periods of immobile silence":** Ibid. **"the brains of the gang . . . and called him Master":** *Gay Sunshine* 18, June–July 1973. **"'Sniffing Keyholes' . . . broken through to something new":** Norse, Harold: introduction to "Sniffing Keyholes" at a poetry reading held at the In and Outs Press, Amsterdam, November 18, 1984. Released by Ins and Outs on cassette as *Harold Norse Of Course.* **"nothing but flow . . . Potent is come":** Norse, Harold: *Beat Hotel.* San Diego: Atticus Press, 1983. **"I recall my enthusiasm . . . was high praise indeed":** WSB: Foreword to Norse, Harold: *Beat Hotel.* **"A voice that is . . . to, come from, everybody":** *Gay Sunshine* 18. **"There is nothing to fear . . . than you, I think":** WSB to AG: June 21, 1960. **"I am leaving . . . Don't like it. Never did":** WSB to AG: March 12, 1961. **"The starting point . . . compile such an inventory":** Gramsci, Antonio: *The Prison Notebooks, a Selection.* Trans. Quintin Hoare and Geoffrey Nowell Smith. New York: International Publishers, 1971. This quote is incomplete in this edition, the last phrase being left out. This is supplied in translation by Edward Said in *Orientalism,* New York: Random House, 1978. **announcement card:** "Cosmographies Harold Norse" was held at the Cave de la Librairie Anglaise from March 17 until April 5, 1961. The announcement card/catalog consisted of a yellow card folded in three with a French translation of Burroughs's text on page one, followed on page three by the original English version. **"Sorry I could not . . . come on down any time":** WSB to AG: April 14, 1961. **Ginsberg's cover blurb:** Ginsberg, Allen: flap blurb for *The Soft Machine,* Paris: Olympia, 1961. This was not used on any subsequent editions of the book. ***The System of Dante's Hell:*** Jones, LeRoi: *The System of Dante's Hell,* New York: Grove, 1963. **"That book was written . . . in a play fine":** GC interviewed by Michael Andre 1972: *Unmuzzled Ox* 5 / 6 New York 1973. **"That will be florins . . . much has to be changed":** GC to AG: October 13, 1961. **"Come along . . . as you can make it":** WSB to AG: May 20, 1961.

10: Fade Out in Gray Room

"Nine Lies-the-Heart . . . a thin smouldering stick": Morrissett, Ann: "An Account of the Events Preceding the Death of Bill Burroughs." *Evergreen Review* 29. March 1963. **"The only problem . . . don't have Alpha waves":** quoted by Carnegie, Alasdair: *The Life and Works of Brion Gysin 1916–1986* [privately distributed six-page pamphlet. Sudbury: Suffolk, March 1990]. **"The Dreamachine should have . . . all of the faces":** BG interviewed by Jon Savage. **dust wrapper design by Ian Sommerville:** Among the others are a fragment of the same collage used on the dust wrapper of the first UK hardback of *Naked Lunch* and a fold-out page in *Gnaoua* magazine, Tangier,

1964. **"With _The Soft Machine_ . . . pages of straight narrative":** WSB interviewed by A. J. Weatherby. _The Guardian_, March 22, 1963. **"It was through Jacques Leiser's . . . to find out how":** Antony Balch interviewed by Terry Wilson in _Here To Go: Planet R-101_. **"[I remember] saying . . . we met Anthony Balch":** BG to Jon Savage. **the "board members":** The others were David Jacobs, Bachoo Sen, Liam O'Leary, Norman Warren, John Gillett, and Andrew Rabanech. The film also "starred" Brion Gysin, Ian Sommerville, and Michael Portman. **"When film technicians . . . most effectively stir the senses":** _Continental Film Review_, May 1961. **"I was the last person . . . William was already there":** BG interviewed by Jon Savage. **Kaja even wrote about the Switchboard:** "In Heaven at 9 rue Git-le-Coeur."